Fodor's EXPLORING

EGYPT

FODOR'S TRAVEL PUBLICATIONS
NEW YORK • TORONTO • LONDON • SYDNEY • AUCKLAND

WWW.FODORS.COM

Revised third edition 2000
First published 1996
Copyright © Automobile Association Developments Limited 2000
Maps copyright © Automobile Association Developments Limited 2000

Published in the United States by Fodor's Travel Publications
Published in the United Kingdom by AA Publishing

Fodor's is a registered trademark of Random House, Inc.

ISBN 0–679–00681–8
ISSN 1520–4944
Third Edition

Fodor's Exploring Egypt

Authors: **Anthony Sattin and Sylvie Franquet**
Series Adviser: **Christopher Catling**
Copy Editor: **Donna Dailey**
Revisions Editor: **Lodestone Publishing Limited**
Original Photography: **Rick Strange and Steve Day**
Cartography: **The Automobile Association**
Cover Design: **Tigist Getachew, Fabrizio La Rocca**
Front Cover Silhouette: **Peter Guttman**
Front Cover Top Image: **Corbis**

Printed and bound in Italy by Printer Trento srl
10 9 8 7 6 5 4 3 2 1

How to use this book

ORGANIZATION

Egypt Is, Egypt Was
Discusses aspects of life and culture in contemporary Egypt and explores significant periods in its history.

Gazetteer
Breaks down the country into regional chapters, and covers places to visit, including walks and drives. Within this section fall the Focus-on articles, which consider a variety of subjects in greater detail.

Travel Facts
Contains the strictly practical information vital for a successful trip.

Accommodations and Restaurants
Lists recommended establishments throughout Egypt, giving a brief summary of their attractions.

KEY TO ADMISSION CHARGES
An indication of an establishment's admission charge is given by categorizing the standard, adult rate as:

Inexpensive	under 10LE
Moderate	10LE–20LE
Expensive	over 20LE

ABOUT THE RATINGS
Most places described in this book have been given a separate rating. These are as follows:

▶▶▶   **Do not miss**

▶▶   **Highly recommended**

▶   **Worth seeing**

MAP REFERENCES
To make the location of a particular place easier to find, every main entry in this book is given a map reference, such as 176B3. The first number (176) indicates the page on which the map can be found, the letter (B) and the second number (3) pinpoint the square in which the main entry is located. The maps on the inside front cover and inside back cover are referred to as IFC and IBC respectively.

Contents

Sylvie Franquet studied Arabic at Ghent, Tunis and Cairo universities and lived in Cairo for six years. She now writes full time and has a column in the Belgian newspaper *De Morgen.*

Anthony Sattin is the author of several books, including *Lifting the Veil*, a history of travelers in Egypt from 1768 to 1956, and *The Pharaoh's Shadow*, an account of his search for Egypt's surviving ancient culture.

They met in Cairo and now divide their time between Europe and the Middle East, traveling, writing and raising two children.

Our Egypt

Foreigners have been arriving on the Nile with books to guide them since Herodotus tried to describe the sights and customs of Egypt nearly 2,500 years ago. Yet for all the words that have been written since then, Egypt and Egyptians remain a mystery.

Sylvie and I visited Egypt for the first time in 1985. We have spent years living there since then and have written hundreds of thousands of words about the country and its people. Egypt continues to surprise, in its past and its present, in country and town, to fulfill our expectations, and to confound us at the same time.

Our Egypt is a place of wonders and revelations, of heartbreak and sadness. A model for historical continuity, it is also a place of surprising change. Part of its present glory rests in the survival of its monuments—pharaonic, Christian, and Arab—many of which are now threatened with destruction. Population growth and a drift into cities have destroyed the sense of community, yet Egyptians remain completely family-oriented. The desert, former refuge of hermits, is now the chosen weekend spot for four-wheel drivers.

Above all, our Egypt is stimulating. Traveling up the Nile along the tourist circuit we have been hassled by guides and hawkers selling their services or tacky imitation antiquities. Stepping away from that well-trodden trail we have always met with the response for which Egyptians are famous—food, help, and a laugh. The government's recent drive against Islamist groups has made it more difficult for foreigners to travel off the main routes. But even in out-of-the-way villages, where people showed concern for our safety by taking us to the village *omda* (head man), we were still offered a meal before being escorted back to the nearest town.

Egypt is a place of superlatives—the oldest, the first, the largest, the most crowded, most remote, most beautiful—and one way or another it also gets visitors talking in superlatives, about how they loved or hated it, how the climate cheered them up or the food got them down. For the long shadow of its historical and cultural significance, the glitter and glare of its present, the warmth of its people, the heat of its sun, and the dazzling beauty of its landscapes, we love it.

Egypt Is

Egypt is defined by its geography. Most of the country is desert, bordered by the Red Sea to the east, the Mediterranean in the north, and the Libyan and Nubian deserts in the west and south. But running through the middle of all this is the world's longest river, the magical Nile.

THE NILE VALLEY Egypt occupies 3.3 percent of Africa's land mass, but 95 percent of Egyptians inhabit only about 5 percent of their country, most of it near the Nile. The Nile runs through rainless Egypt from south to north and irrigates it like the blessed river that Muslims believe runs through the gardens of paradise. It is worthy of praise: flowing out of the lakes of Ethiopia and Uganda, it is over 3,800 miles long, and for the last 1,600 miles of its course through Sudan and Egypt, it has no tributaries and receives very little rainfall. So vital is it to the country that Egypt is defined according to its direction of flow. The south of the country is known as Upper Egypt, while the north is called Lower Egypt, and when asked for directions, Egyptians will often refer to the river: *qibli*, toward the mountains in the south and *bahari*, to the sea in the north.

THE RIVER'S COURSE The ancient Egyptians used the lotus plant, with its thin stem and a fan-shaped bud, as one of the icons to depict their watery lifeline. Seen from the air, the river still looks very much like that. In southern Egypt, the Nile valley is extremely narrow in places where the river passes between harder rock formations that it has been unable to erode. Farther north, where the rock formations are softer, the river averages more than half a mile in width, while its valley stretches some 6 miles from east to west. After passing Cairo, the Nile splits into the branches that have created the Delta.

THE DELTA In antiquity the Nile had seven branches, but now there are only two, which flow into the Mediterranean near Rashid (Rosetta) and Dumyat (Damietta). Between

them lies some of the most fertile land in the country: low-lying, irrigated by a network of canals, and intensively farmed. The Delta has been an inspiration to Egyptians to reclaim land from the desert, but even a river as powerful as the Nile has its limits and beyond its reach lie the rock and sand of the deserts.

THE WESTERN DESERT To ancient Egyptians, the west was the place of

the dead. So it must have seemed appropriate that threats to Egypt's security often came out of the Western Desert, from the Libyans in antiquity to the Germans in World War II.

The desert here is relatively flat, with depressions that have created oases. Ironically, it is to the west that some Egyptian strategists look for the country's development. Oil fields have been found in the northern desert, while the planned Toshka Canal will irrigate huge swaths of the southern desert.

THE EASTERN DESERT Unlike the Western Desert, the narrower stretch of land between the Nile Valley and the Red Sea coast is mountainous. The Red Sea mountains rise to a height of 2,500 feet and, as the ancient Egyptians knew, are rich in gold and other minerals. Although

close to the Nile Valley, the Red Sea mountains were almost considered another country, where hermits went to retreat from the world. The last of the region's seminomadic tribes have now been settled.

HOLY DESERT The Sinai desert offers an even more dramatic landscape than the Eastern Desert. The peninsula is flat along its coastal plains, rough and rugged in the south and the center. The sacred Gebel Musa (Mt. Sinai), where Moses is said to have received the Ten Commandments, rises to 7,497 feet while the neighboring Gebel Katerina is Egypt's highest mountain, reaching to 8,668 feet.

With most of their country covered by desert, Egyptians farm intensively along the Nile

11

Egypt became a republic in June 1953 when the monarchy was replaced. Although a limited form of democracy is practiced, the country is still effectively ruled by a handful of very powerful people who take their orders from the president.

THE STATE Egypt is an Arab republic, headed by a president who has the power to appoint a government and its ministers. The government is aided by the People's Assembly, a legislative body elected every five years. The state proclaims the right of freedom of thought and religious practice. Islam is the state religion and *Sharia* (Islamic law) provides the precedent for state laws.

THE GOVERNMENT Hosni Mubarak won the presidential election in 1999 with around 94 percent of the votes cast. As with each election since he became leader, after President Sadat's assassination in 1981, he was unopposed. Mubarak has been called the most democratic leader Egypt has ever had, but he has been criticized abroad

for not offering real democracy to his people. The president is head of state and of the armed forces and also has the right to appoint all government ministers. In all respects, he runs the country. As a presidential spokesman once explained, the president holds "sovereign power in his hands" with the cabinet "serving as his administrative hand."

When President Sadat's assassin called his victim "pharaoh," he only echoed popular opinion.

POLITICAL PARTIES The National Democratic Party was once the only political organization that had access to power and it still holds the upper hand. But in response to growing unrest, President Mubarak has allowed a wider range of political opinions to be voiced and parties that had long been silent are again being heard. However, he stopped short of lifting the ban on the Muslim Brotherhood and other Islamist organizations. In response, they have built power bases elsewhere, as in such democratically elected bodies as the lawyers' syndicate.

THE ACTUALITY OF POWER Egypt has had only three rulers since the mid-1950s. President Mubarak was the heir-apparent to his predecessor, but he has yet to give his sign of approval to a visible successor, nor, at present, is there a democratic system in place to elect one. His supporters explain that the president is transforming the entire political system. But reforms are slow, there isn't a large educated electorate, and the old guard are unwilling to change the system that put them in power. For now, the prospect of either Islamic extremists or army hard-liners taking over ensures that few grumble loudly.

The Egyptian flag, symbol of a modern Arab republic

12

HUMAN RIGHTS Amnesty International's 1999 report cited "thousands ... held without charge or trial... Torture continued to be systematic... Prison conditions amounted to cruel, inhumane or degrading treatment. At least 73 people were sentenced to death..." Since President Sadat was assassinated, the Egyptian government has ruled with emergency powers, in effect suspending ordinary Egyptian law along with much of its own accountability. It is clear that the authorities have used these powers in their struggle against opposition groups.

FOREIGN POLICY The Ministry of Foreign Affairs is housed in an impressive and very visible headquarters on the Nile in Cairo, an outward and public sign of its importance. Egypt runs a large diplomatic corps and has made the most of the ending of the isolation that followed the Camp David accord (see page 51), especially since the Arab League moved its headquarters back to Cairo in 1990. The country is active

President Hosni Mubarak has become an international statesman and enjoys a close relationship with other leaders of the Islamic world

in international affairs: President Mubarak was Chairman of the Organization of African Unity while Dr. Boutros Boutros-Ghali was the previous secretary-general of the United Nations.

Egypt's importance as a stabilizing presence and a moderate link between the region and world powers was highlighted by its role in the Gulf War and in peace talks between Arabs and Israelis. The U.S. and other Western allies have taken great care and invested considerable amounts of money in Egypt in the hope of preserving this status quo.

The Egyptian government has done much to further relations with other Arab states, particularly with Saudi Arabia and the oil-rich Gulf emirates, while maintaining essential communications with its Arab neighbors who are under pressure, including Syria and Libya.

Egypt is not an Islamic republic like Iran or Saudi Arabia, but Islam is the state religion and both laws and attitudes are shaped by it. The majority of Egyptian people are guided by Islam in all aspects of their lives.

❏ Muhammad had many wives—he married another ten in the last decade of his life. But after he had married the last one, he received a revelation that a man should not have more than four wives, and that he can have the additional wives only if he can afford to support them and their children, and if he treats all of them equally. ❏

IN THE BEGINNING The Prophet Muhammad was born around AD 570 in Mecca and was raised by his uncle, a merchant. According to Islam, during his 40th year Muhammad had a vision in which he received the word of God through the archangel Gabriel. He began to recite what Gabriel was telling him. The divine

Cairene mosques prove to be too small when the faithful gather for the Friday prayers

message soon attracted followers, but some members of his tribe grew nervous of his power and he was forced to flee to Medina in AD 622. This journey, known as *el-Hijrah*, is the starting point for the Islamic calendar. Muhammad's message was popular, but from the very beginning his followers had to fight for the right to worship and to fulfill Muhammad's vision that Islam was meant for all people. Muhammad fell ill and died in AD 632 while preparing for a campaign in the north of the Arabian peninsula.

THE QURAN (KORAN) For 22 years Muhammad recited his revelations to his followers (*el-Quran* means the recitation), but it was only after his death that they were written down, their accuracy confirmed by those closest to the Prophet. Islam rests on the Quran, the word of God delivered directly and in the language of the people, and on the Hadith and the Sunna, the sayings and the actions of the Prophet, which are unanimously agreed upon by Muslim scholars.

SUNNI OR SHI'A Muhammad died without naming a successor and soon after his death Muslims were divided. The Prophet's companion, Abu Bakr, was accepted as the Caliph Rasul-Allah, the Successor of the Prophet of God, but Ali, the Prophet's son-in-law, claimed that he was the natural leader of Muslims. Ali and his son Husayn were both killed, but their followers, members of the Shi'a sect, believed that only Ali's descendants had rights to the throne. The Sunni refused to acknowledge any of the Prophet's descendants as caliph. The majority of Egyptians are Sunni.

THE FINAL WORD The Quran sees Jews and Christians as "people of the Book" who received the message of the one true God but have failed to be true to it. Muhammad is believed to be the successor of Moses and Jesus, and the last of the prophets.

ISLAM EGYPTIAN STYLE Islam is in some ways practiced differently in Egypt, particularly in the cult of the dead. The first Muslims, who arrived from Arabia, were buried simply in the desert, but before long the ancient traditions of tomb-building and grave-visiting were adopted by the Egyptian Muslims. Visible tombs encouraged the elevation of saints, although Islam had attempted to do away with the priesthood and saints, instead promoting a direct communication between the believer and God. Almost every Egyptian village now has its revered saint buried under a white dome or a tree—a strikingly similar custom to the way that each village in ancient Egypt once revered its own god.

It doesn't matter where you are when it's time to pray

15

❏ The Five Pillars of Faith are these rituals, which every Muslim must perform: publicly declaring that "there is no God but Allah and Muhammad is His Prophet," praying five times a day at specific times facing the direction of Mecca, fasting in the month of Ramadan, making the *hajj* (pilgrimage) to Mecca at least once in a lifetime, and paying a religious levy for the ill or the poor, or for the defense of Islam. ❏

About 10 percent of Egyptians are Christian and a minute number are Jewish. Although the State does not persecute minorities, as do some Islamic countries, their relationships with their Muslim neighbors are as turbulent today as they have been throughout their histories.

16

COPTIC CLAIMS Egypt's estimated 6 million Copts are Christians belonging to the national Christian church (there are an estimated quarter of a million Christians of other denominations). The word Copt is a corruption of the Greek *Aigyptos* (an Egyptian), which is in turn derived from Hut-ka-Ptah (house of the Ka of Ptah), the ancient name for Egypt. Egyptians split from the rest of Christianity in AD 451 after church rulers in Constantinople supported the edict of the Council of Chalcedon, which denounced monophysites—those who believed in the single nature of God rather than the Trinity—as heretics.

REAL EGYPTIANS Copts claim to be the direct descendants of the ancient Egyptians, and although the pharaonic world disappeared soon

With religious tension rising, soldiers are on guard outside most Coptic churches

after Jesus was born, they have preserved in their language and customs some traces of that era that survived the Persian, Greek, and Roman occupations. While the Coptic language is descended from ancient Egyptian, it is tempting to see parallels between the ancient religion and Christianity as the strongest link between past and present. It seems only a short step from pharaonic *ankh* to Coptic cross, from Isis suckling Horus to Mary comforting Jesus. Isolated from the rest of Christianity, the religion has evolved on its own, staying close to its original impetus and rituals. Many aspects of the Coptic church service, from the structure of the church (with three altars) to liturgical chants, have very close parallels with pagan religious services.

EGYPT'S JEWS Some of the earliest Bible stories concern the arrival of Jews in Egypt fleeing famine in Canaan, and their subsequent departure under Moses for the promised land. There had been a Jewish community in Babylon-in-Egypt (Cairo) for at least four centuries when the Holy Family is believed to have arrived to escape Herod. The synagogue of Ben Ezra that stands in Old Cairo is the oldest in the country.

Jews also played an important role in Alexandria. Encouraged to settle by the early Ptolemies, they became fully integrated, speaking Greek (the first five books of the Old Testament were translated into Greek for them) and adding to the glory of the city; when it fell to the Arabs in AD 641, the Arab general reported that there were 40,000 Jews in the city.

MODERN TIMES In the 1830s, Edward Lane estimated that there were 5,000 Jews in Egypt (and 150,000 Copts), of

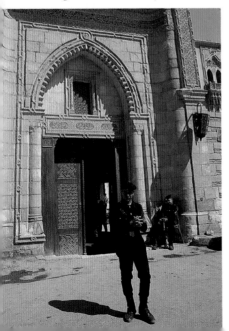

whom 3,000 to 4,000 lived in Cairo. Although their numbers increased under the British, the population was reduced to around 2,600 in 1967. In 1999, there were believed to be fewer than 100 members of the Jewish community still living in the country, and too few of them in Alexandria for regular services to be held in the great synagogue.

RELIGIOUS TENSION Current violence between fundamentalist Muslims and Copts is a new twist in an ongoing struggle. Islam does not preach intolerance, but politics, and groups using religion for their own ends, have led to increasing tension between fundamentalists and Egypt's minorities.

The cross is the proud symbol of Egypt's Coptic minority

The separate identity of the Copts has made them an easy target for extremists, though tension between the communities surfaces in other ways. If you see a new church with a high bell tower, you will probably find that there is a higher minaret under construction nearby. Interestingly, the Coptic church has undergone an extraordinary revival in its fortunes.

There was widespread dismay at Egypt's crushing defeat by the Israelis in 1967 and this, added to a sense of vengeance after the October 1973 war, led to attacks on property owned by the Jewish community.

Egypt's agriculture is guaranteed by a constant water supply and its manufacturers can draw on huge labor resources. The country also controls one of the arteries of world trade and contains some of the world's most important monuments. After years of crisis, economic reforms have created the beginnings of a revival.

INDUSTRIES The Nile made it possible for civilization to develop along the valley, and the Aswan High Dam made it possible to grow three crops a year. But the need to earn foreign currency to service massive international debts led to the growth of crops for overseas markets and made Egypt dependent on imports for up to 60 percent of its food (figures vary and are a matter of dispute). Egypt's main crops include rice, sugar cane, grains, beans, and cotton, on which its 19th-century wealth was based. In fact, agriculture now accounts for only 18 percent of gross domestic product, industry for 30 percent, and services (including tourism and the Suez Canal) for 52 percent.

EGYPT'S RESOURCES Egypt has offshore gas fields along the Red Sea coast, phosphates, precious metals, and small oil reserves (Egypt is not a major oil producer), but its most valuable assets are its immense work force, the monuments from its glorious past, and the Suez Canal. The canal is one of the country's largest earners of foreign currency after remittances from Egyptian workers abroad and will continue to prop up the economy for as long as it is cheaper to transport goods through the canal than via the Cape. Even in antiquity, Egypt's monuments attracted visitors but then, as now, for many people it was a once-in-a-lifetime visit. New tourist developments along the Red Sea coast are attracting

a different sort of tourist, who comes to sun and swim and is more likely to return year after year. Perhaps Egypt's most important resource is its population, the largest in the Arab Middle East. If new regional economic policies come to fruition, many new jobs will be created. With at least 20 percent of its estimated 18 million workers unemployed, Egypt is well placed to gain from this.

WORKERS ABROAD At the time of the Gulf War it was estimated that 1 million Egyptians were working in the region. Egypt's educational system had long been producing a surplus of qualified engineers, teachers, and other professionals who were sought after, especially by other Arab countries. Under President Sadat, all university graduates were guaranteed a job, which led to job-sharing in Egypt, but some of them went to the Gulf, attracted by much better pay. For many years their remittances, sent home in foreign currency, bolstered Egypt's economy, supported their families, and produced a housing boom as new buildings were commissioned for their homecoming. Their return to

Egypt because of the war meant a loss of this revenue and added another million to the large number already without work.

AID Egypt is the second-largest recipient of U.S. aid (only Israel receives more) and is reputed to be the second-largest recipient of all international aid. The country's need for aid is obvious and some of the more visible results—improved infrastructure, communications, health care, and environmental awareness—suggest that some of it is having an effect. Some Egyptians have resented the involvement that aid donors have demanded in the country's policies. The World Bank, in particular, has regularly made suggestions as to how Egypt should be governed, and it has made loans conditional on the government pursuing reforms such as the reduction of food subsidies and the freeing of currency controls. These economic reforms, and the reduction of massive foreign debt, have created a new business environment. Many foreign analysts have listed Egypt as a significant, emerging market and it has now seen a huge influx of foreign investment.

Some farmers still work the fertile soil of the Nile valley in much the same way as their ancient forefathers— a sharp contrast to the bustle of modern city life (below)

Egyptians share a rich heritage, but they can't eat old stones (though some live off them in other ways). For many Egyptians life is a search for the basics, made tolerable because they are comforted by an extended family, consoled by religion and kept smiling by an irrepressible sense of humor.

A boy selling green herbs grown in his parents' garden

GROWING FAST To Egyptians, children are a blessing and a security in their old age. There are now around 65 million Egyptians, but the population has been growing by up to a million every seven or eight months.

Current hardships and longer life expectancy (from 41 years in 1960 to 61 years in 1990) are changing perceptions. In 1960, the average Egyptian family had seven children and it was thought lucky to have as many as ten; by 1990, the average was down to 3.8 children.

FAMILIES Egyptians identify strongly with their country, province, and hometown, but above all, at whatever age, the family is at the center of their life. While the father is still very much the patriarch, a figure to be respected and sometimes also feared, it is usually the mother who rules as well as runs the house. It is also the women who keep up the traditions, preparing customary dishes for feasts and sometimes seeking help from saints or ancient shrines in times of trouble.

YOUNG LOVE On top of all the other obstacles to young love, people in Egypt face the daunting task of finding themselves a home.

At night they sit by the river, thinking about the difficulties. Many will have to wait for years and take on night work to save enough for an apartment, which is why more Egyptian men are marrying later in life. Those who can't wait start married life living in the house of one of their parents.

EDUCATION Like other sectors that depend on government spending, education was underfunded while the Egyptian military rearmed after the wars of 1967 and 1973. The growing population, further stretching resources, has necessitated schools running two or three shifts of classes to accommodate the students.

Although education is compulsory, a lack of enforcement means that many children, especially girls, will stay at home to help out. During the British occupation, several private schools were opened in Cairo and Alexandria, a trend that has continued to educate the children of the growing middle classes. But though illiteracy exists, some 10 percent of Egyptians continue on to university or other higher education colleges.

ELECTRIFYING President Sadat promised to bring electricity to every village in Egypt, and with it came television. Farmers whose days were regulated by the sun now stay up late watching American soap operas.

TV has brought great changes, not least in taste, with more people aspiring to buy imported goods.

GREAT CHANGES After receiving his Nobel prize for Literature, the Egyptian novelist Naguib Mahfouz announced that he could write no

❏ One of the many consequences of the recent economic boom in Cairo is that the disparity between the wealth of the city's millionaires and the village poor has become even more apparent. ❏

more: his subject, the Egyptian character, was changing too fast.

One of the great shifts is in where people live. Fifty years ago most Egyptians lived and worked on the land, their lives ruled by the river. Since the 1952 revolution, especially since the 1970s, a lack of employment for the growing rural population and the prospect of better-paid jobs have lured immigrants to Egypt's cities.

HUMOR It isn't easy living in Egypt. Problems are many, opportunities are few.

One thing that helps is a sense of humor. The Saeedis (Upper Egyptians) are the butt of many jokes. But in Egypt, everything except religion is a suitable subject, even President Mubarak.

Egyptians always have time for a good joke or a laugh

Religious, courteous, and patient, Egyptians have held on to their identity in spite of the massive changes in their society which haven't yet managed to shake their pragmatism.

TRUST IN ALLAH One of Egypt's most commonly used words expresses a trust in God that foreigners find hard to understand. *Insha'allah* (literally, God willing) is used whenever some future event is referred to, as in "We'll meet at eight, Insha'allah."

TOMORROW AND TOMORROW
Time is a commodity in which many Egyptians are rich. When *bokra*

(tomorrow) is referred to, with an accompanying *insha'allah*, it may mean an indeterminate time in the future—not today, maybe tomorrow, maybe later. This applies to things they are promising to do, as well as the many blessings that life has so far failed to bestow upon them.

A LITTLE UNDERSTANDING *Insha'allah* and *bokra* reveal something about the Egyptian character, but another common word *ma'alesh* has even more uses. It means "Never mind." Foreigners rarely use it, but when an Egyptian travels and the plane is late, the food cold, or the only room left in the hotel faces a wall—in other words, when they can't get what they want—*ma'alesh* is their gracious and sympathetic response.

SEPARATING THE SEXES Women can sit anywhere on the Cairo metro and Alexandrian tram system, but there are always cars where men are not allowed. Sexual segregation is not a matter of legislation, but increasingly it is the norm.

COVERING UP Egyptian women tend to cover themselves up outside the house, so when Egyptian men see a girl's bare shoulder, or her figure in see-through clothes, they often consider it a sexual provocation and will stop to stare. Yet when a woman openly breastfeeds her baby in the street they will hardly even notice.

AND FINALLY Egyptians are pragmatic about death. It isn't hidden away, but is part of their lives, sometimes literally: many old houses contain tombs, and some thousands of people are now living in Cairo's cemeteries.

Many Egyptian women prefer to wear a headscarf rather than the traditional face veil

The Egyptian people are renowned for their hospitality. They are also tolerant toward foreigners, but if you really want to fit in and get along, you'll need a few tips on etiquette.

GREETINGS When Egyptians meet, they don't just say hello. Greetings are elaborate. Even if acquaintences are in a desperate hurry, very often one forces the other to stop for tea. In the café they take time to swap stories with the owner before tea is served. The farewells are as elaborate as the greetings. Foreigners who ask after people's health are always appreciated.

CLEANLINESS Muslims are scrupulous about washing before prayer. Even if no running water is available, they will still attempt to wash themselves. They are just as scrupulous about eating and will only use their right hand, the left being reserved for cleaning themselves. Feet are also considered unclean (you don't know where they've been), so when a male Muslim enters a mosque he takes off his shoes and when he sits down facing someone he makes sure the soles of his feet are not showing.

PHOTOGRAPHS If you want to photograph Egyptians, especially women or religious people, you should always ask first (or make yourself understood). Children will sometimes ask for *baksheesh* (a tip), but otherwise you will be either waved away or given encouragement.

GIFTS If you are invited to a house for a meal, it is polite to take your host or hostess a gift. Flowers will not do and wine is usually out of the question, but something that often goes down well is a selection of pastries.

PHYSICAL CONTACT Egyptian men walk hand in hand down a street, but it is rare to see males and females touch in public. Physical contact between foreign couples is frowned upon. If you want to feel at ease, don't kiss or embrace in the street.

Muslims take off their shoes upon entering a mosque

Out of Egypt's early 20th-century struggles has come a profusion of artistic talent. The most populous Middle Eastern country might no longer be "Mother of the World" but it has shown the way for the arts in the Arab world.

THE SPOKEN WORD Traditions of storytelling go back to long before the Arab invasion. Pre-Islamic stories were inevitably epics, long narrative cycles relating the adventures of heroes and the desperate acts of lovers. The *Hilaliya* (the story of Abu Zayd) and *Laila and Majnun* are two examples of stories still in circulation today. The audience, assembled in cafés (or in houses for special occasions), would already know the story but would enjoy the raconteur's embellishments. It was from this tradition that medieval European writers like Boccaccio and Chaucer drew inspiration. Egyptian storytellers were popular until the advent of radio and television.

Theater director Hassan el-Geretly is currently engaged in recording as many of these epic narratives as possible in an attempt to preserve and reinvent the tradition.

LITERATURE Introductions to novels and collections of short stories published in the 1960s and 1970s often cited the influence of European novelists and poets on Egyptian writers. Until the early 20th century, Egyptian literature was still an offspring of an oral tradition. But education, contact with foreign influences, and political struggle led to experimentation by writers like Haykal and those of the so-called New School.

Tawfiq el-Hakim stands out as one of the leading figures of that period, but the writer who dominates the century is Naguib Mahfouz, who started writing in 1928. His winning of the Nobel Prize stirred up controversy in Egypt: it was claimed that other Egyptian writers had achieved more, and some Muslims felt that a man with a *fatwa* (religious edict) calling for his death because what he wrote was considered blasphemous should not be so rewarded. But Mahfouz has captured an Egypt that is only just out of sight.

TRANSLATED WRITERS Many more Egyptian writers are now available in translation. Among the more notable are the older

Many of Mahfouz's characters come from the alleys of Islamic Cairo

generation of Mahfouz, Constantine Cavafy (*Collected Poems*), and el-Hakim. Waguih Ghali's only novel, *Beer in the Snooker Club*, is a bitter view of post-revolutionary Cairo that has never been available in Egypt. Nawaal el-Saadawi is often typecast as a feminist and her works are also controversial. Like Gamal el-Gitani, el-Saadawi writes novels that are allegorical attacks on attitudes and government. Ahdaf Soueif is a younger novelist writing in English about contemporary Egypt.

MOVIES AND THEATER Egyptians are proud of their cultural importance in the Arab world and nowhere is it more obvious than in movies and television. Movies created in Cairo's cinema city, and particularly the work of veteran moviemaker Youssef Shaheen, have helped to shape Arab identity and attitudes. Some of the current stars have a huge following, which allows them to move easily between screen and stage. Entertainers such as Adel Imam or Fifi Abduh, like Umm Kalthoum before them (see page 26), can be seen on stage in Cairo at the same time as movie theaters and television show their movies.

Television has changed the traditional family life

TELEVISION Egyptians are passionate television viewers and with the proliferation of satellite dishes and new land-based channels, the choice is becoming greater. The main TV event of the year is the *Fawazeer* during the month of Ramadan. These programs are full of stories, which are clues to a puzzle. At the end of the month, the person with the right answer wins an attractive prize. (The excitement is only mildly lessened by the knowledge that the answer can be bought on the street in Cairo some days before the end of the month.)

VISUAL ARTS Like all other art forms, painting and sculpture were transformed by Egypt's struggle for nationhood. Modernist artists like Mahmoud Mukhtar, Mahmoud Said, and Muhammad Nagy were working in a period of mixed influences. While Nagy was in Paris with the Impressionist Claude Monet, Egyptologists were uncovering more of the pharaonic past. Egyptian art has developed out of these two

The arts

influences, the innovation of the West and the burden of the past, and contemporary artists continue to explore these themes.

CLASSICAL ARABIC MUSIC The reed pipe, drum, tambourine, oud, and three-string fiddle—these are at the heart of Egyptian music. The greatest names in classical Arabic music are Umm Kalthoum, who brought a previously unknown passion and bravura to the trilling, warbling vocals, and her one-time colleague Muhammad Abdel Wahab, who transformed the traditional thin *takht* music into something more like a big-band sound. While classical Arabic music is still performed today, it has been less popular since the deaths of these performers.

Umm Kalthoum sang about impossible love and passion

UMM KALTHOUM Few performers have had such a devoted following as Umm Kalthoum, the magical *chanteuse* of Arab songs. Egyptians once sat beside their radio sets to hear the *Kawkab el-Sharq*, the Star of the Orient as she was known, sing her latest song about love and passion. Although she died in 1975, the legend lives on: mention her name and Arabs everywhere will smile, and maybe hum one of her tunes.

NEW SOUNDS The latest changes have again been influenced by the west. *Shaabi* (people) music, as sung by Ahmad Adawiya, mixes protest lyrics with a strong back beat, while *el-Jeel* (the Generation) fuses disco beats to local rhythms. The newest sound is fusion, as performed by the likes of Georges Kazazian and Natasha Atlas, and epitomized by the album *Songs from the City Victorious*.

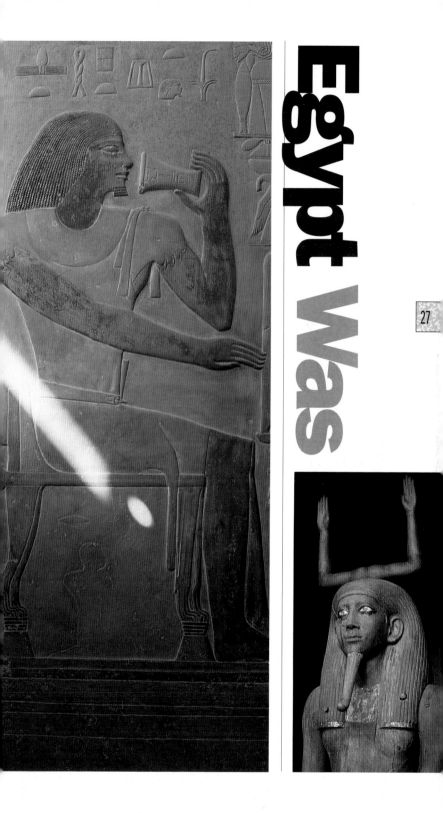

Egypt was

Some 20,000 years ago the weather in Egypt became drier, which turned plains and forests into deserts. The people who had depended on the forests now worked together to cultivate the fertile land along the Nile River. In doing so, they created one of the world's first nations.

THE TWO LANDS The spread of deserts in North Africa forced pre-dynastic hunters to settle around Egypt's oases and along the Nile. As communities developed, they learned that the annual rise and fall of the Nile would allow them to plant crops and therefore guarantee their survival. The need to make the best use of the Nile's flooding led to the creation of local administrators, who exercised power over the individual for the greater good of the community. These administrators became centralized over time and eventually developed into two opposing groups, one in the valley, the other in the delta, each with their own gods, capitals, and leaders. They are known as the Two Lands of Egypt.

THE EARLY DYNASTIC PERIOD Facts about the people who lived along the Nile during this period (ca3100–2686 BC) are few. Even material from the royal tombs, usually rich sources of information, is inconclusive: not

only were the tombs burned, but there appear to have been two of them for each king, one at Saqqara and another at Abydos. The Abydos tombs were probably symbolic, confirming the city's role as Egypt's spiritual center. The tombs at Saqqara were surrounded by graves containing numbers of the pharaoh's subjects who may have been killed to accompany the king on his final journey.

THE OLD KINGDOM The Old Kingdom—the reign of the pharaohs of the 3rd to 6th Dynasties (ca2686–2181 BC)—was a period of growing power and wealth that saw the first great flourish of ancient Egypt.

Tributes are brought to the priest Ptah Hotep, Saqqara

❏ There is no proof that anyone by the name of Menes (or Narmer, as he is also known) ever lived. Whether man or symbol, what is important about him is that around 3100 BC he achieved something rare in Egyptian history by reconciling the opposites and uniting the Two Lands. It was around that time that people from Upper Egypt conquered the north and founded a new capital, Memphis, at the border of the Two Lands, not far from present-day Cairo. They created a unified monarchy and the first Egyptian dynasty. ❏

A picture of contentment: the dwarf Seneb and his family

Imhotep, the architect for the 3rd-Dynasty pharaoh, Zoser, made the jump from the *mastaba* (oblong tomb chamber) to a series of *mastabas* built on top of each other—a step pyramid—which pharaohs of the 4th Dynasty perfected into the shining, limestone-clad pyramids of Giza. The pyramids prove the Old Kingdom's strong central authority, which maintained the large numbers of workers necessary for their construction.

THE END OF THE OLD ORDER

Authority slipped away from the 5th-Dynasty pharaohs (ca2498–2345 BC), as is obvious from the Pyramid of Unas, the last pharaoh of the dynasty. Constructed only three centuries after Imhotep built the Step Pyramid and a little over 200 years after the Great Pyramid was finished, Unas's complex was a work of inferior quality, built with a rubble core and limestone casing. It was restored by a son of Ramses II, but is once again in a state of dilapidation. By the 6th Dynasty, nobles were no longer buried near their pharaoh but in their own provinces, another step toward the end of central authority and therefore of the Old Kingdom.

Funded by the rewards of successful campaigns in Nubia, Libya, and Sinai, and encouraged by a strong central authority whose main posts were occupied by relations of the pharaoh, Egyptians made significant developments, particularly in architecture with the development and perfection of the pyramid.

29

For 150 years, the Egyptian ideal of statehood was torn apart by factional fighting between two main groups, centered around Thebes and Heracleopolis, near modern Beni Suef. Around 2050 BC a strong ruler emerged to unite them. The Middle Kingdom is considered to have ended around 1786 BC with the invasion of the Hyksos from the northeast.

UNIFIED LANDS The 11th Dynasty dates from ca2133 BC, but the start of the Middle Kingdom is associated with the accession of Menthuhotpe I in 2060. He is also known as Sehertowy, or "He who unites the Two Lands." As during the Old Kingdom, political stability brought great rewards. Not only was the country quiet, but Egyptians were able to resume their military and commercial campaigns elsewhere. During this period they were active in Nubia and Qush up the Nile and around the Mediterranean as far as Syria and Greece.

ARCHITECTURAL WONDERS This new kingdom, its capital at Thebes (modern-day Luxor), saw great advances in Egypt's culture, as suggested by the paintings in 11th- and 12th-Dynasty tombs at Beni Hasan. There was also a revival of large architectural projects, one of the most famous being the Pyramid of Amenemhat III (1842–1797 BC) in el-Faiyum. Little has survived, but the pyramid originally stood 190 feet high and was joined by a mortuary temple known as "the Labyrinth", carved from a single rock. Herodotus, visiting Egypt around 450 BC, found it a more impressive structure than the Great Pyramid at Giza.

CULT OF THE DEAD Increasing prosperity meant that people were able to pay for elaborate funerary rites, hoping to ensure a happy afterlife. The cult of Osiris grew in popularity during the Middle Kingdom, pilgrimages to the god's spiritual center at Abydos became central in the annual cycle of festivities and, as with the Old Kingdom pharaohs, it became desirable to have a false tomb, or at least a *stele* (memorial stone) erected at Abydos so that the soul would be able to make the pilgrimage after death.

Top: the Rock Tombs of Beni Hasan. Left: Menthuhotpe II, founder of the Middle Kingdom

The New Kingdom spanned three dynasties (18th–20th Dynasties, 1570–1070 BC) and its ruins suggest that this was the golden age of Egyptian art and architecture. It brought widespread development, from the introduction of the chariot to the start of the Iron Age, and also produced some particularly famous rulers, among them Tutankhamun and Ramses II.

❏ Tuthmosis I (1524–1518 BC) made a radical break with tradition when he decided to hide his tomb. No Old Kingdom pyramid or Middle Kingdom labyrinth for him. He was the first New Kingdom monarch to be buried in a deep, rock-cut tomb that was intended never to be visited, neither by priests nor tomb robbers. The place where he was buried is now known as the Valley of the Kings. From Tuthmosis I's death until the end of the New Kingdom, this was where all but one of Egypt's rulers were buried. ❏

pharaohs Seti I, Ramses II, and Ramses III are also among the finest architectural works to have survived from antiquity.

REVOLUTIONARY IDEALS
Hatshepsut's nephew, Tuthmosis III, was one of the great generals of

The impressive colossus of Ramses II at Abu Simbel

THE EGYPTIAN EMPIRE Middle Kingdom pharaohs lost control of the north of the country to the foreign Hyksos people, who probably came from Syria, but the Theban ruler Ahmosis I overran their capital of Avaris in the Delta and, in 1567 BC, chased them out of Egypt. The great Egyptian empire he founded had its capital at Thebes.

THE IMPORTANCE OF THE TEMPLE
Rather than have the cult of the dead pharaoh centered on his tomb, secret burials in the Valley of the Kings focused attention on the mortuary temple. Queen Hatshepsut (1498–1483 BC), who served as regent for her nephew, Tuthmosis III (1504–1450 BC), and then ruled as pharaoh with him, began a revival of art and architecture with her magnificent funerary temple, built like no other into the side of the hill at Deir el-Bahri. The nearby mortuary temples of the later New Kingdom

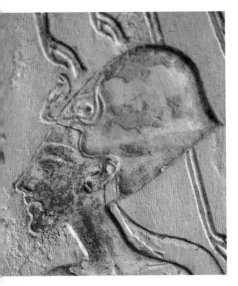

Queen Nefertiti enjoyed high status as Akhenaton's Great Wife

When Akhenaton rejected the religion of Thebes, he also discouraged the old, formal artistic styles of his predecessors and favored instead a naturalism previously unknown in Egypt. It is tempting to see the spirit of his reign expressed in the free and flowing representations of the royal family, full of affection, emotion, and even bodily functions (the first depiction of vomiting), unlike anything else in ancient Egypt. They are among the most beautiful works to have survived from antiquity. The most famous of them is the head of Akhenaton's wife, Nefertiti, now in Berlin's Egyptian Museum.

Egyptian history and under his command the armies were victorious in Africa and Asia. Amenophis III (1386–1349 BC) capitalized on his successes, and brought wealth and power to Egypt and its capital, Thebes.

The priesthood used the massive donations of gold and land to extend its power and influence. It was perhaps as a result of this that Amenophis IV (1350–1334 BC) moved his capital from Thebes to a new city he constructed at Akhetaton (modern Tell el-Amarna). Denouncing the state god Amun (and therefore also the priesthood), he promoted the sun god Aton, whom he worshiped as "the one god" in an early instance of monotheism. He also changed his own name to Akhenaton.

THE PRIESTS' REVENGE The priests of Amun had their revenge on Akhenaton when the crown passed to Akhenaton's son-in-law, the boy king Tutankhaton (1334–1325 BC). Akhenaton's general, Horemheb, and Tutankhaton's tutor, Ay, moved him and his capital back to Thebes, and encouraged Tutankhaton to restore the god Amun and change his own name to Tutankhamun. As a reward, when the young pharaoh died in the

eighth year of his reign, the priests buried him in spectacular style. Tutankhamun's successors, Ay and Horemheb, consolidated the power of the priesthood of Amun but failed to preserve their own dynasty.

A CLASSICAL REVIVAL As well as restoring the old capital and state religion, the 19th Dynasty revived classical art, but in an updated and refreshed form as monuments from the reign of Seti I suggest. Seti, a man of taste and ability, restored the empire by fighting the Libyans, Syrians, and Hittites. His tomb in the Valley of the Kings and his temple at Abydos are particularly beautiful. The Abydos temple confirms the old order: the names of Akhenaton, Smenkhkere, and even Tutankhamun were pointedly omitted from the list of kings.

THE MONUMENTAL BUILDER One pharaoh, Ramses II, particularly stands out as you move around the remains of ancient Egypt. His pre-eminence is partly due to the fact that he reigned for 67 years after Seti I's death. Although not as capable a general as his father, Ramses fought famous wars against the Hittites, notably the Battle of Qadesh (ca1275 BC), which is depicted on many of the buildings he erected. The fact that he married a

A shady "garden" of fine stone columns in Karnak Temple

Hittite princess as part of a peace treaty suggests his victory was not so conclusive. Nor were his artistic achievements as notable as Seti's temple at Abydos, but his buildings at Karnak, Luxor, Thebes, and Abu Simbel ensure his prominence.

THE LAST GREAT PHARAOH Some 40 years and six pharaohs after Ramses II's death, Ramses III inherited a country threatened from the north by Libyans and the Mediterranean "sea peoples." He fought off a succession of external and internal threats throughout his 32-year reign. His mortuary temple at Thebes was built like a fortress and during the centuries of decline that followed Ramses' death, when the priests themselves finally took over the running of the state, it was often used for that purpose.

Egypt had lost its power long before the Assyrians sacked Luxor. After a succession of ineffective rulers weakened the country, Egypt was taken with little effort by Persian armies and then by Alexander the Great. But under the Ptolemies (323–30 BC), who succeeded the young general, Egypt regained some of its glory.

ALEXANDER THE GREAT For the 700 years known as the 3rd Intermediate and Late Dynastic periods (1085–322 BC), Egypt was fought over by a succession of rulers—some native, others from Libya, Nubia, and Persia—who moved the capital from Thebes to Tanis to Sais to Memphis. In the end, Egypt became part of the Persian empire.

When Alexander the Great defeated the Persian king, Darius III, at Issus in 333 BC, Egypt was his. Alexander was an idealist and a colonizer and he wanted to Hellenize the world. He founded Alexandria as a port that would link the old worlds of the pharaohs, of Babylon, and of the Persians and Greeks.

THE FIRST PTOLEMY Alexander died in the East in 323 BC. His Macedonian general, Ptolemy, met Alexander's funerary procession and, it is said, diverted it to Alexandria, where the dead hero was buried at the center of his new city. Ptolemy, who formerly had been governor of Egypt, then became king, adding Palestine, Cyprus, and parts of Asia Minor to his lands.

Ptolemy built temples, to familiar designs, at Edfu and Kom Ombo. These and subsequent works were meant to reassure Egyptians that their gods were being respected and to confirm the Ptolemies' status as rulers by divine right. But although he was energetic in administering and unifying the Nile Valley, Ptolemy I's real interest lay to the north. Alexandria, which he had helped Alexander to lay out and which he himself had built, was becoming geographically and intellectually the heart of a new world: ancient Egypt was dead.

THE GLORY OF ALEXANDRIA During the reign of the Ptolemies who followed, Alexandria became a world city. Their navy controlled the Mediterranean and trade flowed through the city both from the east and the north.

But while the rulers of ancient Egypt had channeled their resources into the pyramids and other visible monuments, the Ptolemies used theirs to encourage science, religious thought, and literature. Alexandria's reputation as a place of the intellect, centered on the fabled Mouseion (library), shone as brilliantly as her Pharos lighthouse.

CLEOPATRA The dynasty is named after its men, but apart from the first couple of Ptolemies, it is the women who come across as being the most exceptional, and none more so than Cleopatra (51–30 BC). She was the last ruler until the modern era of an independent Egypt.

She was properly called Cleopatra VII Philopater, wife to her brother, Ptolemy XIII. In an attempt to save Egypt for herself, Cleopatra used what she considered her most suitable weapon, her femininity. When Julius Caesar defeated the Egyptian navy and her brother/husband was drowned, Cleopatra married her younger brother, Ptolemy XIV, and became Caesar's mistress, bearing him a son, Caesarion. After Caesar's death, she became the lover of his successor, Mark Antony. The arrival of Caesar Augustus brought about the deaths of Antony, Cleopatra, and Ptolemaic Egypt.

Top: the Temple of Isis, Philae
Right: relief in the Ptolemaic temple of Hathor, Dandara

Unlike Alexander, the Romans had to fight to take Egypt and continue fighting to keep it. Alexandria consolidated her role as a center of art and intellect, but much of the country suffered from the new rulers' indifference to anything but the size of the harvest.

AUGUSTAN EGYPT The Roman emperor Augustus captured a rich prize when he defeated Mark Antony and Cleopatra. Ptolemaic administrators had helped Egypt grow prosperous and the Romans left much of the system intact. But whatever happened elsewhere in Egypt, Alexandria and the Delta were too close to the Mediterranean, and therefore to Rome, to be left alone.

Augustus made changes. Greek continued as the official language, but he dismissed the Greek senate of Alexandria. Among other moves, he granted Alexandrian Jews autonomy. There were riots in Alexandria after fighting between Greeks and Jews escalated. When Roman soldiers intervened, fires broke out in the harbor and the Mouseion's library burned down.

RULE FROM ROME Augustus ensured that Egypt was the emperor's private land, ruled by the emperor's deputy. Egyptians were subjected to a census and taxed, according to their numbers, in the form of grain. It was a valuable commodity for the emperor of a grain-poor country to control.

Augustus and the emperors who succeeded him maintained a sense of continuity in Egypt. Work was resumed on the great temples begun by the Ptolemies, older temples were restored, and new buildings, like Trajan's beautiful 2nd-century kiosk at Philae, started. Roman leaders

Emperor Augustus, first Roman ruler of Egypt, in stern repose

were happy to follow the example of Alexander in being identified with the Egyptian pantheon.

Everything was done to encourage the idea that nothing had changed, except that now Egyptians were obliged to worship a divine Roman, rather than a divine Macedonian or Persian. There were even tangible benefits: around AD 115 the emperor Trajan had the Red Sea canal recut, linking the Nile to the Red Sea, and eastern trade flowed through Egypt, past the Roman garrisons at Babylon-in-Egypt (Cairo) and Alexandria.

THE HABIT OF RELIGION Egyptian civilization was old before Rome was founded and the habit of religion ran deep. This, and the newer spirit of philosophical thought, produced extraordinary results when St. Mark arrived in Alexandria to spread the word about a new religion: Christianity. Dates vary, but some time in the 1st century AD, Egyptians began converting; by late in the 2nd century, Christianity was firmly established alongside Judaism and the pagan cults.

In Egypt, Christianity attracted many converts, perhaps because religious texts had been translated into Coptic and therefore appealed to a

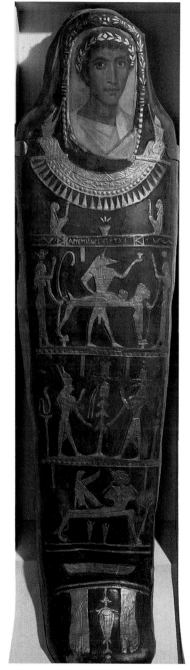

much wider audience. Christianity spread just as Roman emperors such as Decius moved against it; Egyptian stoicism clashed with Roman intolerance and Egypt provided the Church with early martyrs.

THE COPTIC CHURCH In AD 391, less than 80 years after Emperor Constantine declared Christianity the state religion, Christians attacked the temple of Serapis in Alexandria, burning its library and smashing its gods. But there was a growing division among Christians concerning the nature of Jesus. Was he a man who became part of the Trinity? Monophysites believed that he was God at all times and that the Arians, to whom Father and Son were two gods, were no better than pagans worshiping Osiris and Horus.

37

The debate continued into the 5th century, when an edict from the new imperial capital, Constantinople, declared that Christ was one person with two natures. Egyptians couldn't accept this and, ever since, the Coptic Orthodox Church has stood alone.

The simple beauty of an early Christian painting, now in the care of the Coptic Museum in Old Cairo

A fusion of Egyptian and Greek motifs on a Roman mummy case

At the beginning of the 7th century a new force appeared, with dramatic suddenness, in the old imperial world. Arab Muslims came to spread the word and rule the world, and they ended up changing Egypt forever.

38

❏ The Arabs were desert people and old habits died hard. Amr was terrified by the prospect of going on a boat, but the caliph, Omar, took his fear of water one step further. Amr suggested maintaining the capital at Alexandria, Omar refused because there would be water between himself and his army. Amr retraced his steps and returned to his camp at Babylon-in-Egypt. ❏

MESSAGE FROM THE EAST

Muhammad, born in AD 570, was a member of the Quraysh tribe of Mecca, Arabia. In his 40th year he received revelations from the archangel Gabriel. Islam, the religion based on Muhammad's Quran (the recitation of these revelations), began to unite the various tribes of the Arabian peninsula until Muhammad's death in 632. Muslims were then led by the caliphs (from the Arabic *khalifah*, meaning follower), Abu Bakr (*d.* 634), Omar (*d.* 644), and Othman (*d.* 656).

THE NEW FORCE The people of this new religion were energetic in spreading their message and, happy to do God's work and gain power and wealth in the process, Arab armies moved north. The Byzantine and Persian empires, weakened by plagues and infighting, were in no state to resist the new force. Between AD 636 and 649, the Arabs took all of the Persian and much of the Byzantine empires; by the end of this period of rapid expansion they had reached the Oxus River, the Caspian and Black seas, crossed the whole of North Africa (only stopping there, as the general said, riding his horse into

the Atlantic, because there was no more land), and then turned north into Spain.

AMR Amr Ibn el-As visited Egypt as a trader in his youth. In 639 he returned at the head of 4,000 horsemen, with whom he defeated a Byzantine army near the ruins of ancient Heliopolis. After a seven-month siege, troops at the fortress at Babylon-in-Egypt, key to the Nile and the eastern trade, surrendered in April 641. When Alexandria opened its gates a few months later, Egypt became another province of the Arab empire.

ARAB RULE Amr met little opposition to his rule once the Byzantine armies had been defeated. The native Egyptians, whether bitter over the Christian controversy that had left the Copts isolated or merely indifferent to another foreign ruler, made no protest. For some there were benefits. The Arabs had no desire to force converts to their religion and people were free to worship as they chose, on payment of a tax. No doubt Amr's popularity was helped by charging Jews and Christians taxes as "people of the Book."

E. M. Forster called him "one of the ablest and most charming men that Islam ever produced" and Amr proved to be as able a governor as he was a general. He left Alexandria to the ravages of time and salt water, and made his capital at his old camp at Fustat, outside Babylon on the Nile, the seed from which Cairo has since grown.

TULUN By 868, when Ahmed Ibn Tulun was sent to administer Egypt, the caliphs were losing their grip on the empire. Ibn Tulun seized the opportunity to exploit their

weakness and founded the first independent dynasty in Egypt since Cleopatra: the Tulunids. In his new capital, el-Qatai, north of Fustat, Islamic architecture came of age. Ibn Tulun's son, Khomaruya, embellished the capital, making it the stuff of fantastic tales, but less than 40 years after Ibn Tulun's

Ibn Tulun Mosque, Cairo, is impressive for both its grand scale and its extreme simplicity

arrival, the caliph's troops were back in control. El-Qatai was destroyed and only Ibn Tulun's mosque, one of the most perfect Islamic buildings, has survived.

Empires are always either growing or shrinking. While the caliphs in Baghdad were losing power, rival leaders in Tunisia were preparing to take it from them. Their rule was one of the most fantastic in Egypt's Islamic history.

40

❏ On August 5, 969, the Fatimid general Gohar laid out the plan for a new capital city. Ropes with bells were slung around the perimeter. At the most auspicious moment, to be determined by Gohar's astrologers, the bells would ring and the ground would be dug. But a raven landed on the ropes, the bells rang, and the building of the city began. At that moment, the planet Mars was ascendant. In Arabic it is called el-Qahir, so the new city was called el-Qahira (the triumphant), which Europeans corrupted to Cairo. ❏

THE FATIMIDS The Abbasid caliphs in Baghdad staked their right to power on their descent from the first caliphs. The Abbasids had been energetic about eliminating rivals but somehow, a powerful group had formed around the Fatimid rulers, people who claimed descent from Ali, the fourth caliph, and his wife Fatima, Muhammad's daughter. Their rivalry led to a split in theology, for the Abbasids were Sunni and the Fatimids were Shi'a Muslims. When the Fatimid ruler, el-Muizz, invaded Egypt, his army met with little resistance. Disillusioned by their rulers, Egyptians welcomed change.

THE FATIMID SUCCESSION
The Fatimid empire included North Africa, Sicily, parts of Syria, and the Hejaz. It contained great wealth, which the caliphs

El-Azhar Mosque

Crusaders make a treaty with Saladin

increased by good management. Fantastic palaces were built, as well as Islam's first university-mosque, el-Azhar. Its purpose was to educate Muslims in the way of the Shi'a, a task in which it failed; but, as the historian ibn Khaldun observed, by the time that was apparent, the dynasty had passed from innovation to exhaustion.

> ❏ Salah ed-Din is hard to separate from his legend, although his recorded achievements need no elaboration. He turned his back on the Fatimid palaces and built a citadel above Cairo. He assumed the title of sultan, reinstated Sunni rites in Egyptian mosques, and left religious authority in the hands of caliphs in Baghdad. By calling for and leading a *jihad* (holy war) to rid the Holy Land of Christians, he gave Muslims a common cause. He recaptured Jerusalem and provoked the Third Crusade. In the peace treaty of 1192, the Crusaders' presence in the area was reduced to a minor holding on the Mediterranean coast. Salah ed-Din drew a Muslim buffer across the great trade routes between Europe and the East. He died in 1193 and was buried in Damascus. ❏

AYYUBIDS On September 10, 1171, prayers were offered in Cairo's mosques for the Sunni caliph in Baghdad, not the Shi'a caliph dying in the fortress-city. Fatimid rule ended without a fight. Three years earlier, the Fatimids had been powerless to stop a Crusader army from attacking Egypt and only the intervention of forces from Damascus saved Cairo.

The Syrian troops were led by a young Kurd called Salah ed-Din, son of Ayyub. Having made the country safe, he founded a new dynasty in the name of his father and brought Egypt back into direct contact with the Muslim world.

Salah ed-Din, known as Saladin

From the first Arab invasion to the downfall of the Fatimid caliphs, power in Egypt had always been legitimized by descent from the prophet Muhammad and his followers. With the coming of the Mamluks, succession in Egypt became a fierce and often bloody test of strength and ruthlessness.

THE MAMLUKS Mamluks were slaves, mostly Turks, who were brought to Egypt, converted to Islam, taught how to fight, and given their freedom. At this point they usually joined the army of an emir. The most promising were given official posts as cup bearer, horse master, treasurer, and so on. Without hereditary sultans, the country was ruled by the most powerful Mamluk emir, his right enforced by his Mamluk soldiers. The system encouraged loyalty and ruthlessness and succeeded admirably in its intention of providing Egypt with a supply of men to fight invaders in the north and east.

❏ The first "dynasty" of Mamluk sultans (1250–1382), mostly Turks or Mongols, were called Bahri (or river) Mamluks because their barracks were on the river at Roda Island. They were succeeded by the Circassian Burgi (tower, or citadel) Mamluks (1382–1517), who were garrisoned in Salah ed-Din's citadel. ❏

A MUSLIM QUEEN Between the last Ayyubid and first Mamluk sultans, Egypt was briefly ruled by a queen (a rare thing in Islamic history). When Sultan el-Salih Ayyub died fighting the Crusaders in the Delta in 1249, his son by an earlier marriage was in

The scale of Sultan Hasan's madrasa was unprecedented

Syria. The death was concealed by his wife, Shagar el-Durr (Tree of Pearls), until the prince returned. Once back in Cairo he was murdered and his stepmother was proclaimed queen.

When the Ayyubid caliph in Damascus heard the news he said, "Woe to the nations ruled by women," and sent an army to remove her. To help her face the challenge, Shagar el-Durr married her Mamluk lover, Aybak—insisting first that he divorce his wife—and on his victory he became sultan. Eventually, he, too, ran afoul of this formidable woman and she had him killed in 1259. In retaliation, his Mamluks handed her to Aybak's first wife, who had her beaten to death with wooden bath clogs.

A MATTER OF TASTE Although their lives were filled with violence, Mamluks displayed good taste in their monuments. Inheritance of position was forbidden and inheritance of wealth was frowned upon, so the successful Mamluk had plenty of money to spend during his often short lifetime. Arab historians recorded the opulence of their houses, but Mamluks also expressed their power and hopes for remembrance after their death through public buildings. The inscription outside Qalawun's mosque in Cairo glorifies his name and lets us know how quickly it was built, speed being necessary so that the great project would be finished before the sultan met his end.

Much of the present-day appearance of Islamic Cairo was shaped during this period. Schools, hospitals, markets, caravanserai for visiting traders, and public fountains were built and endowed, the Mamluks perhaps hoping to obtain good favor in heaven for their charitable works. The rest of the country also benefited from Mamluk taste and talent. More citadels are now being uncovered across the Sinai desert.

THE COMING OF THE OTTOMANS
The Ottoman Turks, another tribe that came out of central Asia, took Constantinople in 1453 and by the 16th century, they were threatening to move south to Egypt. The Mamluks, weakened by their own squabbling, were unequal to the fight and, only 19 years after the late flowering of Mamluk architecture under the Sultan Qaytbay, the Ottomans were in Cairo. The last Mamluk sultan was hanged from Bab Zuwayla and another long period of foreign domination began.

43

The Ottomans showed little interest in Egypt. It was just one part of an immense empire, and their desire was that it should be quiet and pay taxes. Their gain was Egypt's loss.

EGYPT'S MANY LOSSES The independent Mamluk ruler of Egypt was hung in front of his people in 1517, and the last Abbasid caliph died in Cairo in 1538. By then, Europeans had sailed to the Americas and India and broken the Mamluk monopoly on eastern trade. Egypt, once a wealthy, independent state controlling a vital trade route, now found itself with reduced revenues and facing demands for tribute from an indifferent foreign ruler.

A LAND OF LEGEND Under the Ottomans, who periodically banned Christian ships from the Red Sea for fear of their involvement with the holy places, Egypt became isolated. In its seclusion, something strange happened: the monuments along the Nile were forgotten abroad, as well as the churches, mosques, and palaces. A country and people that Europeans had little difficulty in understanding some centuries earlier became a place of myth and legend. The 18th-century explorers, like James Bruce, who came looking for the source of the Nile, found themselves laughed at when they recounted their tales of travel—such things surely could not be!

MAMLUKS AND JANISSARIES
Authority in Egypt was officially held by a governor appointed in Istanbul; it was enforced on the ground by janissaries—Ottoman troops recruited from the Balkans. But with no one to replace the tax-collecting, administrating Mamluks, the Ottomans had no choice but to perpetuate the system of purchasing and training slaves. A power game developed between janissaries and Mamluks, which weakened both of them and threatened to ruin the country.

It was then that the British and French, looking for faster access to their eastern colonies, considered the possibilities of passing overland through Egypt. The landing of Napoleon Bonaparte and a French army in 1798 brought an end to Egypt's isolation and, in effect, to Ottoman rule. Napoleon brought learned men as well as soldiers to Egypt. The *Description de L'Egypte*, the result of their researches, was the first attempt to systematically record Egyptian monuments.

A mashrabiya lattice window of the 16th- and 17th-century Bayt el-Suhaymi, one of Cairo's finest merchant houses

44

Like the Ottomans, the French and British were drawn to Egypt because of its command of eastern trade routes. But while their sights were set elsewhere, a Macedonian-born commander in the Ottoman army had his eye on controlling the Nile.

❏ Muhammad Ali's main rivals were the Mamluk *beys* (nobles). In March 1811, his position secure, he invited 470 Mamluk *beys* and their followers to a banquet in Cairo's Citadel. As they left, he ambushed them. According to local legend, all were killed but one, who escaped over the walls on his horse. ❏

THE EUROPEAN WARS For nine years (1798–1807), Egypt saw a succession of foreign armies coming up the Nile shores in what the contemporary historian el-Jabarti called "a period of great battles, of ghastly events, of disastrous facts, of frightful calamities, of constantly growing evils." The French arrived as liberators under their idealistic general. The British followed them, also as liberators. Then the Ottoman sultan in Constantinople sent an army of mercenaries.

Visitors at the foot of the Giza Pyramids, ca1895

MUHAMMAD ALI After the French army had been forced out of Egypt in 1801, the Ottoman troops attempted to change the balance of power by eliminating the Mamluks. But there was no money to pay troops in Cairo and a contingent of Albanian mercenaries mutinied. Their revolt became a rallying call for the many who were dissatisfied with Ottoman rule. In 1805, the people of Cairo insisted that Muhammad Ali, commander of the Albanian troops and the most powerful figure in Egypt, be made their ruler.

45

THE MAKING OF MODERN EGYPT
Muhammad Ali brought direct rule back to Egypt after three centuries and founded a dynasty that lasted until the revolution of 1952. During his reign as pasha from 1805 to 1848, Egypt was transformed, roads and railroads laid, canals cleared, agriculture encouraged, industries started, and the military reorganized. While his motives weren't entirely altruistic—he made himself owner of all land in Egypt—it was his inspiration that laid the foundations of modern Egypt.

Egypt was too important for the 19th-century European powers to ignore. The Suez Canal, the cotton harvest, access to Africa, and its potential as a market for European goods meant that foreign governments were unenthusiastic about Egyptian independence.

❏ After Tawfiq's succession, a faction of the army objected to British and French control of Egypt's finances. To appease them, one of their officers, Ahmad 'Urabi, was offered a cabinet post. But that didn't stop riots breaking out. On July 11, 1882, British ships bombarded Alexandria and a month later 20,000 British troops landed under the pretext of restoring peace. 'Urabi and his supporters were defeated at the battle of Tell el-Kabir. ❏

RAILROAD OR CANAL The vigor of Muhammad Ali's reign died with him. His successor, Abbas (1848–1854), sacked his foreign advisers and canceled their projects, although the British-built railroad was continued between Alexandria, Cairo, and Suez. Abbas's successor, Said (1854–1863), was more sympathetic to French interests and granted De Lesseps the Suez Canal concession, but under terms that proved financially disastrous for Egypt. In order to meet the terms, Said had to borrow money from abroad, a move that subsequently made Egypt financially dependent on European backers.

EGYPT DEVELOPED In 1866, three years after coming to power, Muhammad Ali's grandson, Ismail, negotiated with the Ottoman sultan to change the succession to ensure that his own children inherited his position, and for permission for Egypt to maintain its own army.

More important still were his plans to redevelop Cairo. Ismail had lived in Paris as a student, and when he returned there in 1867 he was so impressed by Haussmann's transformation of the old medieval city that he decided that his old Arab capital should be redesigned along similar lines. In the next couple of years, Ismail initiated a building boom that has left Cairo with broad boulevards, palaces, public gardens, Cairo central station, an opera house, and scores of other buildings. Ismail explained his intentions at the opening of the Suez Canal in 1869 when he announced his belief that Egypt now belonged to Europe, not Africa. It did, but not as he imagined.

Queen Victoria's initials on the British Embassy gates, Cairo

THE VEILED PROTECTORATE Egypt earned enormous profits in the 1860s by meeting the shortfall in cotton caused by the American Civil War. But there wasn't enough to finance Ismail's plans, compensate for financial mismanagement, and service Egypt's growing overseas debts. Egypt was broke and had already sold her shares in the Suez Canal to Britain by 1879, when the British and French governments persuaded the Ottoman sultan to depose Ismail. The throne passed to Tawfiq (1879–1892) and his son Abbas II Hilmi (1892–1914), but by 1882 a British consul-general and a corps of British civil servants were running the country in the name of the *khedive* (viceroy).

THE INDEPENDENCE MOVEMENT
There is no starting point for the independence movement. It grew among all classes of Egyptians, fueled by increasing resentment at foreign presence and intervention in Egypt's affairs. When Turkey allied

The belvedere of the Edwardian-Moorish Old Cataract Hotel, on the Nile in Aswan

itself to Germany in World War I, Egypt, still officially Turkey's colony, was finally annexed by the British. In 1918, Egyptians approached London, not Istanbul, for their independence.

THE WAFD Saad Zaghlul, a British-appointed minister for education, demanded the right for an Egyptian delegation to attend the international Paris peace conference of 1919. The British refusal led to an uprising. The force of that protest showed that discontent with British rule was widespread. Zaghlul and his Wafd (Delegation) party were at the forefront of the independence movement, and they won a landslide victory in the 1924 elections after Egypt declared itself independent. But the British remained, pulling their troops back to Suez Canal bases in 1936 and still hesitating over withdrawal 18 years later.

As the dissatisfaction of Egyptians came to a head after World War II, the country became increasingly unstable. In 1952, the Egyptian army moved to restore stability and 150 years of rule by Muhammad Ali's dynasty ended.

AFTER WORLD WAR II Egypt remained officially neutral throughout the war, although factions in the government showed support for the Nazis in the hope they would rid Egypt of the British. With the Germans defeated and the British still in place, Egypt was in turmoil.

King Farouk, who had come to the throne in 1936, alienated his subjects with his decadence and political mismanagement. The old establishment was corrupt and nepotistic, and the Wafd party had lost its credibility as champion of independence in 1942, when British tanks surrounded the royal palace to ensure the appointment of a Wafdist prime minister. Meanwhile, other parties were becoming increasingly active and the Muslim Brotherhood, originally a reformist Islamic group, adopted a political agenda encouraging violent struggle.

THE FREE OFFICERS Several army officers were also opposed to the government and the British. The first aim of the Free Officers, Muhammad Naguib and the young Gamal Abdel Nasser among them, was to force the British out of Egypt. Meanwhile another disaster struck: in 1948–1949, Egypt and its Arab neighbors went to war with the newly created state of Israel and returned home after a crushing defeat. Rumors of Egyptian soldiers fighting with defective arms increased sympathy for the dissidents. In 1948, the Muslim Brotherhood struck out and assassinated the prime minister, but a couple of months later the Brotherhood's founder, Hassan el-Banna, was killed, large numbers of his supporters were arrested, and the group was officially outlawed in Egypt.

BLACK SATURDAY The British base at the Suez Canal was one of the world's largest military establishments and, as the situation within Egypt deteriorated, it became a target for patriotic groups. On January 25, 1952, retaliating against these attacks, British troops surrounded a police post at Isma'iliya and ordered the auxiliaries inside to surrender. They refused, and 41

Anti-British rioters attacking foreign interests in Cairo

Egyptians were killed in the fight. On the following day—known as Black Saturday—foreign interests were attacked throughout Egypt. Cairo's famous Shepheard's Hotel and the Turf Club were obvious colonial targets, and both were destroyed.

THE REVOLUTION On the night of July 22, the Free Officers and their supporters took over key posts and both the old government and King Farouk were toppled in a bloodless coup. It was a popular move, greeted with widespread celebrations. General Naguib was appointed president and prime minister of the new republic, with Nasser as his deputy.

THE NASSER YEARS Nasser was president by May 1954 and within six months had negotiated the withdrawal of British troops. The terms were something of a compromise, but agreement had been reached and he was seen as his country's savior, the man who could guarantee Egyptian independence. Encouraged by this, he pushed through plans for building the Aswan High Dam and proposed to

President Nasser joined forces with President Tito of Yugoslavia to form the Non-Aligned Movement

finance part of it by nationalizing the Suez Canal, in which Egypt owned no shares. The move prompted a joint British, French, and Israeli invasion. When Nasser stood up to them they were forced by international pressure to withdraw, and he became an Arab hero.

❏ On July 26, 1952, King Farouk was escorted aboard the royal yacht to sail into exile. His extravagances didn't end there, though. Living in Switzerland, he maintained his reputation as a gambler and a cigar smoker. King Farouk died in exile, but was allowed back to Egypt for a quiet burial in a tomb with others of his dynasty, in Cairo's City of the Dead. His son, King Fuad II, who was a child-king for 11 months until the monarchy was outlawed, lives in exile in Europe. ❏

After three damaging wars with Israel, Egypt risked the anger of its Arab partners by talking to the enemy. The resulting Egyptian-Israeli peace treaty made peace possible.

50

1967 In six days during the summer of 1967, Israeli forces defeated the combined armies and air forces of Egypt, Jordan, Syria, and Lebanon. The Israelis took Sinai, crossed the Suez Canal, and were ready to march on Cairo when cease-fire terms were agreed. Nasser, autocratic but ever popular, resigned after the defeat, but mass demonstrations brought him back and he continued as president until his death in 1970. More than 3 million people attended his funeral.

SADAT'S REVOLUTION
Vice-President Anwar Sadat assumed power on Nasser's death. A Free Officer, he was neither as charismatic nor as popular as his predecessor, and there were doubts about his ability as leader. But within two years of becoming president, Sadat was secure enough to push through sweeping changes, and Soviet links were cut as Egypt turned toward the West.

Sadat's next move was more unexpected: in October 1973, Egypt attacked Israeli forces in Sinai. While the October War was not the great victory Egyptians sometimes claim, the Israeli defensive line in Sinai was breached and Egyptian forces were

still intact when the cease-fire was arranged. The myth of Israeli invincibility had been destroyed. As both the Israeli and Egyptian militaries managed to end the war with their pride intact, the way was left open for reconciliation.

OPENING DOORS In November 1977, Sadat shocked Arab leaders and Egyptians, too, by speaking at the Israeli Knesset in Jerusalem. Many Egyptians saw it as an act of weakness and betrayal, but it led to the peace agreement with Israel, signed in 1979 at Camp David, and to Egypt receiving massive aid from the USA. Arab countries isolated Egypt, removing the Arab League headquarters to Tunis. This further encouraged

Egypt and Israel had been at war for over 30 years when the Camp David treaty was signed

❑ Egypt became embroiled in the Cold War when it turned to the Soviet Union for funds after the USA refused help with building the Aswan High Dam. Mementos of the Soviet years litter Egypt—the Mugamma building in Cairo is one—but Arab socialism never strayed toward the Soviet model. ❑

Sadat's open door policies, attracting foreign investment and easing currency restrictions to revive Egypt's war-torn economy.

SADAT'S DOWNFALL Sadat's economic policies created great wealth, but only for a minority; they widened the gap between rich and poor that the revolution was supposed to close. Inflation made the situation worse and conditions were so tense that when food subsidies were lifted in 1977, there were riots in the cities until the government changed its mind. The lack of foresight that led to the riots suggested that Sadat had lost touch with his country.

While economic policies led to social unrest, the president's easing

❏ By the terms of the March 1979 accord, signed at Camp David under President Jimmy Carter's patronage, Israel and Egypt recognized each other's rights according to international law. The treaty has been widely criticized for not being explicit on important issues, and both Israelis and Egyptians have complained of a "cold peace". But without Camp David as a precedent, other Arab-Israeli negotiations would have been more difficult to arrange. ❏

President Hosni Mubarak

51

of political repression had more damaging effects for him. The Wafd regained some of its credibility as a viable opponent of the government, the Muslim Brotherhood came out of hiding, and a host of other parties attracted supporters. On October 6, 1981, at a ceremony to celebrate Egypt's victory in the 1973 war, Sadat was assassinated. Egyptians cite his standing up to greet the soldiers who had come to kill him as proof of how little he understood the anger he had stirred.

The Sphinx and the
Pyramid of Cheops, Giza

Quba
Palace

Merryland

Airport

**Masr el Gadida
(Heliopolis)**

Nasser's
Tomb

Baron
Empain's
Villa

ABBASIYA

MADÎNET
NASR

Cairo
Stadium

EL
WAYLI

Sadat's
Tomb

**EL QÂHIRA
(CAIRO)**

Gebel   el   Muqattam

Madînet
el Muqattam

```
0        1        2 km
0              1 mile
```

D

E

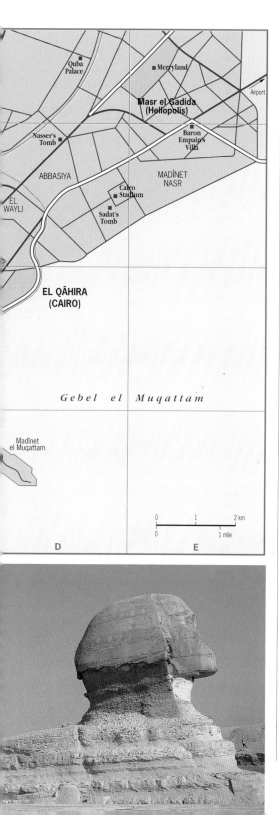

Gazetteer
Cairo

Cairo

FIRST SIGHT Many flights into Cairo (el-Qahira) arrive at night. From the air, Africa's largest city appears as a galaxy of movement and light, but by day, its size and complexity can be disorienting and that glittering night vision can seem illusory. However, in spite of the population explosion, industrial development, economic hardship, and now terrorism, Cairo does still retain some of the qualities of the "Mother of the World."

GETTING ON TOP OF THE CITY One of the best ways to make sense of Cairo on arrival is to get on top of it. From the viewing platform on the Cairo Tower, or the terrace outside Muhammad Ali's mosque at the Citadel, it is possible to follow the city's lifeline, the Nile, identify its various landmarks, and see how the desert hems it in. Another way to reach an understanding is via the city's origins.

BEFORE CAIRO There were settlements along the Nile long before what we know as Cairo came into existence, but you have to look hard to find them. Little remains at the early dynastic Egyptian capital of Memphis, 14 miles away, or at the Old Kingdom religious center of Heliopolis. Persians and Romans left more of a mark, building fortified posts (the ruins at Babylon-in-Egypt) at what is known as Old Cairo, where the river was more easily crossed, and where a canal from the Red Sea joined the Nile. But it wasn't until the Arab conquest that the seeds of modern Cairo began to sprout.

At sunset thousands of muezzins call the believers for prayers

The lights of Cairo seem to go on for ever, bisected by the dark Nile

OLD CAIRO When the Arab general Amr took control of Egypt in AD 641, the capital was at Alexandria. Amr would have been happy to keep it there, but the caliph, Omar, in Baghdad refused to allow the Nile to come between him and his general. So Amr went back and built his settlement where he first pitched his tent. The site, near the Roman emperor Trajan's fort at Babylon-in-Egypt, became known as Fustat (the camp).

ISLAMIC CAIRO At the end of the 9th century, the Abbassid ruler Ibn Tulun constructed el-Qatai, a new settlement. What we know as Islamic Cairo wasn't founded until 969, when the Fatimid caliphs from Tunisia usurped Baghdad's power and built their fabled palace enclosure, el-Qahira. When Salah ed-Din ended Fatimid rule in 1171, he recognized the difficulty of protecting the Fatimids' royal enclosure and built the Citadel on an outcrop of the Muqattam Hills. It has housed one of Cairo's most important garrisons ever since.

MODERN CAIRO The 19th-century ruler Muhammad Ali believed his family would remain in power as long as they continued to live in the Citadel, but his grandson ignored his advice. Ismail did much to develop Cairo along the lines of Europe's great cities and set an example by building himself the palace of Abdin down among the new developments in 1874. Five years later he was forced to abdicate. The "Europeanization" and "Americanization" of the capital has continued without much interruption for more than a century, which is why, at first sight, downtown Cairo looks so familiar to tourists.

DON'T BE FOOLED BY APPEARANCES However familiar the city may seem, it is unique in its makeup. Built and rebuilt over a thousand years, it is home to people of the Nile Valley, the Delta, and the deserts, as well as a sizable population of foreign businessmen, scholars, and refugees. Each community has its own gathering place. Downtown Cairo is the place where the city's sophisticates used to meet, which is why it looks familiar, but you don't have to go far from the center to find yourself in an entirely different world. That is part of the city's attraction and one of the reasons why, if you can bear the pollution, it is so rewarding to climb down from the terrace or tower and walk around.

55

WHAT'S IN A NAME?
The western name for the city—Cairo—comes from the Arabic *el-Qahira* (the victorious), supposedly given to the Fatimid city because Mars, the victorious planet, was ascendant when the city was founded. However, in Arabic both the city and the country of which it is the capital are known by an older name, Misr.

Pharaonic Cairo

▶▶▶ El-Haram (the Pyramids of Giza) 52A1

11 miles southwest of central Cairo. Site open daily 7 AM–dusk;
Pyramid of Cheops closes at 4 PM; Solar Boat Museum open
daily 9–4. Admission: Plateau: expensive;
Pyramid interior: expensive; Solar Boat: expensive

Already in ancient times, the Pyramids of Giza were considered one of the Seven Wonders of the World. Today they are the only "wonder" to have survived the ravages of time, almost intact. They are, without doubt, the most famous and probably the most photographed monuments in the world. But in spite of all the superlatives, a first visit to the pyramids can be disappointing, perhaps because they have become so familiar that when you stand in front of them they can seem smaller or less impressive than expected. Pictures usually show the pyramids in the middle of the desert, but suburban Cairo has crept up to the foot of the Giza Plateau and takes away from the splendor of the view. It takes time, walking around them or watching them from the desert, before you realize how grand they are. The best time to visit is around sunrise or sundown when it is cooler and the light is at its best, or at night when most of the camel drivers, touts, and soft-drink sellers have gone home.

The Great Pyramid of Khufu (Cheops)▶▶▶ (4th Dynasty) is the first pyramid to appear as you approach them along Pyramids Road. As it is the oldest and largest pyramid in this group it is hard to avoid some statistics. Cheops' pyramid is built with around 2.3 million limestone blocks, each weighing an average 2.75 tons—6.8 million tons in all. Originally 482 feet high, the loss of its shiny outer casing has lowered it to 449 feet. From the entrance, a long, narrow, and low corridor descends into an unfinished room (sometimes closed), probably intended as a burial chamber. It is not clear why this chamber was abandoned. An ascending corridor leads to another unfinished room known as the Queen's Chamber

GETTING IN
You need a separate ticket to explore the secrets inside the Great Pyramid. It is a hot and exhausting business, so take water and wear comfortable clothing: for much of the climb you will be bent double or crawling on hands and knees.

56

The Pyramids of Giza (from left to right): Mycerinus, Chephren, and Cheops

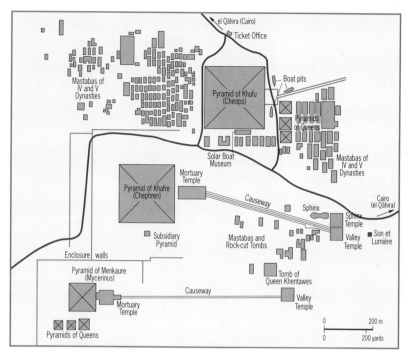

Mastabas of IV and V Dynasties

Ticket Office

el Qâhira (Cairo)

Boat pits

Pyramid of Khufu (Cheops)

Pyramids of Queens

Solar Boat Museum

Mastabas of IV and V Dynasties

Mortuary Temple

Pyramid of Khafre (Chephren)

Causeway

Sphinx

Cairo (el Qâhira)

Sphinx Temple

Subsidiary Pyramid

Mastabas and Rock-cut Tombs

Valley Temple

Son et Lumière

Enclosure walls

Pyramid of Menkaure (Mycerinus)

Causeway

Tomb of Queen Khentawes

Valley Temple

Mortuary Temple

Pyramids of Queens

0   200 m

0   200 yards

and through the magnificent 154-foot-long Great Gallery to the main burial chamber. In the undecorated King's Chamber, built in red granite, the sarcophagus lies empty: the mummy was never found.

Surrounding the pyramid, only fragments of paving from Cheops' mortuary temple were found, while the causeway and valley temple are buried under the village of Nazlet el-Samman, making excavation difficult. The three smaller neighboring pyramids belonged to Cheops' queens or sisters. Five boat pits have also been found, of which three were empty and one contained a dismantled solar boat, now housed in the specially constructed Solar Boat Museum. In 1987 another boat was found, perfectly preserved under a canopy of limestone blocks. It has been left under the sand.

The enigma of the sands: who built the Sphinx, when and why?

The Sphinx▶▶▶ is called *Abu 'l-Hol* (the Father of Terror) in Arabic, which sums up the mysterious aura surrounding this strange figure with a lion's body, a human face, and a royal beard. Tradition suggests that Chephren found an outcrop of soft limestone where his father Cheops had quarried stone for his pyramid and had the Sphinx carved on it, in his own image. However, some archeologists have claimed that the Sphinx was built by people of a lost civilization who lived over 2,600 years before Chephren. Herodotus, who visited the pyramids around 460 BC, doesn't mention the Sphinx, probably because it was already buried in the sand. A *stele* (memorial stone)

Cairo

The unavoidable, ever-present camel drivers

between the front paws tells the story of how Tuthmosis IV (18th Dynasty) dreamed that if he cleared away the sand he would become pharaoh, a dream that came true. The Sphinx's nose fell off after Turkish and French troops used the face for target practice. Today all the sand has been cleared away, but the Sphinx is threatened by incompetent restoration, rising ground water, and pollution.

The Pyramid Complex of Khafre (Chephren)▶▶▶ (4th Dynasty) is well preserved as it was partly buried under the sand until 1853, when the French archeologist Mariette started excavating. The exceptional diorite statue of the pharaoh (Egyptian Museum, Room 42) came from the limestone and granite valley temple just behind the Sphinx. Some believe that the pharaoh's corpse was brought to the valley temple to be mummified, while others believe that it was mummified in Memphis and brought here for the "Opening of Mouth" ceremony. Mourners carried the mummy along the causeway, still partly visible, to the mortuary temple at the foot of the pyramid. Among the stones used for this temple, the largest was 45 feet long and weighed 180 tons.

Originally both the Pyramid of Chephren and the Great Pyramid were covered with polished limestone, but only the upper part of Chephren's retains traces of this covering. Perhaps because of this, and because it stands higher on the plateau, Chephren's pyramid looks taller than the Great Pyramid, although at 447 feet (originally 469 feet), it is slightly smaller. The pyramid has two entrances, both closed to the public. An empty sarcophagus was found in the undecorated burial chamber.

The Pyramid Complex of Menkaure (Mycerinus)▶▶▶ (4th Dynasty) is the smallest of the group. The 203-foot-high pyramid marks the decline of centralized power and the end of the great pyramid-building era. The pyramid was started by Mycerinus, Chephren's successor, and finished by his son. This is often called the Red Pyramid because of its red Aswan granite casing.

The interior, now opened to the public, contains an unfinished chamber, probably used for storing the royal canopic jars (which held the mummified viscera), and an underground burial chamber where human remains (now believed to belong to a 26th-Dynasty king) were found in a basalt sarcophagus.

The pyramid is flanked by three smaller subsidiary pyramids and, to the east, stand the remains of the funerary temple.

Ride

A desert ride

One of the most pleasant ways to experience the desert and see some rarely visited monuments is to ride by horse or camel from Giza to Saqqara. The ride takes around three hours, one way, and is best started early in the morning to avoid the searing heat of the midday sun. Beware of the desert wind in winter. You can rent camels near the Sphinx, but they are usually more expensive and less comfortable than horses from the stables nearby (MG and AA stables are recommended). Make it clear from the start that you want to take the desert route past Zawiyet el-Aryan. As you head for the desert, leaving the green cultivated land to your left, there are marvelous views of the Giza pyramids behind you.

After little more than an hour, you reach the **Zawiyet el-Aryan pyramids▶**. The 4th-Dynasty Unfinished Pyramid never made it beyond its granite foundations; the Layer Pyramid (probably 3rd-Dynasty), with layers of small blocks, looks as though it was intended to form a step pyramid. After half an hour, you'll come to the twin **Sun Temples of Abu Ghurab▶**, dedicated to Ra, the sun god of Heliopolis, which stand at the edge of agricultural land. The courtyard of the Sun Temple of Nyuserre (5th Dynasty) contains an alabaster altar where cattle were sacrificed, and the base of a solar obelisk. Beyond the ruined Sun Temple of Userkaf are the four 5th-Dynasty pyramid complexes of Abusir. Although the **Pyramid of Sahure▶** is badly damaged, it is possible to crawl through a narrow passage to the burial chamber.

Farther along are the pyramid complexes of Nyuserre, Neferikare, and Neferefre; the first and the last were never finished as the pharaohs died young. The Step Pyramid of Saqqara is now in front of you, half an hour away. Beyond Saqqara are the four Pyramids of Dahshur.

Travelers riding around 40 centuries of Egyptian history

The Great Pyramid in Giza is one of the world's most famous monuments, but few realize that it was surrounded by more than 80 others along the Nile near Cairo. Until recently, little was known about the way pyramids were built and there are still disagreements as to what purpose they were intended to fulfill.

PYRAMIDAMANIA
More than 80 pyramids were built between Giza and el-Faiyum. Many of them have crumbled, but for the dedicated it is still possible to visit others, including: the Pyramids of Zawiyet el-Aryan (see page 59), pyramids in North and South Saqqara (pages 62–65), the Pyramids of Dahshur (page 59), and the Pyramids of Hawara, Lahun, Lisht, and Maidum (Meidum), all near el-Faiyum (page 117).

Houses of Eternity A 12th-century Arab historian wrote that "All things fear time, but time fears the Pyramids." That is how the pyramid builders wanted it because they believed that the well-being of their *ka* (soul) in the after-life depended on their corpses being preserved intact. The accepted theory is that the Houses of Eternity, as the pyramids were called, were built as enormous, impregnable tombs designed to protect the body and provide accommodation for the visiting *ka* (often represented in paintings and sculpture as a bird). Pyramids were served by temples at which rituals and offerings were made for the dead.

How to build a pyramid The perfect triangular form of the Giza pyramids evolved during the 3rd Dynasty. Earlier dynasties built tombs below ground and covered them with *mastabas* (mounds of mud brick and plaster). The 3rd-Dynasty architect Imhotep had the means and the inspiration to build his *mastabas* in stone and then to mount them one on top of the other, creating the Step Pyramid at Saqqara. His master stroke is the earliest known large stone building. From there, it was just a short step to the smooth-surfaced, gilt-capped pyramids at Giza: it took less than 200 years to perfect the pyramid form.

Each limestone block of the Pyramid of Cheops was precisely placed to prevent pressure building up at any one point

A design fault in the structure of the "Collapsed Pyramid" of Maidum sent stresses outward rather than inward

Statistics continue to astound admirers of the pyramids. The Great Pyramid, 449 feet high, was built out of 2.3 million stone blocks that are estimated to weigh 6.8 million tons. Recent excavations have produced an even more impressive fact: the pyramids were built not by slaves, as was previously thought, but by willing laborers, paid with lentils, onions, and leeks and led by a few thousand skilled craftsmen.

Only periods of wealth and stability could provide the necessary authority and administration for such an undertaking; it is not by chance that pyramids were first built when Egypt was newly unified, nor that building stopped when centralized power broke down at the end of the 6th Dynasty. Perhaps the act of building pyramids was itself a unifying factor, a visible symbol of a common goal, an expression of a hierarchy: pharaoh up on top, a broad base of peasants supporting him from below.

COSTLY BUSINESS
"Now, the sum that was spent on radishes, onions, and garlic for the workmen, is marked in Egyptian characters on the Pyramid... If these things be so, how much besides may we calculate was spent on the iron with which they worked, and on bread and clothes for the workmen..."
Herodotus (ca460 BC)
The Histories

The enormity of the building task at Giza is awe-inspiring

Of stars and staircases The perfection of the construction of the pyramids' begs the question which has yet to be answered conclusively: what purpose do they serve? This enigma continues to exercise imaginations and intellects around the world. Archeologists are almost united in accepting that pyramids were built as tombs, and as homes for the pharaoh's *ka*, his living soul in the afterlife. But they disagree about other functions.

Some have loaded the pyramids with symbolism, claiming that their sides represent the sun's rays and that the steps of the Saqqara pyramid represent a staircase to heaven. Earlier Arab travelers thought they were filled with treasure, while 18th-century Europeans believed they were the ancient granaries in which Joseph stored the corn that saved Egypt from famine. A modern theory suggests that the layout of the pyramids mirrors stars in the Orion constellation and that the size of the pyramids reflects the brightness of the stars to which they refer, all of this being an attempt to unite the dead pharaohs with Orion, the constellation of Osiris, the god of the afterlife.

Cairo

PICNIC IN THE DESERT

Until the new Rest House opens, there is nowhere on site to buy food or drinks. As it takes at least a day to visit the highlights of Saqqara, it's a good idea to take a picnic. Egyptians often like to eat in the ruins of the 6th-century Monastery of Jeremiah, just off the parking lot, but if it's not too hot then an even better picnicking spot is available in the desert beyond Zoser's mortuary temple. From there you can admire Imhotep's genius while having lunch and then, as a sweet dessert, visit some exquisite *mastabas*.

62

The forever-young king, Ramses II, resting in Memphis

▶▶ Memphis   52B1

Open: daily 8–5 (4 in winter). Admission: moderate

The ruins of Memphis, in the sleepy village of Mit Rahina, give little idea of the glory of the world's first imperial city, but still make a pleasant excursion into the countryside.

The legendary King Menes (ca3100 BC), who united the southern valley and the northern delta, was the first pharaoh to wear the double crown of Upper and Lower Egypt. Symbolically, on the exact spot where the valley met the delta, he founded his new capital. Memphis became a magnificent city and its importance as a commercial center and as the cult-center for the God Ptah (the creator of the gods and the world) helped it retain its importance, even after the capital was moved to Thebes and later to Alexandria. The temple of Ptah was the city's most impressive building, but like the other temples and public places it was destroyed long ago. Memphis's houses and palaces, built like so many village houses today in mud brick, have also disappeared.

The site of Memphis is now a pleasant open-air museum. A limestone colossus of Ramses II as a young king, housed in a concrete pavilion, and a fine New Kingdom sphinx are the star exhibits. Both of them probably stood in front of the temple of Ptah. Other sculptures found on the site lie scattered around the garden, but the more important pieces are displayed in the Egyptian Museum (see pages 88–91).

▶▶▶ Saqqara   52B1

Open: daily 8–5 (4 in winter). Admission: expensive

The necropolis of Saqqara, on a desert plateau 3.5 miles to the west of the ancient capital of Memphis, contains the tombs of Old Kingdom royalty and nobility. The burial site, about 4 miles long and a mile wide, was one of the

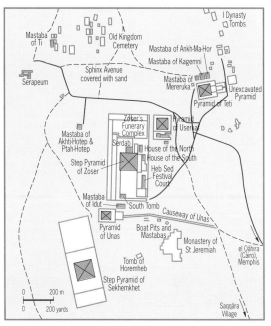

The first large stone building in the world: the Step Pyramid of Saqqara

largest and most important in Egypt and remained in use for more than 3,000 years, but much of it has still to be excavated. The necropolis is divided into two main areas, North and South Saqqara. As the most interesting monuments are in the northern part, only visitors with time and dedication venture south to see the collapsed pyramids.

The Step Pyramid Complex of Zoser▶▶▶ is the largest funerary complex in the necropolis. The Step Pyramid was completed for King Zoser around 2650 BC by the architect Imhotep, who was later deified for his achievements. This was not only the first pyramid to be built, but also the world's first large stone building and therefore a starting point for architecture. Imhotep began by building a single stone *mastaba*, the traditional funerary monument, and then added four and then another six smaller *mastabas*, one on top of the other. The finished structure, a stepped pyramid covered in a shiny white limestone, stood 204 feet high and measured 358 feet by 411 feet around its base. Inside, a 92-foot-deep shaft leads to the burial chamber and several galleries. The original entrance is now blocked and access is only possible through a later forced entrance (and with special permission from the Department of Antiquities).

The pyramid is surrounded by a vast funerary complex, which was enclosed by a limestone wall. Little of the wall is visible today, apart from the reconstructed entrance gate. A colonnade leads from the gate to a wide courtyard

EARLY GRAFFITI
Inside the corridor of the House of the South is some of the world's earliest graffiti, dating back to the New Kingdom. The visitors, who were scribes writing in a cursive hieroglyphic script, scribbled their admiration of Zoser's achievements.

Ptah-Hotep inspects the gifts and tributes that are brought by the estates from North and South

THE HEB SED FESTIVAL
Traditionally this five-day festival was held in Memphis after 30 years of a king's reign; occasionally it took place more frequently as a symbolical renewal of the king's vitality. All the rituals had to be performed twice, once as the King of the South and once as the King of the North. In one ceremony the king ran between the two altars representing each region in a symbolic reunion of the country. Officials came from all over Egypt to witness the festival and renew their allegiance.

with the Step Pyramid in the north. Ahead is the South Tomb, a deep vertical shaft that may have stored the king's viscera. To the right of the colonnade is the Heb Sed Court, seen nowhere else in Egypt and now completely rebuilt. Inside the court, site of the Heb Sed festival, a double row of dummy chapels represents the shrines of Upper Egypt and Lower Egypt. Farther north are the House of the South and the House of the North, which are thought to represent the archaic shrines of Upper and Lower Egypt. Nearby is the Serdab, containing a copy of a statue of King Zoser.

The Pyramid of Unas▶▶, the last king of the 5th Dynasty, is small and badly preserved, but there are some fine hieroglyphic inscriptions on the alabaster and limestone walls of the burial chamber. These are known as the Pyramid Texts, a collection of the first written versions of ancient funerary prayers and instructions. The deterioration of the reliefs led to the pyramid's permanent closure in 1998. The causeway, a 1,100-yard-long covered corridor that runs from the mortuary temple to the pyramid, is one of the best preserved in Egypt. The pyramid is surrounded by *mastabas* (tombs) of the king's relatives; the Mastaba of Idut, his daughter, has some of the finest reliefs.

The **Mastaba of Mereruka▶▶** (6th Dynasty) is the largest *mastaba* in Saqqara and contains 32 rooms. Mereruka was a vizier (high official) to King Teti and married the king's daughter, who is also buried here with their son, Meri-Teti. Among the decorations there are lively scenes of Mereruka painting on an easel, of hunting, farming, and dancing. The chapel in the middle has a fine statue of the tomb's owner and beautifully carved reliefs of funerary scenes and, to the left, of domestication of animals. Nearby are the tombs of two other viziers to King Teti; the Mastaba of Kagemni, with decoration very similar to Mereruka's, and the Mastaba of Ankh-Ma-Hor, with the famous depictions of toe surgery, circumcision, and a variety of craftsmen at work.

The **Double Mastaba of Akhti-Hotep and Ptah-Hotep▶▶▶** (5th Dynasty) is of interest for the way that it shows the different stages in the decoration of a tomb. In the corridor when you enter, you can see how, before the reliefs were carved, the red drawings were first corrected in black by a master artist. The tomb chamber of the priest

Ptah-Hotep has some of the most exquisite Old Kingdom reliefs, with very detailed depictions of children's games and Ptah-Hotep being manicured while surrounded by musicians. It is interesting to note that one of the games shown here, a jumping game called *Khaki el-Wizza*, is still played by Nubian children today. The tomb chamber of the priest's father, the vizier Akhti-Hotep, has similar but less refined decorations.

The **Mastaba of Ti►►►**, a 5th-Dynasty royal hairdresser who through marriage became overseer of the royal farms and mortuary temples, has an amazing variety of detailed scenes depicting life in ancient Egypt. The most famous relief is an unusual allegorical version of a traditional scene in which Ti and his wife go sailing in the marshes while hunting hippos (who here represent Evil) and fishes and birds (here representing Chaos). There are also fine reliefs of servants feeding cranes, of craftsmen, and of musicians cheering Ti at his offering table.

The **Serapeum►►** is without doubt the eeriest place in Saqqara. It was discovered by the French archeologist Auguste Mariette in 1851. In these cool, dark, underground rock-cut galleries, mummified Apis bulls were buried like royalty because the people of Memphis believed them to be reincarnations of their god Ptah and identified them with Osiris. The oldest gallery, now closed, dates back to the 19th Dynasty, the second to the 26th Dynasty, while the main chamber is Ptolemaic.

65

Above: the ubiquitous camel driver of the pyramids

Left: Ti, the royal hairdresser who climbed up the social ladder

UNTOUCHED TOMB
Mariette discovered only one chamber in the Serapeum that had escaped plundering. It was walled up during the reign of Ramses II (19th Dynasty), and after 3,700 years nothing had been disturbed. Not only was the mummy of the bull found, but there were also footprints left in the sand and a finger mark left in the mortar when the ancient workman put the last stone in the wall. The tomb is now closed again.

TRIP ON THE RIVER
Avoid traffic jams and take an inexpensive riverbus to Old Cairo, leaving from Maspero station, across the road from the Television Building. When the air isn't too thick and the windows not too dirty, it is a pleasure to zigzag across the river, passing an obelisk on the embankment, then fishing boats, yacht clubs, a fountain in mid-river, Qasr el-Aini Hospital, Manyal Palace, the Nilometer, *feluccas* (sailing boats), and then the high-rises of Maadi where the landscape opens up. Get out at Misr el-Qadima station and ask directions to Mari Girgis, a five-minute walk.

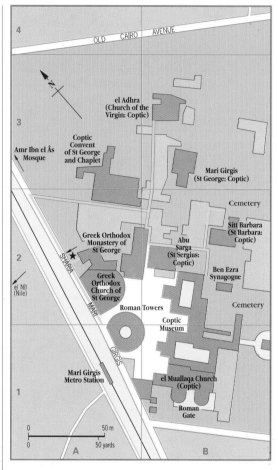

The architectural details of the mosque, synagogue, and churches in this area show many similarities

Old Cairo

►► Abu Sarga (St. Sergius Church)   66B2

St. Sergius is probably the oldest of the churches in the Coptic enclave, dated to the 5th century and typical in having 12 columns (one for each Apostle) separating the nave from the aisles. It was restored, along with several other buildings in the area, in the 12th century. To the right of the altar, steps lead down to the crypt where Coptic tradition claims the Holy Family rested after fleeing from Herod.

►► el-Muallaqa Church   66B1

Sharia Mari Girgis. Donations welcomed
This church, dedicated to the Virgin Mary, is called the "Hanging Church" because of its position, built over the bastions of a Roman gate. It is reached from the stairway at the end of a pleasant courtyard, passing through a vestibule where you can buy videotapes of papal sermons and liturgies, crosses, and plastic shrines to the Virgin Mary. Copts claim that the church dates back to the 4th century, but the present building is unlikely to be older than the 7th century.

The interior, with the ceiling resembling an ark, is intricately decorated with cedar panels. The three *haikals* (altars) are hidden behind beautiful screens inlaid with bone and ivory. The carved marble pulpit, supported by 12 columns representing the Apostles, is the finest in Egypt. To the right of the entrance is a 10th-century icon of the Virgin and Child with Egyptian features. Coptic masses are held on Fridays (8–11 AM) and Sundays (7–10 AM).

▶▶ Amr Ibn el-As Mosque   66A3

Sharia Sidi Hasan el-Anwar. Admission: inexpensive
This was the first mosque in Egypt, built in AD 641 by the Muslim general Amr Ibn el-As after he conquered Babylon-in-Egypt. The mosque provided the foundation of Fustat, the first Arab city in Egypt, which quickly became one of the wealthiest cities in the world. In 1168, its own inhabitants burned Fustat when they were threatened by the Christian king of Jerusalem. Whatever is left now lies among the rubble behind Amr's mosque.

The mosque was originally a simple, mud-brick building, but it was enlarged as Islam became more established in Egypt, and in 827 it was doubled to the present size. Later embellishments and restorations have left none of the original building intact. The façade was most recently rebuilt in 1983. The oldest part is to the right of the sanctuary. To the left is the tomb of Abdallah, Amr's son, buried in their house, which was later incorporated into the mosque. The columns in the *qibla* (prayer niche) hall have been salvaged from various neighborhood churches.

▶▶ Ben Ezra Synagogue   66B2

Egypt's oldest synagogue has been restored in all its splendor, but nothing can bring back its Jewish community. Amm Shehata, selling Andy Warhol-style souvenir postcards, is the only Jew left here.

The Copts sold the 4th-century Church of St. Michael to the Jews in the 11th century and it was restored in the 12th century by Abraham Ben Ezra, the rabbi of Jerusalem. The synagogue resembles an early basilican church and its

THE LAST JEW
Egypt's Jewish community is disappearing. Most Jews left for Israel long ago and the ones who stayed behind are old and usually poor; often there are not enough people to hold a service. Amm Shehata saved the Ben Ezra Synagogue from falling down, and for 20 years he has overcharged visitors for his wacky postcards so that he could keep up the repair work. God must have heard his prayers as, a few years ago, big money was spent by a North American sponsor and the Egyptian government to restore the synagogue to its former glory. Amm Shehata is still around and, fortunately, still sells his postcards.

67

Ben Ezra Synagogue has been restored to its former glory

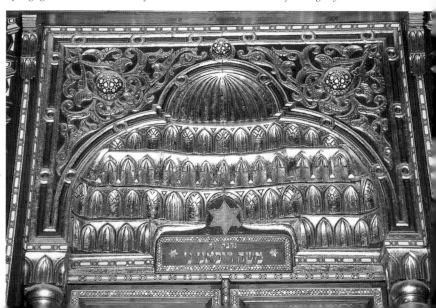

HELL ON EARTH
Between the mosque of Amr and the cemetery walls is a bizarre sight: a moonscape where hovels made out of clay and recycled rubbish lie under a cloud of black smoke. It looks like hell on earth and it is hard to imagine any human life in this strange place, but as you walk in, treading carefully, you will be welcomed and shown around by brightly dressed children. This back end of the city is home to an interesting community of potters who burn refuse in their ovens to fire everything from water pipe stems and kitchenware to sewage pipes.

Artifacts such as this Coptic papyrus show how early Copts used techniques and traditions of the ancient Egyptians to express their faith

decoration would not be out of place in one of the nearby churches or mosques. Jews claim that this is where Jeremiah preached in the 6th century BC, while Copts believe Moses was found here in the bullrushes.

▶▶▶ Coptic Museum   66B2

Sharia Mari Girgis. Open: Sun–Thu 9–5, Fri 9–11, 1–4. Admission: moderate

The two Roman towers and the sections of wall built around AD 130, to the right of the garden of the Coptic Museum, are all that remains of Babylon-in-Egypt. At the end of the garden is the elegant building that, since 1908, has served as a museum of religious and secular Coptic artifacts. Coptic art flourished in the period between the Greco-Romans and the arrival of Islam (AD 300–1000).

The first floor, in the New Wing, is arranged chronologically. Starting on the left of the entrance hall (Room 2), early Christian reliefs suggest how the pharaonic *ankh* (looped cross) evolved into the cross. Room 3 contains excellent frescoes; one from el-Bawit monastery (6th century) shows Christ ascending to heaven in a chariot and the Virgin and Child with the Apostles.

In Room 6, amid the fine artifacts from the 6th century Monastery of Jeremiah in Saqqara, is the earliest known stone pulpit, probably influenced by the Heb-Sed throne in Saqqara. Room 8 contains a splendid wooden screen from St. Barbara's Church, reminiscent of Fatimid woodwork. A 10th-century fresco in Room 9 shows Adam blaming Eve for the Fall.

On the second floor, Room 10 contains *ostraca* (flat pottery fragments used as writing tablets), manuscripts, and the papyri (text written on papyrus) from the Gnostic Gospels of Nag Hammadi. Some fine examples of Coptic textiles are found in Rooms 10–12, including a 4th-century towel and a tapestry showing joyous musicians (Room 10), a linen cloth decorated with Isaac's sacrifice in cartoon style (Room 11), and a fine silk robe embroidered with images of the Apostles (Room 12). Room 13 contains icons and fine Alexandrian-style carved ivories. Among the artifacts on exhibit in the last rooms are Nubian paintings salvaged from the villages now flooded by Lake Nasser.

Back in the courtyard, you can see part of the Roman wall and gate from Babylon. Steps lead down to the level of the Nile and to vaulted corridors, once used as prisons and stables. The Old Wing, which contains beautiful *mashrabiya* (carved wood) work with Christian motifs, pottery, and glass, is now closed for extensive restoration.

▶ Sitt Barbara (St. Barbara Church)   66B2

This church was dedicated to St. Cyrus and St. John in AD 684, but it is now known for the saint whose 3rd-century relics are held in the sanctuary to the right of the altar. Legend has it that Barbara's pagan father denounced his beautiful daughter when she chose to become a nun, after which she was tortured and executed by the Romans. Skylights give the church a lighter feel.

The Chaplet of the Convent of St. George

Walk

Enclave of devotion

This is a two-hour walk through the narrow streets of Coptic Cairo. Although the area is usually quieter than an Egyptian village, on Sundays and Coptic holidays the streets are crowded with worshipers. See the map on page 66.

Start at Mari Girgis (the Monastery of St. George), the seat of the Greek patriarch and scene of one of Cairo's largest Coptic celebrations, the *moulid* (festival) of Mari Girgis. Although it is closed to the public, you can visit the round Greek Orthodox **Church of St. George▶**, a modern building that sits over a Roman tower. If you want to visit the tower, you can reach it from the steps just outside the church. Downstairs from the church, in the chapel, priests wrap a heavy chain around the heads and waists of believers while the priests chant prayers in

remembrance of the persecution of St. George by the Romans.

Returning to Sharia Mari Girgis, take the steps to the right, through a passageway and out onto an old cobblestone street. To your left is the Coptic **Convent of St. George**, closed to visitors except for the **Chaplet▶**, which is full of icons, heavy incense fumes, and people chanting. In a side room, the nuns offer chain-wrapping and moral guidance.

Continue to the end of the street, noticing the old houses, and turn left into a narrow lane. A woman often offers bunches of basil, as the **Church of the Virgin** here is known as Qasriyat el-Rihan (Pot of Basil). Walk back and follow the arrow to **Abu Sarga,** the Coptic Church of St. Sergius (see page 66). Here you will find a crypt in which the Holy Family is believed to have stayed during their flight into Egypt.

Continue along the street, with the **Ben Ezra Synagogue** (see page 67) on the right and **Sitt Barbara** (see page 68) on the left. Walk until the end of the street and stroll around the peaceful Christian cemetery.

Cairo

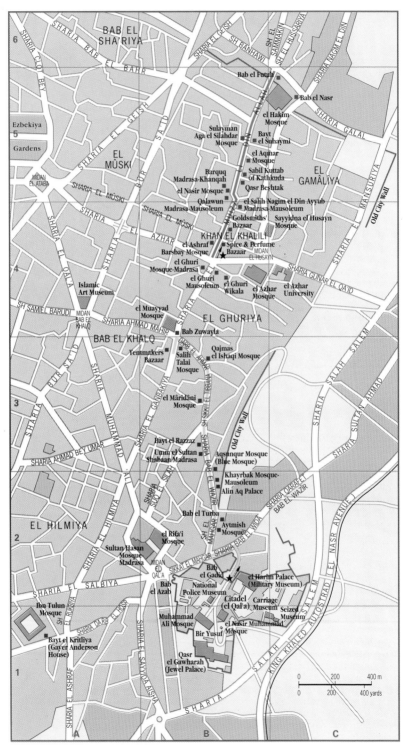

BAB EL SHA'RIYA

SHARIA BAB EL BAHR

SHARIA EL GEISH

SH. BANHAWI

SHARIA EL SAMMAKIN

SH. EL HUSSARIYA

SHARIA NAGIM EL DIN

Bab el Futuh

Bab el Nasr

el Hakim Mosque

SHARIA GALAL

Ezbekiya Gardens

MIDAN EL ATABA

EL MÜSKI

SHARIA EL SA'ID

BUR SA'ID

Sulayman Aga el Silahdar Mosque

Bayt el Suhaymi

el Aqmar Mosque

EL GAMÂLIYA

SHARIA EL MÜSKI

SHARIA EL MÜSKI

Barquq Madrasa-Khanqah

el Nasir Mosque

Qalawun Madrasa-Mausoleum

Sabil Kuttab of Kathkuda

Qasr Beshtak

el Salih Nagim el Din Ayyub Madrasa-Mausoleum

Old City Wall

SHARIA EL MANSURIYA

SHARIA EL AZHAR

'Goldsmiths' Bazaar

Sayyidna el Husayn Mosque

KHAN EL KHALILI

el Ashraf Barsbay Mosque

Spice & Perfume Bazaar

MIDAN EL HUSAYN

SHARIA GUNAR EL QA'ID

SHARIA EL QALA

el Ghuri Mosque-Madrasa

el Ghuri Mausoleum

el Ghuri Wikala

el Azhar Mosque

el Azhar University

Islamic Art Museum

SH SAMI EL BARUDI

el Muayyad Mosque

EL GHURIYA

MIDAN BAB EL KHALQ

SHARIA AHMAD MAHIR

Bab Zuwayla

BAB EL KHALQ

SHARIA EL GANBAKIYA

Tentmakers Bazaar

Salih Talai Mosque

Qajmas el Ishaqi Mosque

Old City Wall

SHARIA SALAH SALEM

SHARIA DARB EL AHMAR

SH HMIS

el Mâridâni Mosque

Bayt el Razzaz

Umm el Sultan Shabaan Madrasa

Aqsunqur Mosque (Blue Mosque)

Khayrbak Mosque-Mausoleum

Alin Aq Palace

SHARIA QARAFET BAB EL WAZIR

SHARIA AHMAD BEY UMAR

SHARIA MUHAMMAD

ALI

SHARIA SUQ EL SILAH

SH EL WAZIR

Bab el Turba

Aytmish Mosque

SIKKAT EL MAHGAR

SHARIA BAB EL WIDA

SHARIA SULTAN AHMAD

EL HILMIYA

SHARIA EL HILMIYA

el Rifa'i Mosque

Sultan Hasan Mosque Madrasa

MIDAN ED QAL'A

Bab el Gadid

el Harim Palace (Military Museum)

SHARIA EL SALBIYA

Bab el Azab

National Police Museum

Citadel (el Qal'a)

Carriage Museum

Seized Museum

Ibn Tulun Mosque

SH EL FAR'A

SHARIA DARB EL HSR

Muhammad Ali Mosque

Bir Yusuf

el Nasir Muhammad Mosque

KING KHALED AUTOSTRAD

EL NASR AVENUE

Bayt el Kritliya (Gayer Anderson House)

SHARIA EL SAYYIDA AISHA

Qasr el Gawharah (Jewel Palace)

SHARIA EL ASHRAF

SHARIA

SALAH SALEM

0   200   400 m

0   200   400 yards

Islamic Cairo

▶▶ el-Azhar Mosque and Madrasa   70B4

*Sharia el-Azhar. Open: daily 9–7. Closed: Fri 11–1.
Admission: moderate*

El-Azhar (meaning "the most blooming"), founded in AD 970, was the first mosque built in the Fatimid city of el-Qahira and claims to be the oldest university in the world. As the foremost center of Islamic theology, and with its sheikh the highest theological authority for Egyptian Muslims, el-Azhar also plays an important role in the country's politics.

The mosque is a confusing but harmonious blend of periods and styles. It is entered through the Barber's Gate, where students had their heads shaved. To the right of the central courtyard is a 14th-century *madrasa* (theological college) with a beautiful *mihrab* (prayer niche), and *riwaq* (free apartments) for students. The sanctuary hall originally contained only five rows of columns and the old *mihrab* is still there. It is here that students memorize the Quran, sitting in a circle around their sheikh. To the east is the Chapel of the Blind, whose blind students were notorious for their religious fervor. There are wonderful views of the city from the roof and minarets.

▶▶ Bab el-Futuh, Bab el-Nasr, and the   70C5
city wall

Admission: inexpensive

The monumental gates (AD 1087), along with the remaining city walls, are a masterpiece of Islamic military architecture. Bab el-Futuh (Gate of Conquests), with its twin oval towers, marks the northern end of the Fatimid city. You may need to look for the gate's custodian to gain entry, but he is never far from the entrance. Inside is a huge vaulted room with stairs leading up to the wall, which has good views over the Bab el-Nasr cemetery. Inside the wall is a 220-yard tunnel with fine masonry, which allowed covered passage from one gate to the other. Bab el-Nasr (Gate of Victory) was built on a plan similar to that of Bab el-Futuh and is decorated with shields, the symbols of victory.

Students in the courtyard of the el-Azhar Mosque

METROPOLIS OF THE UNIVERSE
"He who hasn't seen Cairo cannot know the grandeur of Islam. It is the metropolis of the universe, the garden of the world, the nest of human species, the gateway to Islam, the throne of royalty: it is a city embellished with castles and palaces and adorned with monasteries and dervishes, and with colleges lit by the moons and stars of erudition."
Ibn Khaldun, 14th-century Arab historian

EARTHQUAKE
The series of earthquakes that hit Egypt in 1992 left their mark on Cairo's Islamic monuments, many of which remain under scaffolding, waiting for grants for their repair. Work will continue throughout this century.

Muslims don't have to go to a mosque to pray, which is why some mosques function as more than mere prayer halls.

Muezzins used to call for prayer from the top of the minarets, but now a tape recorder does the job

MOSQUES CLOSED TO NON-MUSLIMS
Outside prayer time, all Cairene mosques are open to non-Muslims (sometimes for a fee and a tip) with the exception of the mosques of Sayyidna el-Husayn and Sayyida Zeinab, which will only admit Muslims.

ESSENTIAL MOSQUE GLOSSARY
Liwan – a hall opening on to a courtyard
Qibla – direction of prayer toward Mecca
Mihrab – an alcove or niche indicating the qibla
Minaret – thin tower above a mosque from which the muezzin used to call
Minbar – a stepped chair or pulpit from which sermons are delivered
Muezzin – man who calls to prayer

The religious obligation Muslims are allowed to perform their prayers wherever they happen to be when they hear the *muezzin*. When they pray they should be in a state of purity (all mosques have some sort of washing facilities) and should pray on clean ground, facing Mecca. Egyptian hotel bedrooms usually have an arrow facing east, but mosques make the point more strongly with a *mihrab* to indicate the *qibla* (see panel).

Early mosques The world's first mosque was in the court-yard of the Prophet's house in Medina and offered nothing more than some shade. Early Egyptian mosques were rarely more elaborate, but they were larger. Ibn Tulun's 9th-century mosque is perfect in its simplicity, but its decoration is elaborate. It was intended as a congregational mosque, for social and administrative use.

Conflicting traditions Sunni Islam forbids the representation of the human form, which is why Egypt's mosques do not contain many pictures, though they make up for it in the variety of decoration. Islam also discourages the cult of the dead, but many rulers, from a companion of the Prophet to the last Shah of Iran, are buried in Cairo's mosques and their tombs attract worshipers.

A quiet corner Egyptian mosques are often used for more than just prayer. Although they are crowded and noisy at prayer times, at other times they are quiet enough for people to lie down and sleep. They offer a spot for meditation away from the bustle of the city.

An elaborate domed ceiling, Muhammad Ali Mosque

▶▶ Bab Zuwayla 70B4

Sharia Darb el-Ahmar. Admission for the mosque: inexpensive
From the platform between the twin towers of Bab
Zuwayla (AD 1092), which marked the southern end of the
Fatimid city, Mamluk sultans watched the departure of
the annual procession to Mecca. In the 19th century it
became known as the Bab el-Mitwalli, after a saint called
Mitwalli el-Qutb performed miracles near the gate. It was
then also a place of execution.

The two minarets rising above the towers belong to the
Mosque of el-Muayyad (AD 1420), which contains the
mausoleum of Sultan el-Muayyad and his son. The courtyard contains a garden with palm trees, a good place to
rest after seeing the spectacular view from the minaret.

▶▶▶ Bayt el-Suhaymi 70B5

19, Haret Darb el-Asfar. Currently closed for restoration.
This splendid and remarkably well-preserved merchant's
house offers a rare insight into the sumptuous lifestyle of
the 16th and 17th centuries. Behind the plain façade, the
cool, peaceful courtyard comes as a surprise after the
street. The house is a labyrinth of rooms on different
levels. As in all Islamic houses of the period, there is a strict
division between the male, public areas and the female,
private, and "forbidden" areas. Male guests were entertained with music and dancers in the grand, first-floor
reception room. The richly decorated, second-floor reception room of the harem has beautiful *mashrabiya* (carved
wooden) screens that overlook the courtyard and the
terrace opposite, where men gathered on summer
evenings. Beside the private bathroom (rare at that time) is
a room containing a whalebone, believed to make barren
women fertile. At the time of writing, the house was
undergoing a major restoration.

*The busy and crowded
area around Bab
Zuwayla accentuates the
peace of the courtyard of
the el-Muayyad Mosque*

1001 NIGHTS
Cairo, as one of the cities
of the *Thousand and One
Nights*, has preserved
many of its medieval buildings. It is exciting to
wander off into the narrow
lanes and stumble upon a
crumbling palace or a
small mosque, which can
be explored at the cost of
a small *baksheesh* (tip) to
the guard. Take time to
stroll around, sipping tea
and listening to stories
wherever they are offered,
and you might find yourself
slipping back in time to a
world of fairy tales.

There is little in the rest of Cairo to prepare you for a visit to the cemeteries known as the City of the Dead. Many thousand Cairenes are now living around some spectacular Islamic architecture, their numbers swelled on weekends and feast days by pilgrims and other visitors.

ANCIENT MOTIFS
Even in so revered a place as the Imam el-Shafi'i's tomb, ancient Egyptian traditions mix with Islamic practice: the dome above the tomb is topped with a boat, familiar from ancient tombs as the transport of the soul on its final journey. The Imam's boat used to be filled with grain to attract birds—which, to ancient Egyptians, represented a man's soul—but the present-day guardians are now loath to climb up there to fill it.

74

Pharaonic traditions Egyptians were traditionally buried in the west, toward the sunset, but Islam shifted the focus of devotion eastward toward Mecca, and the conquering Arabs buried their dead in the desert to the east. As their settlements spread farther north, forming what is now the older part of Cairo, the cemetery grew around its eastern edge. Muslims believe that the soul is independent of the body and the corpse need not be cared for, but Egyptians are traditionalists and, as in ancient Egypt, guardians and prayer reciters live in the cemeteries to ensure the spiritual and physical welfare of the deceased.

Growth of the cemetery The cemetery grew quickly after AD 1399, when Sultan Barquq chose to be buried not in the palace grounds but in the desert near some pious sheikhs. His son built schools, mills and bakeries, baths, rooms for merchants, and a market around the tomb. Barquq's example was followed by Sultan Qaytbay and the cemetery soon developed into a suburb, a place of commerce and a retreat from the city. In recent times, Cairo's population explosion has increased the numbers living in and around the tombs, estimated at up to half a million people.

Important monuments The cemeteries' most important monuments are found in two groups. Barquq's complex, in the northern cemetery, was built between AD 1400 and 1411 and is known as a *khanqah*, an institution for

The great are buried beside the unknown in the City of the Dead

mystics and holy men. Barquq and his son, Farag, lie in one tomb chamber, and in another are two of Barquq's daughters. They rest beneath Cairo's earliest large stone domes. Nearby, Qaytbay's complex (1472–1474) is a perfect example of late Mamluk architecture, elaborately decorated in stone, marble, glass, and wood. Even the outside of the dome over Qaytbay's tomb is beautifully carved.

The southern cemetery is older and larger, and hidden among its new apartment buildings are some of the earliest Muslim graves in Egypt. The most important—and the largest—Islamic mortuary complex in Egypt is that of the Imam el-Shafi'i, descendant of the Prophet and founder of one of the four rites of Sunni Islam. The complex, enlarged and restored several times since his death in AD 820, is seen as a place of *baraka* (blessing). Muslims come from around the world to pray at his tomb, kiss the sandalwood screen and an ancient marble pillar, and leave written requests for the saint. Behind the Imam's complex is the Hosh el-Basha, resting place of some of Egypt's 19th-century royal family and of the Mamluks who were killed in 1811 to secure the family's position.

The dome of Qaytbay's Mausoleum, among the finest of Mamluk masonry

The living cemetery Tomb squatters now cover all of the cemeteries and have made them into crowded suburbs. On Fridays and holidays (particularly the Aid el-Fitr at the end of Ramadan), people from elsewhere in the city come to spend time at the graves of family or friends, reward the guardians, and enjoy themselves. As there are many saints buried in the cemeteries, *moulids*—feasts on saints' days (see pages 146–147)—are frequent. The day of Imam el-Shafi'i, at the beginning of the Islamic month of Sha'ban, is one of the largest and most colorful. People come from across the city to shop at the weekly Friday market on and around Sharia el-Imam el-Shafi'i.

WALK WITH CARE
The best way to see the City of the Dead is to walk, but as the cemeteries are difficult to police, they are hiding places for criminals and deserters. Beware of straying too far from the main streets. Also, the earthquake of 1992 left many tomb chambers in a precarious state, and some graves are in danger of collapsing underfoot.

The Citadel

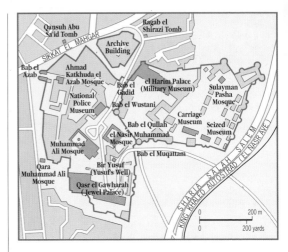

ORIENTAL INHOSPITALITY
One evening in 1811, Muhammad Ali invited more than 400 Mamluks for dinner and, breaching the conventions of hospitality, locked the gate of Bab el-Azab and had them shot as they tried to leave. The victims were buried in the Hosh el-Basha, the crypt of Muhammad Ali's own family, near the Mosque of Imam el-Shafi. Muhammad Ali became the sole master of Egypt.

GENERAL VIEW
The best view of the Citadel's imposing walls and towers, built with limestone from the Muqattam quarries and with blocks taken from the Giza pyramids, is from Sharia Salah Salem.

Some Cairenes are still bitter about the fact that they gave the French an ancient obelisk for a clock that never worked

▶▶ **Aqsunqur Mosque (Blue Mosque)**   *70B3*

Sharia Bab el-Wazir. Open: daily 9–5. Admission: inexpensive
The Blue Mosque (AD 1347) contains the mausoleum of its builder, Amir Aqsunqur, to the left of the pleasant courtyard. Beside it stands the mausoleum of his brother-in-law, Sultan el-Ashraf Kuchuk (the Little One), who ruled for five months before being assassinated at the age of six. To the right is the tomb of Ibrahim Aga, who added the beautiful panels of blue tiles in 1650. The *qibla* (direction of Mecca) hall has a fine marble *mihrab* (prayer niche) and one of Cairo's oldest surviving *minbars* (pulpits).

▶▶▶ **Citadel (el-Qal'a)**   *70B2*

Bab el-Gadid. Open: daily 9–5. Admission: expensive
The Citadel and the minarets of Muhammad Ali's mosque tower high above Cairo's skyline. The original buildings, started in 1176 as part of Salah ed-Din's grand fortification plan, were torn down by Sultan el-Nasir and by Muhammad Ali to make way for their own mosques and palaces.

The **Mosque of Muhammad Ali**▶▶ looks spectacular from anywhere in Cairo, but on closer inspection it is often disappointing. Although modeled on the Blue Mosque in Istanbul, it misses the integrity and simplicity of Cairo's great mosques. Its enormous dome, supported by four semidomes, gives a sense of space but the decoration inside is garish and overdone. Muhammad Ali is buried under a marble cenotaph to the right of the entrance. The alabaster courtyard is overlooked by a French clock given by Louis Philippe (in exchange for the obelisk now adorning Paris's Place de la Concorde) and from the terrace beyond there are magnificent views over the city and the pyramids.

To the south is what remains of Muhammad Ali's **Qasr el-Gawharah (Jewel Palace)**▶, damaged by fire in 1972. It was Sultan el-Nasir who made the Citadel the seat of power, and it remained so for 700 years, but the striped **Mosque of el-Nasir Muhammad**▶ (1318–1335), with its faience minarets, is all that survives from his reign. Behind the mosque is **Bir Yusuf (Yusuf's Well)**▶, 318 feet deep, which was linked to the Nile through natural channels. Muhammad Ali's Harim Palace has been turned into the uninteresting Military Museum. Farther north is the

Carriage Museum▶, formerly in Bulaq, with royal carriages on show and the curious Seized Museum▶, displaying antiquities seized from people who tried to smuggle them out of Egypt. Back toward the entrance is the bizarre National Police Museum▶, providing information on a range of topics about criminality.

▶▶▶ Gayer-Anderson House (Bayt el-Kritliya) 70A1

4, Midan Ahmed Ibn Tulun.
Open: daily 8–4. Closed: Fri 12–1. Admission: moderate

The entrance to the Bayt el-Kritliya (the House of the Cretan woman) is to the left of Ibn Tulun's Mosque (see page 80). It is now part of the Islamic Art Museum and the ticket price includes a guided tour around the house. The Englishman Gayer-Anderson, a doctor to the royal family, lived here from 1935 to 1942. He restored the house—originally two houses, joined by a passage—and furnished it with oriental objects he collected on his travels. The *haremlek* (women's quarters) are 17th-century, with a beautiful reception room, several private rooms, and a roof terrace where the women went to catch the breeze. A passage leads to the *salamlek* (men's quarters). The richly decorated reception room on the first floor is one of the finest in Cairo. The names of other rooms—the Queen Anne Room, the Damascus Room with splendid wood paneling, the Persian Room, and so on—are the fantasies of an English Orientalist.

As in Bayt el-Suhaymi, the house suggests that wealthy Cairenes were able to enjoy a far more luxurious lifestyle than their 16th- and 17th-century European contemporaries.

No effort was spared in the elaborate baroque decoration of Muhammad Ali's mosque

The Gayer-Anderson House; the women of the harem watched the men from behind the second-floor screens

The silhouette of the pagoda in the Citadel at dusk

Leave the Citadel along Sharia Bab el-Gadid and turn right at the post office onto the tree-lined Sikket el-Mahgar. The **Mosque of Aytmish el-Bagasi** (AD 1383) is 200 yards down on the right, with a *sabil-kuttab* (fountain and school) on the corner. The alley (right) leads to **Bab el-Turba**, an old gate to the Bab el-Wazir cemetery and the **Mausoleum of Tarabay el-Sharifi** (AD 1503).

Return to the main street (now called Bab el-Wazir). The ruins to the right were once the imposing **Palace of Alin Aq** (AD 1293), later occupied by Khayrbak (AD 1502–1520), who built his **mosque-mausoleum** next to it. Farther down is the **Blue Mosque** (see page 76), while on the left, beyond the **Madrasa of Umm el-Sultan Shabaan** (AD 1368), is **Bayt el-Razzaz**, a 15th-century palace with splendid *mashrabiya* (carved wood) screens on the third floor.

Past the small square, on the left, is the **Mosque of el-Maridani** (AD 1339–1340), whose peaceful courtyard encourages a rest. The *qibla* hall, behind the beautiful *mashrabiya* screens, is said to have treasure hidden, to rebuild the mosque when it falls down. The **Mosque of Qajmas el-Ishaqi** (AD 1481), to the right where the street becomes Sharia Darb el-Ahmar, is richly decorated with magnificent stained-glass windows and colored marble. Opposite **Bab Zuwayla** (see page 73) is the **Mosque of Salih Talai** (AD 1160), attractively simple, and the entrance to the **Suq el-Khiyamiyyah**, or Tentmakers' Bazaar (AD 1650), a covered market where men make elaborately appliquéd tents.

Walk

From the Citadel to Bab Zuwayla

This two-hour walk from the Citadel to Bab Zuwayla follows a street that changes its name several times. Formerly a cemetery outside the Fatimid city, then a pleasure garden in the reign of Salah ed-Din, the area prospered when the Citadel became the seat of power in the 14th century. See the map on page 70.

Walk

To the Northern Gates

Sharia el-Muizz li-Din Allah was originally called the Qasaba, which ran
through the heart of the Fatimid city.
It would take days to see every monument en route, but an afternoon will
do to get the feel of it. See the map
on page 70.

Start on the Khan el-Khalili (the
bazaar) side of Sharia el-Azhar and
walk along Sharia el-Muizz. The alley
to the left, before the Mosque of el-
Ashraf Barsbay (AD 1425), leads to the
Spice and Perfume Bazaars.
Cross the crowded Sharia el-
Muski to the
**Goldsmiths'
Bazaar**, with
hundreds of
jewelry workshops
behind the shopfronts.
Above an entrance to Khan
el Khalili, where the street
changes its name to **Suq el-
Nahhasin** (Coppersmiths'
Bazaar), is the **Madrasa-
Mausoleum of el-Salih
Nagm el-Din Ayyub** (AD
1250), with Cairo's
only surviving
Ayyubid minaret.
From here you
get a magnificent
view of the
imposing

*Making the
tarbouche*

Mamluk complexes of Qalawun, el-
Nasir, and Barquq (see page 84).

This part of the Qasaba is still
known as **Bayn el-Qasrayn** (Between
the Two Palaces), although nothing
remains of the fabled Eastern and
Western Palaces that stood at the city
center. Before the road forks, the little
alley to the right leads to **Qasr
Bashtak** (AD 1339), which once had
five floors, with running water on each
one. On the fork is the **Sabil-Kuttab of
Kathkuda** (AD 1744), with a tiled *sabil*
(fountain) on the ground floor and a
Quran school on top of it.

Take the street to the left. Farther
along on the right is the **Mosque of
el-Aqmar** (the moonlit), built in 1122,
the first with a decorated stone
façade. On the left beyond the Darb
el-Asfar is the **Mosque of Sulayman
Aga el-Silahdar** (AD 1839), with a
blend of Mamluk style and European
baroque and rococo.

Farther north the street
widens into the lemon,
garlic, and onion market,
ending at the **Mosque of
el-Hakim** (see
page 80) and
the **Bab el-
Futuh** (see
page 71).

THE CAPRICIOUS CALIPH
There are many stories about the behavior of Caliph el-Hakim. As a reputed misogynist, he imposed a 24-hour curfew on women and forbade the manufacture of women's shoes. He liked to roam the streets at night, which perhaps explains why he decreed that the night was the time for work, the day for pleasure and rest. Although el-Hakim was an energetic persecutor of Christians, intellectuals were free to discuss every possible subject in his House of Science.

Fine plasterwork in the Mosque of Ibn Tulun

Over the years the fabric merchants have expanded their shops into the foundations of the Madrasa el-Ghuri, making it a safety hazard

▶▶ Ghuriya Complex 70B4

Sharia el-Azhar. Wikala open: daily 8–midnight.
Admission for wikala: inexpensive

Getting out of a taxi at the pedestrian bridge over Sharia el-Azhar, you can't miss the Ghuriya, a complex built by Sultan el-Ghuri, the Mamluk sultan whose defeat began 400 years of Ottoman domination. Both the striped mosque-*madrasa* (theology school) (AD 1505) to the right and the domed mausoleum were badly damaged during the 1992 earthquake, although rumors suggest that adjacent shops have also weakened their foundations. The *wikala*, in the small street around the corner from the mausoleum, is the best preserved of Cairo's *caravanserais* (caravan hostels). Now converted into artists' studios, it is an oasis of peace and quiet, but imagine it in its heyday full of animals stabled on the first floor and traders bargaining loudly with their clients above.

▶ el-Hakim Mosque 70C5

Sharia el-Muizz li-Din Allah. Open: daily 8–6.
Admission: inexpensive

The notorious Fatimid caliph, el-Hakim bi-Amr Allah (Ruler by God's Command), built his mosque between 990 and 1013, but the two unusual minarets and some Quranic inscriptions are all that remain of the original construction. Over the years it has been used as a prison, a stable, a museum, and, under Nasser, a school. It has since been restored beyond recognition, with the addition of shiny marble and gilt, by the Bohras, an Ismaili sect originating in Bombay who claim to be the true descendants of el-Hakim. During his life el-Hakim declared himself divine while his disciple el-Darazi, founder of the Druze sect, preached that el-Hakim was the Messiah.

▶▶▶ Ibn Tulun Mosque 70A1

Sharia el-Salbiya. Open: daily 8–6. Admission: inexpensive

If there is time to see only one mosque in Cairo, it should be this one. Ahmed Ibn Tulun built it near the Muqattam

hills between 877 and 879. It is the oldest intact mosque in the city, impressive both for its grand scale and its extreme simplicity, and a rare survivor of the classical period (9th and 10th centuries) of Islamic architecture. The entrance, through a *ziyada* (enclosure) later used as a bazaar, leads to a vast courtyard 300 feet square and covered simply with pebbles. The pointed arches are of red brickwork and stucco. Below the ceiling of the mosque runs a 1.2-mile-long sycamore-wood frieze which is inscribed with one-fifteenth of the Quran. The strange spiral minaret was probably inspired by the minaret of Samarra in Iraq, where Ibn Tulun grew up, although romantics allege that he absentmindedly rolled up a piece of paper and used it as the design for a minaret.

▶▶ Islamic Art Museum   70A4

Midan Ahmad Mahir (Bab el-Khalq). Open: daily 9–4.
Closed: Fri 11:30–1:30. Admission: moderate

The museum's collection of Islamic art from the 7th to the 19th centuries is the most extensive of its kind in Egypt. The new entrance, through a garden at the side, leads to Room 7, but as most of the 23 rooms are arranged chronologically you should start with Room 1, opposite the old entrance. Note the lack of representations of animals or humans—no statues, for instance—which Sunni Muslims consider idolatry. The Fatimids, who were Shi'a Muslims, had no such restrictions and freely used birds, animals, and scenes from daily life to decorate stucco and woodwork (Room 4). In the archway between Rooms 4 and 5, note the Ottoman colored windows (ask the attendant to illuminate them). Room 5, devoted to the Mamluk period, contains a fine 14th-century mosaic fountain. Another fountain in Room 10 sits beneath a domed ceiling whose windows would have allowed women to watch entertainment below. In the Room of Masterpieces (Room 13), linger over the decorated door from the mosque of Sayyida Zaynab. In Room 21 are glass lamps, with some fine ones taken from the Madrasa of Sultan Hasan.

Traders in the grain market, Islamic Cairo

81

ASK THE GUARD
The Islamic Art Museum is undervisited so not all the exhibits are lit, but the guards will switch on lights when asked. Note that tips are not allowed here.

THE CITY OF EL-QATAI
Ibn Tulun, remembering the grandeur of his hometown, Samarra, built his new capital, el-Qatai, on a spur of the Muqattam hills. The Tulunid dynasty only lasted from AD 868 to 905, and of Ibn Tulun's extravagant pleasure palaces, lavish gardens, enormous mosque and *maidan* (square) in the middle of the city, where he played polo with his captains, only the mosque has survived.

Sufi mystics imported the coffee bean from Yemen long before the 16th century, after finding that the presence of the stimulant caffeine helped them to prolong their recitations. Since then qahwa *(the Arabic word for coffee and café) has been an essential and fascinating part of life in Cairo.*

WELCOME TO WOMEN
It is possible that foreign women will feel uncomfortable in some of Cairo's cafés, but there are some atmospheric places that are particularly female-friendly. These include: el-Fishawi, el-Sukkariya, and Naguib Mahfouz, all in Khan el-Khalili; Mahran, in the alley beside 6 Sharia Qasr en-Nil, downtown; Musicians Café, Sharia Muhammad Ali, Ataba.

82

The flexible forum There are cafés that have remained intact over the past 200 years and are monuments in themselves, but even they will confound the expectations of visitors hoping to find grand European-style coffee houses. The Cairene café is a much more flexible place, often starting out as nothing more than a bench or two, a water heater, a charcoal burner, a radio, and fluorescent lighting, but capable of spreading chairs and thin copper-topped tables across pavements and around buildings in search of space or shade.

Much more than coffee Some cafés will stay open until the early hours of the morning, so it is not surprising that they offer a range of drinks to satisfy the needs of different times of day or night. Besides coffee and *shay* (tea, served strong and sweet) there are thick hot drinks for winter nights, but food cannot be counted on and alcohol is never served. (For more details on café drinks, see page 103.)

The men's room Most of Cairo's cafés are frequented by men only, some of whom are looking for things that are missing at home, like the companionship of a game of cards or *tawla* (backgammon) and the heady pleasures of a *sheesha* (water pipe). Cafés are also the hunting grounds of hawkers selling everything from wallets, sunglasses, and shoeshines to a chance of paradise if you buy a Quran. They used to be the stage of professional storytellers who retold legends as old as the *Thousand and One Nights*, but they and the musicians who accompanied them lost their places to radio and television. Nowadays the most compelling stories are usually enacted among the audience.

▶▶▶ Khan el-Khalili   70B4

This maze of bazaars is squeezed into a small area between Husayn's mosque (see page 85), Sharia el-Muizz, and Sharia el-Muski. Amir Jarkas el-Khalil, a horse-master, built it in 1382 as a *khan* (caravanserai) and Sultan Qansuh reconstructed most of it in the 16th century, leaving a façade and an original gate, the Bab el-Badistan, toward the middle of Sikket el-Badistan. It used to attract foreign merchants, but most of the Jews, Greeks, and Armenians have left and nowadays you are most likely to bargain with Egyptians.

The main artery, Sikket el-Badistan, begins with souvenir shops, but there are antiques and jewelry shops past the Bab el-Badistan. Gold is sold by the weight in the Goldsmiths' Bazaar in Sharia el-Muizz, where it borders Khan el-Khalili. Although the price for gold is fixed, just watch the Egyptian women bargain as they buy their wedding dowry. You may do the same. Haret Khan el-Khalili is the place for silver and leather work. In the narrow alley off Haret and Sharia Khan el-Khalili, a few shops sell the famous Muski glass.

Sharia Khan el-Khalili, with good carpet shops, leads to the end of Sharia el-Muski, where the clothes for belly dancers glitter in the afternoon sun. In Sharia el-Muizz, left of the mosque of Barsbay, a tiny alley leads to the Perfume Bazaar. Remember that it is all part of the experience to be tempted into buying the essential oils of jasmine, amber, Opium, and Chanel No. 5 and to feel a little sheepish when your great bargain leaves marks on your clothes. Cairenes come here for cotton sheets, towels, and fabrics. Farther down the alley, your nose will lead you to a wonderful covered spice market. If you want to equip an Egyptian café, or just buy a water pipe, take a look on Sharia el-Muizz past Barquq's Madrasa.

Above: Spice shops sell spices used in cooking and a wide array of herbal remedies

Opposite: Almost every street in Cairo has its own café where locals meet for business during the day and for a game or a chat after work

WALK IN AL-MUSKI
Almost everything is sold on Sharia el-Muski, the street that starts to the east of Midan el-Ataba and runs parallel to Sharia el-Azhar, to Midan el-Husayn. Cars seem to be banned on this street, more by the crowds than by law, but occasionally a pushcart will endanger your safety. It is a real bazaar and it is wonderful to get lost in the crowds of women and Upper-Egyptians who buy here for their small shops back home. It makes a pleasant stroll in the late afternoon.

BY NIGHT
To appreciate the grandeur of the Islamic buildings, walk on Sharia el-Muizz late at night. The sight of the minarets rising up from the deserted streets, lit by the moon, is truly moving. It is quite safe to roam the main streets at night, and people always return greetings when you say "Salaam alay-kum."

The rebuilt façade of the mosque of el-Husayn, central landmark of Islamic Cairo

84

▶▶▶ Qalawun, el-Nasir and Barquq complex

70B5

Bayn el-Qasrayn on Sharia el-Muizz. Open: daily 8–5. Admission: inexpensive (for each mosque)

The 607-foot façade of this complex, built by three of the most important Mamluk sultans, is a spectacular sight both for its grandeur and harmony. The first building in the complex that you come to from el-Azhar was built in 1285 by Sultan Qalawun. The original *maristan* (hospital), which served as a lunatic asylum until the 1850s, is now partly beneath and beside the new eye hospital. A second entrance farther on leads to a corridor with the badly damaged *madrasa* (theology school) to the left and, to the right, the sultan's mausoleum, a rarely visited jewel of Mamluk architecture. The tomb chamber, reached through a little courtyard and an intricately carved stucco arch, is sumptuously decorated and overwhelmingly grand. It is hard to imagine that all this was built in only 13 months.

The second part of the complex, begun in 1296 by Sultan Kitbugha, was finished in 1304 by one of Qalawun's sons, el-Nasir Muhammad. El-Nasir was an obsessive builder, with 30 mosques, a canal north of Cairo, and an aqueduct from the Nile to the Citadel to his credit. His *madrasa* and mausoleum, following the plan of his father's, is under restoration, but you can admire the delicate stucco work on the elegant minaret. El-Nasir is buried in his father's mausoleum; his own son is buried here.

Next door are a *madrasa* and *khanqah* (religious hostel) built in 1384–1386 by Sultan Barquq, the first Circassian Mamluk sultan. The heavy bronze-plated doors, with silver inlay under a panel of black and white marble, lead to a cruciform *madrasa*. Behind the doors in the corners are stairs leading to living quarters (*khanqah*) for Sufis and students. The beautiful ceiling in the *qibla liwan*

Sultan Barquq's tomb, a masterpiece of Mamluk architecture

(vaulted hall facing Mecca) to the right is supported by pharaonic porphyry columns. Barquq is buried in the City of the Dead, while his daughter Fatima is buried in this splendid tomb chamber.

FAULTY TOWERS
As if the architecture weren't imposing enough, Sultan Hasan wanted to emphasize the entrance by adding two further minarets to the mosque. One was erected, but it collapsed in 1360, killing 300 people, so the other one was never built.

85

▶ Sayyidna el-Husayn Mosque 70C4

Midan el-Husayn
The mosque of el-Husayn is closed to non-Muslims, but as it is one of the most sacred mosques in Cairo there is always plenty of activity outside it. Husayn, grandson of the Prophet Muhammad, was killed in 680 in Iraq. His head is believed to be buried here, although this is disputed. Muslims from all over the world come to pray. The mosque is so sacred that alcohol cannot be served in the area, and bread baked nearby is believed to be blessed. The *moulid* of el-Husayn, celebrated for two weeks in the Islamic month of Rabi el-Tani, is one of Egypt's greatest festivals and attracts up to 1 million Egyptians.

Minarets and domes are among the most striking of Cairo's architectural features

▶▶▶ Sultan Hasan Mosque-Madrasa 70A2

Sharia el-Qal'a. Open: daily 8–5. Admission: moderate
The scale of this architectural masterpiece was unprecedented when Sultan Hasan started work in 1356 and it is still one of world's largest mosques. The vast complex, covering about 2 acres, includes a cruciform mosque, a tomb, and *madrasas* (theology colleges) for the four Quranic schools, as well as a market, a well, and apartments.

The mosque is best visited in the morning, when the sun brightens the dark mausoleum. Beyond the entrance portal and dark corridor, the magnificent space and light of the open courtyard are dazzling. The height of the vaults, already overwhelming, is emphasized by low-hung mosque lamps. Huge doors on either side of the *mihrab* (prayer niche) lead to the somber mausoleum; the original door to the right is made of bronze and inlaid with gold and silver. The mausoleum was placed here so that it would receive blessings from Mecca and overlook the Citadel. Sultan Hasan was never buried here; his body disappeared after he was assassinated, two years before the mosque was completed. The guard often demonstrates the fine acoustics by chanting "Allahu akbar" (God is the Greatest).

Cairo

The Cairo World Trade Center is a world apart from the relatively poor neighborhood of Bulaq

DESPAIR AND FRUSTRATION
If you need to extend your visa (see Travel Facts, page 255), you can join the stream of people going through the right-hand door of the Mugamma, up the right-hand stairs, asking at which of the 1,001 windows they should line up and then hearing that it might be better to come back on another day, or week, or with another photograph. And you're the lucky ones, because things have become much easier for foreigners. Egyptians suffer more and the spiral staircase has witnessed more than one suicide out of total despair and frustration. The building has also been the subject of several movies.

Shoe shops abound in downtown Cairo

Modern Cairo

▶ **Birqâsh**   *207D1*

Admission: inexpensive

Until 1995, the camel market was held in the Cairo suburb of Imbaba. The market has now been moved 22 miles northwest of the city, on the edge of the Delta. Friday and Monday are the main market days, with most trade being done early (6–9 AM). If you get there in time you will be rewarded with the sight of Egyptian and Sudani camel traders battling it out and beating any of the camels which dare to hobble in the wrong direction. Some of the animals are raised in Sinai, but most are still brought from Sudan along the Forty Days Road, the Egyptian stretch of which is usually crossed by truck or train. Many of the camels go straight to the abattoir from Birqâsh. To get there, catch a "meecro" bus, from the old camel market at Imbaba, go by private taxi, or join the Sun Hotel tour (tel: 02/578-1786) at 7 AM on Friday.

▶ **Bulaq**   *87A2*

Bulaq was once an island cut off from the city, but accumulated Nile silt connected the island to the land by the 15th century, when Bulaq became an important port and industrial center. Two mosques have survived from that era: the **Mosque of Qadi Yahya▶** (1489) and the **Mosque of Abu el-Ela▶** (1485), of which only the minaret and the mausoleum are original. The rest is 19th-century, but well worth visiting for its beautiful *minbar* (pulpit) and *mihrab* (prayer niche). Under the Ottomans, Sinan Pasha built his **Mosque of Sinan Pasha▶▶** (1571), which boasts the largest stone dome in Cairo, but nowadays it lies somewhat forlorn between workshops. Although Port Said and Suez took over as ports after the opening of the Suez Canal, Bulaq is still bustling with trade, especially in second-hand car parts and clothes and fabrics. The recent **Cairo World Trade Center▶** on the Corniche focuses its attention on expatriates and wealthy Cairenes on the island of Zamalek.

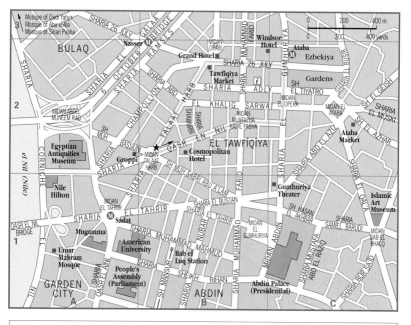

Among 1,001 shoe stores

This two-hour walk in downtown Cairo is ideal for getting accustomed to Cairene crowds and noise, before the inevitable cultural shock that comes with getting lost in the medieval part of town.

Start from the heart of the city center, Midan Talaat Harb, better known by its pre-revolution name, Midan Sulayman Pasha. **Groppi**, the famous coffee house, still stands out as a reminder that 50 years ago these were elegant streets with café-terraces under the trees. The façades are rapidly crumbling, but it's still worthwhile looking at their neoclassical and neo-pharaonic details.

On Sharia Qasr en-Nil, newly planted trees disappear among shoppers, office workers, beggars, and hawkers. Most of the shops here have European names. The **Cosmopolitan Hotel**, an art-nouveau beauty, is down the second street on the right. To the left is **Sharia Shawarbi**, a popular pedestrian precinct with good music shops. Cross Sharia Sherif and walk up to the elegant square of **Mustapha Kamil Pasha**. Look back toward the Nile Hilton for the long views like those in Paris. Continue along to Midan el-Opera, where a modern parking lot has replaced the opera house, built for the inauguration of the Suez Canal and burned down in 1971. In the center of the square are the once magnificent **Ezbekiya Gardens**. At the junction with Sharia Adly, the old Continental Savoy Hotel has been reduced to offices and a vaccination center. Turn left onto 26th July Street, and on the second street on the right is the **Windsor Hotel**, with an old-fashioned bar, and nearby, the el-Hati restaurant where Nasser once ate kebabs. Return to the main street until you reach Sharia Emad el-Din, with cinemas and theaters. Continue on to the Grand Hotel, have a look across the street at the charming **Tawfiqiya market**, and then turn left onto Sharia Talaat Harb, where there are more cinemas, and many more shoe stores, and you will find yourself back at the square from which you started.

The Egyptian Museum—founded in Bulaq in 1858 by the French archeologist Auguste Mariette—moved to this neoclassical building on Midan el-Tahrir in 1902. In spite of dust and old-fashioned displays, it contains some of the world's most extraordinary antiquities. The first floor is arranged chronologically.

88

HELP YOURSELF
In the fall of 1996, an enterprising Cairene did just that. Realizing that the museum had no alarm and that nighttime security went no further than locking the front door, he hid himself at closing time and spent all night choosing which antiquities to take. When staff opened up in the morning they noticed cases had been opened. The thief was caught outside, with Tutankhamun's gold dagger amongst his hoard. He admitted having been inspired by the film *How to Steal a Million*. The museum began installing cameras of its own.

Old and Middle Kingdom The Narmer Palette (left of the entrance in Room 47) marks the beginning of Egyptian art and history and records the unification of Upper and Lower Egypt by King Menes (ca3100 BC). Among Old Kingdom masterpieces (Rooms 46 and 47) are statues of King Zoser, the first pyramid builder, and of King Mycerinus, from his valley temple in Giza; a panel from Userkaf's temple showing birds in the marshes (2475 BC) (back wall); statuettes of scribes (Case C), and the hunchbacked gnome Khnum-Hotep (Case B).

The "Sole Companion and Master of the Secrets of the House of the Toilet," Tepem-Ankh (5th Dynasty), is on guard in Room 41, near the Maidum reliefs. Some of the most striking figures (Room 42) are the 5th-Dynasty, painted limestone scribe; the wooden Sheikh el-Balad, with rock crystal and alabaster eyes, and a diorite King Chephren (4th Dynasty), protected by Horus. Six wooden panels (Room 31) come from the tomb of the earliest-known dentist, Hesire (3rd Dynasty). Room 32 contains the lifelike geese of Maidum, painted on plaster (4th Dynasty); the perfect statues of Prince Rahotep and his wife Nofret (4th Dynasty) and, more unusual, the happy family group of the dwarf Seneb.

New Kingdom The painted head of Hatshepsut (Room 11) and masterpieces of the 18th Dynasty (Room 12) reflect the power and energy of a period of imperial expansion. Tuthmosis III's sandstone chapel from Deir el-Bahri was dedicated to Hathor, and an enormous gilded statue of the cow goddess stands in front of it, suckled by Tuthmosis's son Amenophis II. Amenhoptep, the man responsible for building the Colossi of Memnon at Thebes (Room 12), is shown in youth as a fat scribe and later as a mystical, thin octogenarian. The long gallery (Room 7) contains granite sphinxes of Hatshepsut, damaged by her stepson Tuthmosis III.

The Geese of Maidum, often copied on papyri sold to tourists

Amarna period A model of an Amarna house (Room 8) gives a rare insight into ancient Egyptian

domestic architecture, while the four massive statues of Akhenaton (18th Dynasty) in Room 3 reveal a revolution in art, as there had been in politics and religion. The informality of the *stele* (inscribed stone) showing Akhenaton and Nefertiti playing with their children is unlike anything else produced in ancient Egypt, while cuneiform tablets—"the Amarna letters"—and several busts give a wider but incomplete picture of this remarkable period, which lasted one lifetime and came to an end with the accession of Tutankhamun.

Detail from one of the many sarcophagi displayed in the museum

Later periods In the Late Dynastic and Late periods, Egypt was often controlled by foreign rulers and King Taharqa (Room 25) was clearly a Nubian from the Sudan. Beyond Room 30, Greco-Roman influences create a strange hybrid art, most typically (Rooms 49 and 50) with the bust of Serapis; the sarcophagus of Petosiris (4th century BC), inlaid with glass mosaics, and the Persian-period dwarf, a dancer at the Serapeum Apis ceremony.

OPENING TIMES
The Egyptian Museum is open daily 9–5. On Fridays it is closed for prayers from 11:15 to 1:30 PM. Admission: expensive. Tel: 02/575-4319

The Atrium From the stairway the scale and magnificence of this group of larger objects from all periods is striking. The 17th-Dynasty group of Amenophis III, his wife Tiy, and their three daughters appears soft and sensual in spite of the statues' size. At the center is part of a painted floor from Akhenaton's palace in Tell el-Amarna. Egyptians from all periods loved embellishment and decorations; even pyramidions (pyramid capstones) were carved and inscribed. These pyramidions from Dahshur are probably similar to the ones that sat on top of the Giza pyramids.

IF TIME IS SHORT
If you allowed one minute for each exhibit, it would take nine months to see every object in the museum. Most package tourists are allowed two hours: two or three half days would be more useful. A tour should include: on the first floor, Old Kingdom masterpieces (Rooms 48, 47, 46, 42, 32), Hathor Shrine and New Kingdom statues (Room 12), the Amarna gallery (Room 3), large stonework (the Atrium); on the second floor, Tutankhamun's treasures and the mummy room.

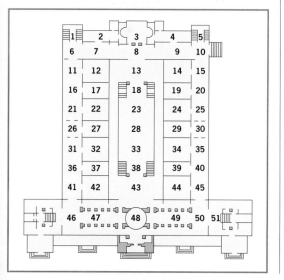

Left: first floor plan

Most of the exhibits on the second floor have come from tombs. There are always crowds to see the famous Tutankhamun collection, but most of this floor is under-visited, which makes it pleasant to browse around if you have the time. The exhibits are arranged more or less chronologically, starting with Room 43 and moving in a clockwise direction.

The blue faience hippopotamus seems to strike a chord in most visitors' hearts

THE FACE OF ETERNITY
"The more I walk along, the more I listen, the more I move around the columns, the more I experience the feeling of a dark world which fastens on to ours and which will not loosen the suckers through which it takes its life. Whatever it may cost, they find it necessary to confirm their existence, to perpetuate themselves, to incarnate, to reincarnate, to hypnotize nothingness and to vanquish it. Fists closed, eyes wide open and fixed, the Pharaohs march against the void, put it to sleep, braving its powers."
Jean Cocteau, 1949

Old and Middle Kingdom Room 43 has a very fine wooden head of a woman from Lisht, the much-copied blue faience hippopotamus and, just outside Room 42, a striking panel of faience from Zoser's pyramid in Saqqara. The alabaster vase in Room 42 is exquisite, and the black Palermo Stone yielded important knowledge of the Old Kingdom as it contains a list of pharaohs from the 1st to the mid-5th dynasties and the main events of that period. Wooden Middle Kingdom sarcophagi fill Room 37; the finest ones belong to Sepi, decorated inside with images of his favorite objects, and to General Mesah, including his neck pillow, sandals, and his model army. Room 32 and 27 have wonderful models of sacred boats and scenes of daily life in ancient Egypt.

Mummy Room There is an additional fee for the Mummy Room (Room 52), which opened in 1994 after many years under lock and key. It contains the mummies of some of the mightiest pharaohs in history. The mummies on display, all found in a cache in Deir el-Bahri in 1875, include great 18th-Dynasty pharaohs like Amenophis I and Tuthmosis IV, and the 19th-Dynasty Seti I and Ramses II.

New Kingdom Room 22 contains interesting artifacts from New Kingdom tombs including *ushabtis* (small tomb figures), scarabs, painted linen cloth, and headrests.

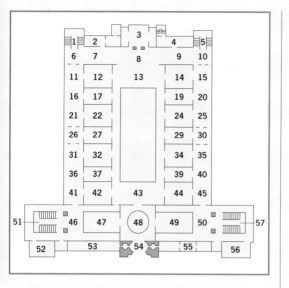

COLLECTIONS ABROAD
European and American involvement in the redis-covery of ancient Egypt, particularly the activities of early "entrepreneurs" such as the 19th-century rivals Giovanni Belzoni and Bernadino Drovetti, who exported sculpture, paintings, papyri, and even small monuments, made possible the creation of important col-lections of antiquities outside Egypt. Museums in Berlin, London, New York, Paris, and Turin today house remarkable treasures and are well worth a visit.

Left: second floor plan

The papyri in Room 17 are from the Book of the Dead. The artifacts found in royal tombs in the Valley of the Kings (Room 12), including a case of wigs for priests, suggest how grand the tombs and their contents must have been before they were robbed. The corridor from Room 41 to Room 11 features mainly New Kingdom sarcophagi, many of which still contain their mummies.

Tutankhamun Collection This collection of 1,700 objects found in the small tomb of the boy-king Tutankhamun is overwhelming. Every item is a highlight and even the smallest objects are finely and delicately executed. Rooms 7 and 8 contain four gilded shrines that fit one inside the other, enclosing the sarcophagus with the mummy (still in his tomb in Thebes) and a canopic chest (Room 9) with jars for the king's viscera. The golden funerary mask (Room 3), inlaid with semiprecious stones, is startlingly beautiful and incredibly perfect, as is the golden coffin. The rest of the room and part of Room 9 are filled with the fine jewelry, sandals, socks, sequins, and other objects that cover Tutankhamun's mummy. Other rooms are filled with exquisite funerary furniture, games, hunting bows and arrows and, in front of Room 45, the two *ka* (soul) statues of the king that guarded his tomb for more than 3,000 years.

And more Rooms 53 and 54 contain prehistoric and pre-dynastic artifacts, with a collection of dusty, mummified animals. Rooms 24 and 29 contain painted *ostraca* (pot-tery fragments) with scenes of the Book of the Dead and depictions of daily life. The household objects in Room 49 look amazingly like objects on sale in the *souks* (markets) today. Room 4 has a dazzling collection of jewelry from the 1st Dynasty to the Byzantine era, among which is a divine 6th-Dynasty golden head of a falcon. Last but not least are the beautiful, almost photographic Faiyum Portraits (Room 14), made of pigment mixed into molten wax, which were strapped onto mummies (AD 100–250).

Goddesses protect the golden canopic chest that contains Tutankhamun's viscera

Cairo Tower, a symbol of the success of modern Egypt

▶▶▶ Downtown (Wust el-Balad)   87A1

This is the center of Cairo, enclosed by the Nile, Garden City, Bulaq, and the Ataba district. Khedive Ismail had the area rebuilt in the 1860s for the inauguration of the Suez Canal. The main square, Midan el-Tahrir (Liberation Square), has some imposing landmarks: the **Museum of Egyptian Antiquities▶▶▶** (see pages 88–91); the **Mosque of Umar Makram▶** where funerals of important people are held; the **Mugamma▶**, the Kafkaesque temple of bureaucracy; and the **American University▶**. The 500-room **Abdin Palace▶** was also commissioned by Ismail; the royal family moved down from the citadel in 1873. Most of the sumptuous palace is closed, but rooms of arms, armor, and antiques have been opened.

▶▶ El Dokki   52B2

A residential area on the Nile's west bank, Dokki has become home to the **Mr. and Mrs. Mohamed Mahmoud Khalil Museum▶▶▶**, Egypt's finest collection of European paintings. The Khalils, who used to live here, put together an important collection of 19th century European art, with works by Gaugin, Monet, Picasso, Rodin, Toulouse Lautrec, and many others.

▶▶▶ Gezira   52B2

Gezira (Arabic for island) is the largest and most exclusive island in Cairo. It is split into two distinctive parts by the 6th of October Bridge: Gezira proper and Zamalek (see page 95). The first landmark beyond the Qasr en-Nil Bridge (el-Tahrir Bridge) is the **Opera House▶▶**, a $30 million gift from Japan, built in 1988, in a daring combination of oriental and western styles. The complex houses the **Museum of Modern Art▶**, devoted to works by Egyptian artists since 1908.

Farther along Sharia el-Tahrir are the **Gezira Exhibition Grounds▶**, and the **Mukhtar Museum▶**, devoted to the works of the sculptor Mukhtar (1891–1934), whose monument, *The Renaissance of Egypt*, stands at the entrance to Dokki. The 613-foot-high **Cairo Tower▶▶** was built between 1957 and 1962 with Soviet help. An elevator takes you to a lackluster restaurant (it revolves only by popular demand), cafeteria, and viewing platform, with spectacular views over Cairo.

▶▶ Giza   52A1

Giza, in ancient times a stopover between Memphis and Heliopolis, is now a rapidly expanding governorate between the Nile and the pyramids. In the 1860s, the area affected by the Nile floods was drained, and Khedive Ismail built his hunting palace (now the Mena House Hotel) and the Pyramids Road, now infamous for its sleazy nightclubs, which are popular with visiting Gulf Arabs. The land that now contains **el-Urman Gardens▶** and the **Zoological Gardens▶▶** once formed the Khedival Gardens, laid out by the Frenchman Deschamps. The avenue between them leads to Cairo University, founded in 1908 as a counterpart to el-Azhar University and now one of the country's most prestigious centers of learning. Wagons-Lits night trains leave from Giza Train Station for Upper Egypt.

▶▶ Heliopolis (Masr el-Gadida)   *53E4*

At the end of the 19th century, as Cairo became too small for its fast-growing population, the Belgian Baron Empain had the idea of building a garden city in the desert, connected to Cairo by a tram line. Baron Empain's empty villa, designed by the French architect Marcel as a Cambodian temple, with a revolving tower to follow the sun, stands abandoned along the main road to the airport. Marcel also designed the 300-room Heliopolis Palace Hotel in a traditional Islamic style; it is now the official presidential residence. Nowadays the desert is nowhere near, but the elegant avenues with Moorish buildings are still there, mainly around Midan Kurba and Sharia el-Ahram. The center of Heliopolis has become the playground for foreigners and wealthy Cairenes, while low-rent housing pushes farther and farther into the desert. To the north is Merryland, one of the first and also the biggest amusement park in Cairo, to be avoided on weekends.

ANCIENT HELIOPOLIS
The City of the Sun, called On by the ancient Egyptians, was the most important theological center of the Old Kingdom, dedicated to the sun god Ra. During the New Kingdom Karnak became preeminent and when Alexandria became the new intellectual center in the 3rd century BC, the glorious city of On more or less disappeared. After centuries of pillaging, nothing is left beyond the Obelisk of Senusert I on a square in Matariya.

A Zamalek tower block

93

The Metro in Cairo, the first in the Arab world, is unlike anything else in the city: it works, it is unnervingly clean, it is easy to use, well organized, quick, and rarely crowded. So if the hustle and bustle of Cairo gets the best of you, look for the "M" signs and go underground.

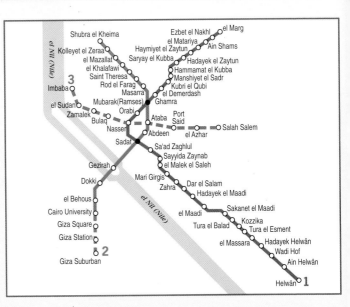

The route The existing lines run from el Marg and Shubra on the northern suburbs, through the center to Giza and Helwan. A western extension to Imbaba is now under construction. The first car of every train is reserved for women only. Hang on to your ticket, as you will need it to exit the station. Here are a few interesting stops along the way:

Ain Shams► (Spring of the Sun) provides water for the Virgin's Tree, under which the Holy Family allegedly rested on their flight into Egypt. It used to be a popular spot for Christian pilgrims, but is now another stronghold of Islamic fundamentalism.

El-Matariya► was the site of the ancient temple of the sun god Ra, but all that is left is the Obelisk of Senusert I on Midan el-Misallah.

Mubarak► is the stop for Ramses (Cairo Central) railway station.

Sadat►► is Midan el-Tahrir (see page 86).

Mari Girgis►►► is for Old Cairo (see page 66).

El-Maadi► is a wonderful place for an afternoon stroll amid the old villas set in lush gardens.

Ain Helwan► leads to a wax museum devoted to moments in Egyptian history, a Japanese Garden, and a spa with sulfurous baths that was fashionable as a winter resort in the 1920s.

▶▶ Roda   52B1

The "Garden Island" was rural until the 1950s but has rapidly become yet another crowded residential area. The Meridien Hotel on the northern tip of the island has beautiful views over the Nile and the center of Cairo. Farther south is the **Manyal Palace▶▶**, built in 1903 in a charming blend of oriental and occidental styles by Prince Muhammad Ali, King Farouk's uncle. The palace is now an excellent museum displaying the private possessions of the prince. The hotel occupying part of the gardens is currently closed. There has undoubtedly always been a **Nilometer▶▶** on the southern tip of the island to measure the rise and fall of the river, but the one that stands there now dates back to 861. The kiosk is a modern reconstruction of a Turkish original. The Center for Art and Life is housed in the *salamlek* (men's quarters) of the former Monastirli Palace, which was built in 1830.

▶▶ Zamalek   52B3

Zamalek, on the northern tip of the Gezira Island (see page 92), is often called the Manhattan of Cairo. Many old villas and luxurious flats in this exclusive, tree-lined residential area are occupied by diplomats, wealthy Egyptians, and expatriates. Zamalek is now bisected by 26th July Street, around which most of the shops are concentrated, and a large part is taken up by the Gezira Sporting Club, founded in the 1880s by the British Army. Opposite the club is the old Gezira Palace, built in 1869 for Empress Eugenie and now incorporated into the Marriott Hotel. Beside this is the Islamic **Ceramics Museum▶▶** whose prize exhibits were taken from the Islamic Museum, the royal family's collection, and from Prince Amr Ibrahim, whose home this once was. Many of Cairo's trendy restaurants and bars are in this part of town (see Directory, pages 271–283), as well as several cultural centers and the **Netherlands Institute of Archaeology and Arabic Studies**, which has excellent public lectures on Thursdays (see page 97).

This complex, geometrically patterned screen is typical of the eclectic architecture lavished upon the Manyal Palace

A LATE AFTERNOON WALK
Starting at the back of the Marriott Hotel, turn right onto Sharia Marsaf, pass the square, and at the British School take a left and then a right. On 26th July Street, turn left and stop for a juice or cappuccino in Simmonds. At the lights outside Simmonds, turn right onto Sharia Brazil and continue straight on (it becomes Sharia Muhammad Mazhar). At the Iraqi Embassy, turn left onto Sharia Marashli, then take the first right onto Sharia Ahmad Hishmat, then turn right again until you reach the Nile. Walk to the left along Sharia Abu el-Feda, where the river is lined with houseboats, and take a left at the overpass to return to 26th July Street.

Europeans came to Cairo as traders in the 13th and 14th centuries because Egypt, along with Venice, controlled one of the principal routes to the East. As they built their own empires beyond the Red Sea, they fought for influence in the city to gain political and financial rewards.

96

HOTEL COMPANY

William Thackeray wrote of an evening in Cairo's Hotel d'Orient (long since gone): "One of the Indians offers a bundle of Bengal cheroots and we make acquaintance with these honest bearded white-jacketed Majors and military commanders, finding England here in a French hotel kept by an Italian, at the city of Grand Cairo, in Africa." *Notes of a Journey from Cornhill to Grand Cairo* (1846)

Right: James Bruce, who went in search of the source of the Nile in 1768
Below: picnicking on the Great Pyramid, now a forbidden pleasure

Explorers and travelers When the Scottish explorer James Bruce visited Cairo in the 1760s he was forced to stay in a religious house in Old Cairo. Napoleon Bonaparte, who landed on a beach outside Alexandria in 1798, declared that the conquest of Egypt would have an incalculable effect on the world's civilization and trade. It also affected Egypt, and by the 1850s visitors like Lady Lucie Duff Gordon were able to live wherever they chose.

At that time, attention was focused on Egypt's present possibilities as well as its past wonders. The overland route between Alexandria and Suez, via Cairo, which was developed in the early 19th century under Muhammad Ali, gave

Europeans a faster passage to India and the Far East than the old route via South Africa. In 1839, 275 passengers crossed between the Mediterranean and the Red Sea. Within eight years there were over 3,000 of them and, by then, there was also a sizable European community offering hotels and other services for travelers.

A city of Europe, not Africa Europe had a great influence on the development of 19th-century Egypt. At the opening of the French-inspired Suez Canal in 1869, Khedive Ismail wanted to show Europe's rulers that Cairo belonged to Europe, not Africa. He initiated a building boom that defined the face of modern Cairo. Streets were laid out by European architects along European lines and the narrow alleys of the old Arab city were avoided by fashionable Cairenes, though not by romantic foreigners. At Abdin, in the center of the growing metropolis, the khedive built himself a grand palace that was fit for a European monarch.

The veiled protectorate After Ismail's abdication in 1879, Britain controlled Egypt by influence and, on occasion, as in 1884, by military intervention. Though the British were loath to annex the country, they nevertheless established in Cairo many familiar colonial institutions. In the British Agency (now the embassy, which retains Queen Victoria's initials on the gates) there were grand balls with dancing on what was regarded as "the finest sprung dance-floor in the East." There were horse and flower shows in the Gezira Club, golf drives and hunts elsewhere. The exclusive apartment buildings around the Gezira Club in Zamalek, with names like Park Lane and Dorchester, and the remaining hotels (the Windsor with its colonial-style bar, the Mena House Oberoi, the Cairo Marriott—formerly the Gezirah Palace Hotel—and the Heliopolis Palace Hotel, now used as the president's official residence) are part of the surviving legacy of that time of European dominance.

Revolutionary activities The 1952 revolution that overthrew Egypt's monarchy was also an attempt to free the country from foreign control. More than 2 million Allied troops are reckoned to have passed through Egypt between 1939 and 1945, and there were almost 90,000 British troops stationed along the Suez Canal when Cairo's Shepheard's Hotel was burned in 1952. The crisis brought about by the nationalizing of foreign interests, including the Suez Canal Company, and the British-Israeli invasion of 1956 saw Europeans fleeing the city. But they were soon back—the Russians in particular—and many of the buildings of the late 1950s and early 1960s, like the monolithic Mugamma in Midan el-Tahrir, reflect the era of Soviet influence.

Modern Cairo Cairo is now host to nationals from many countries around the world. The many Europeans among them have opened clubs and centers to encourage an understanding of their cultures, while many of the older European-style institutions, like the Gezira Club in Zamalek, are enjoyed principally by better-off Cairenes.

WESTERN CULTURAL CENTERS IN CAIRO
American Cultural Center: 5 Sharia Amerika Latina, Garden City (tel: 02/354-9601). British Council: 192 Sharia en-Nil, Aguza (tel: 02/303-1514). French Cultural Center: 1 Sharia Madrasa el-Huqquq el-Faransia, Munira (tel: 02/355-3725). German Cultural Center (Goethe Institute): 5 Sharia Abd el-Salam Aref, downtown (tel: 02/575-9877). Greek Cultural Center: 14 Sharia Emad el-Din, downtown (tel: 02/575-3962). Italian Cultural Center: 3 Sharia Sheikh el-Marsafi, Zamalek (tel: 02/340-8791). Netherlands Institute of Archaeological and Arabic Studies: 1 Sharia Mahmud Azmi, Zamalek (tel: 02/340-0076).

Ornate garden entrance to the Gezira Palace, now the Cairo Marriott Hotel

Shopping

Fixed prices and a bargain Shopping in Egypt is like entering an Aladdin's cave. There are three different places to do it, but wherever you go, you'll need time. Bazaars and markets are the most enjoyable, but also the most time-consuming and nerve-racking. The rule is to bargain, and bargain hard.

Start by halving the asking price, unless it seems ridiculously high, in which case start lower. To get a feel for prices, look around first and decide what an item is worth to you. Bear in mind that bargaining is a game and Egyptians are wonderful players—an invitation to drink tea is often one of their finest opening moves, though it is certainly not an obligation to buy. Secondly, there are small retail shops with fixed prices (usually written in Arabic, so learn those numerals!).

There are department stores that also have fixed prices and credit card facilities. Even this easier option can take considerable time: choose what you want, take the invoice to the cashier, and then go to yet another desk to collect your purchase.

Handicrafts Egypt has always been famous for its handicrafts, but unfortunately the quality has deteriorated, as many products are now made to be sold cheaply. The main crafts to look for are *mashrabiya* (carved woodwork), mother-of-pearl inlay work, pottery, alabaster (cheapest in Luxor), brass and copper ware, handmade glass, and the obligatory painted papyrus. The best place to shop is in the bazaars at **Khan el-Khalili** (see page 83) or, if you have time, in the workshops around el-Azhar.

Antiquities and antiques Most antiquities offered to tourists are fakes, which is just as well because genuine antiquities can only be exported with a license from the Department of Antiquities. There are antiques shops on Sharia Qasr en-Nil (downtown), around the Marriott Hotel in Zamalek, and in the Khan el-Khalili.

Carpets and appliqué work Carpets are not an Egyptian specialty, but camel-hair rugs are inexpensive and colorful. The best place to look is **Haret el-Fakhamin**, an alley behind the Mosque of el-Ghuri (see page 80). The **Tentmakers' Bazaar** outside Bab Zuwayla is a must. The appliqué tents are typically Cairene, used for weddings and funerals, and you don't have to buy a whole tent, as appliqué comes as cushion covers as well. The Copts were once famous for their weavings and the tradition has been continued in the **Wissa Wasif School** in Haraniya, a village near the pyramids. Find them downtown at **Senouhi**, 5th floor, 54 Sharia Abd el-Khaled Sarwat.

Jewelry If you are on an organized tour you will be offered *cartouches* with your name in hieroglyphics, but Cairo has more than that. Shops in the **Goldsmiths' Bazaar** in the Khan al-Khalili and jewelers in the five-star hotels are the obvious places to look for serious jewelry. Shops like **Senouhi** (see above) and **Nomad** in the Marriott Hotel sell interesting silver Bedouin jewelry.

98

ARABIC NUMERALS
It is very useful to recognize Arabic numerals, especially when reading prices and bus numbers.

1 = ١	8 = ٨	
2 = ٢	9 = ٩	
3 = ٣	10 = ١٠	
4 = ٤	20 = ٢٠	
5 = ٥	100 = ١٠٠	
6 = ٦	1001 = ١٠٠١	
7 = ٧		

PAPYRUS
Ancient Egyptians wrote on sheets of papyrus, but the craft of making it disappeared in the 10th century. Dr. Ragab rediscovered the ancient technique and is, in a way, responsible for the millions of papyrus sheets that are thrown at you wherever you go in Egypt. His Papyrus Institute, on a houseboat between Cairo's Gezira Sheraton and University Bridge, shows how papyrus is produced and sells papyri at high but fixed prices. Cheap papyri bought in the street are often made from banana leaves.

Clothes and fabrics On Safari, in the World Trade Center or in the Marriott, is an Egyptian chain selling good-quality, locally styled clothes. Their shirts (also in the **Shirt Shop**) are a good deal, as are clothes at Mobaco. For traditional Egyptian clothes like *gallabiyas* (men's long robes) look in Khan el-Khalili or **Nomad** (Marriott Hotel). **Atlas**, in Sikket el-Badistan in the Khan el-Khalili, sells excellent hand-woven fabrics as well as tailor-made clothes. **Salon Vert**, on Sharia Qasr en-Nil, downtown, and the government-owned **Ouf**, in the alley beside the Madrasa of Barsbay on Sharia el-Muizz, are good for simple cotton sheets, towels, and fabrics. **Tanis** (World Trade Center) has top-quality, locally designed fabrics and furnishings. International chains like Benetton, New Man, and Naf Naf sell good-quality cotton clothes made in Egypt. You can find them downtown or at the **World Trade Center**, 1191 Corniche el-Nil in Bulaq.

A man working on an appliqué in the Tentmakers' Bazaar

Food

Hotel restaurants in Egypt, as elsewhere, cater to tourists and the result is often bland and uninspiring cooking. The choice of restaurants outside Cairo and Alexandria is often limited, but if you know where to go, in Cairo the whole world is at your palate.

Street food All over the city you will be assaulted by wonderful smells coming from colorful food carts and corner stalls. Unfortunately, most of them don't have running water and, however tempting the food, it is only recommended for the adventurous or the hardened of stomach. If you feel confident about this (after all, Egyptians eat at these stalls all the time), then the delights awaiting you include sandwiches with fried shrimps, stewed liver or brain, and the more obvious *fuul* and *taamiya* (see page 102) or *shawarma* (pressed lamb kebabs roasted on a spit).

Egyptian fast food Many Cairenes eat lunch in small local restaurants that will often specialize in just one particular dish. Men are always in the majority in these places, but one part of the restaurant is often reserved for families or women. Among the typical Egyptian dishes these places serve you might find *kushari*, *fuul*, and *taamiya* served with eggs or *torshi* (see page 102) and, less common, *fateer* (a light pizza made of phyllo pastry topped with eggs, minced meat, peppers, and cheese or the sweet version with raisins, jam, and sugar). Other places sell roasted chicken, kebabs, *kofta*, a spicy ground meat patty, or fried fish. Most of these restaurants are far from luxurious, but they are usually inexpensive, clean—with sawdust on the floor to confirm it—and definitely worth trying out.

Restaurants Cairo is one of the Middle East's main meeting places and in all areas of the city frequented by foreigners, there is a wide range of restaurants, from simple Levantine to superb Lebanese cuisine, from bland, internationalized French to exquisite nouvelle cuisine and Far Eastern delicacies. Downtown has middle-priced restaurants, while the expensive places are in the five-star hotels and in Zamalek and Mohandeseen. In the more upscale establishments it is worth noting that a service tax will be added to your bill, sometimes up to 22 percent.

Basic rules Tap water is heavily chlorinated and safe to drink, but bottles of mineral water are widely available. Baraka (blessing) is the most widely available brand, though water from Siwa is popular. When buying water, check that the plastic seal is intact: unsuspecting tourists have been sold bottles refilled with tap water.

As most places have running water and hygiene standards are improving, there should be no reason not to indulge your culinary fantasies, as long as you bear in mind some basic rules. Avoid eating raw salads, ice creams, fruit you haven't peeled yourself, and food that has been stewing for several hours, like *shawarma* and cheap buffet meals. Try to make sure the food has been properly washed, and drink plenty of water to replace fluids.

A place to rest and watch the world go by in the middle of Khan el-Khalili

Food markets Most Cairenes still buy their fruit and vegetables fresh from the market or from the local grocery store, but the new, big supermarkets are proving increasingly more popular with the upper and middle classes of the population.

The majority of fruit and vegetables are locally grown, always fresh and full of flavor, but there seems to be a growing belief that imported fruits taste better, which is rarely true. The best fruit and genuine market atmosphere is still to be found in places such as the covered **Ataba market** (off Midan Ataba, downtown) and **Tawfiqiya market** (off 26th July Street, downtown). Salesmen vocalize loudly, selling pyramids of lemons, oranges, very red tomatoes, artichokes, mangoes, and strawberries. The smells can be overwhelming with stands pitched between entire cow carcasses dangling from hooks, cages of pigeons and hens that are slaughtered to order, and fish merchants selling pungent smoked mackerel. Women come from the outskirts of Cairo to sell home-grown lettuces and herbs while nursing their babies.

In Zamalek, 26th July Street has high-quality fruit and vegetable stores where much of the fruit is imported. This is also the place to buy locally grown organic fruit and vegetables.

Oranges are plentiful in Egypt and very sweet

The influences of Greece, Turkey, Lebanon, Syria, and France reflect Egypt's long history, but Egyptian cuisine has its own character, so bon appetit *or, as Egyptians say,* Bi-l-Hana wa-sh-Shiffa *(with pleasure and health).*

102

Traditional Egyptian mezze and salads served in a Cairo restaurant

Sweets and pastries are always a welcome present when visiting an Egyptian family

Beans, beans, beans Egypt's staple diet is bread and boiled fava beans (*fuul*). The bread is either *aish shami*, a white pita bread, or wholewheat *aish baladi*. *Fuul* is often eaten mashed with lemon juice and cumin. *Taamiya* are deep-fried fava-bean balls, often served with *torshi* (pickled vegetables) and *tahina* (sesame paste). *Kushari* (a mixture of macaroni, rice, lentils, chickpeas, and fried onions) makes a cheap lunch or dinner.

A table of *mezze* When Egyptians eat together they often share a selection of *mezze* (small dishes), eaten with bread. Popular dips are *tahina* (pureed sesame seeds), *baba ghanoug* (eggplant puree with tahina), and *hummus* (mashed chickpeas). *Salata baladi* (country-style salad) has finely chopped tomatoes, parsley, cucumber, and lettuce with cumin and lime. There are excellent vegetable dishes like *shakshuka* (Egyptian ratatouille with eggs) or *waraa aynab* (stuffed vine leaves) and *mahshi* (cabbage or zucchini stuffed with rice). Meat is often grilled (*mashwi*) like kebab (of lamb or beef) or *kofta* (meatballs). *Hamam* (pigeon), comes grilled or in a stew, stuffed with wheat.

Sweet delights *Umm Ali* is a traditional dessert of cracker bread, raisins, nuts, coconut, and cream, soaked in hot milk. *Roz bi-laban* (rice pudding), *mahallabiya* (cornflour pudding), and the ubiquitous *crème caramel* are plainer. The most popular oriental pastries are *basbusa* (semolina cake dripping in honey and nuts), *baklawa* (phyllo pastry, honey, and nuts), and drier *kunafa* (angel hair with cream or nuts).

"Once you drink water from the Nile," Egyptians will tell you, *"you will always come back to Egypt."* Most tourists stick to mineral water, but if you want a taste of the country, try out the wide variety of hot and cold drinks.

Hot drinks *Shay* (tea) is drunk with heaps of sugar, *bi 'l-naana* (with mint) or *bi-laban* (with milk), while *qahwa* (Turkish coffee) has varying levels of sweetness: *saada* (without sugar), *ariha* (little sugar), *mazbut* (medium), and *ziyada* (syrupy). Western-style coffee is called French or American; instant coffee is always called Nescafé. *Sahlab*, delicious on a cold winter evening, is a thick milky drink of arrowroot, cinnamon, and nuts. *Karkadeh*, a red infusion of hibiscus flowers, is available hot or cold in Cairo but is more popular in Aswan and the Sudan. Most cafés will serve herbal infusions like *'irfa* (cinnamon), *yansun* (anis), and the bitter *helba* (fenugreek).

Fruit juices *Asir* (fruit juice) is sold in colorfully tiled juice bars—the pyramids of fruits on the counter tell you what's in season. There is usually *asir burtuqan* (orange juice), *moz* (banana), *manga* (mango), *farawla* (strawberry), *gazar* (carrot), *asab* (sugarcane), *gawafa* (guava), and the delicious *asir ruman* (pomegranate). To be reckless, try the juices sold by street vendors with enormous jugs, *asir laymun* (lemon), *tamar hindi* (tamarind), or *er soos* (licorice).

Forbidden pleasures Since the privatization of Egypt's national brewery, Stella Beer is now available in several strengths (Local, Premium and Export) and on draft. A rival product, Sakkara, has also appeared on the market. All are of a previously undreamed-of quality. Improvements at the privatized Gianaclis Winery have made their wines quite palatable, and a rival wine, Obelisque, made from imported grapes, is also popular. Apart from the often excellent Zibeeb (Egyptian Ouzo), local spirits, with names such as Dry Din, Johnny Talker and Ricardo, should only be bought for the labels.

ALCOHOL IN EGYPT
Religious tension is making much of Egypt dry, but while you may not be offered them, it is usually possible to get alcoholic drinks in hotels and restaurants if you ask for them specifically. During Ramadan it is illegal to serve alcohol to Egyptians, be they Copts or Muslims, and you may be asked for your passport in some establishments. Many bars close for the month.

Small nightclubs with popular singers and belly dancers abound on and around 26th July Street in downtown Cairo

UP TO DATE
For listings of events, especially in foreign languages, look in the daily *Egyptian Gazette* or the government-run English *Al-Ahram Weekly* and the *Middle East Times*. The magazine *Egypt Today* lists events all over Egypt as well as reviews and articles on the performances. They also list occasional lectures at the American University or the weekly lecture (every Thursday at 6 PM) at the Nederlands Instituut in Zamalek.

Nightlife

Neither Arabian dream nor nightmare, there are plenty of possibilities to fill your evenings. Cairenes come out after sunset to catch the Nile breeze, which usually refreshes the city on summer evenings. There is entertainment until the early hours, and it is a special pleasure at the end of a long night out to see the sun come up while the call for dawn prayers echoes across the city.

Watering holes There are plenty of bars around 26th July Street and Sharia Alfi in downtown Cairo for some local color. The trendiest bars to be found in town are **Tabasco** (8, Midan Amman, Mohandeseen) and **Piano Piano** in the World Trade Center (Corniche en-Nil, Bulaq). **Harry's Pub** in the Marriott Hotel in Zamalek is popular with expatriates, as are **Deals** (2, el-Maahad el-Swissri Street, Zamalek) and neighboring **Aubergine** and **Zinc**. Downtown, foreign correspondents favor the rooftop **Odeon Palace Hotel** (6 Sharia Abd el-Hamid Said), and Egyptian actors and intellectuals meet on the terrace of the **Le Grillon Restaurant** (8 Sharia Qasr en-Nil). For live jazz, reggae and rock that goes on late, try the **Cairo Jazz Club** (197, 26th July Street, Mohandeseen).

Discos and nightclubs Nightclubs often offer an early evening program of oriental dance for tourists and a late-night one for Egyptians and Gulf Arabs (see page 106). Discos in some five-star hotels, like **Jackie's Joint** in the Nile Hilton and **Regina** in the Gezira Sheraton, admit only members and residents. **Tamango** (Atlas Zamalek Hotel, Mohandeseen) and **Exit** (Atlas Hotel, downtown) are still popular, but the two places of the moment are **El Gato Negro** (32, Sharia Jeddah, Dokki)—usually packed by midnight—and the **Crazy House** (1, Sharia Saleh Salem), unexpectedly situated on the edge of the City of the Dead and open until the ghoulish hour of 6 AM. Thursday night is liveliest. The seedier **Africana** (Pyramids Road, Giza) is the best for African sounds.

Movies and theater Cairo is the center of Arab motion pictures and theater and there is a wide variety of shows. Most theater is in Arabic, although it is often easy to follow the story; occasional performances in English are announced in the *Egyptian Gazette*. Going to a movie downtown can be an interesting experience, with a mostly male audience eating, drinking tea, and cheering or insulting the main characters. Foreign movies are often censored and subtitled in Arabic. Foreign cultural centers show uncensored movies, usually classics to be enjoyed in quieter surroundings, while newer movie theaters at the Cairo Sheraton and Ramses Hilton hotels are excellent. Check the *Egyptian Gazette* or *Egypt Today* for addresses and programs.

Concerts The main venue for musical events is the prestigious **Cairo Opera House** on Gezira (tel: 02/342-0598), with performances by the Cairo Symphony Orchestra, and foreign artists, often sponsored by embassies. Programs for the Opera House and for concerts in the cultural centers are published in *Egypt Today* and English-language newspapers. Tickets for the Opera House should be bought a few days in advance. Coat and tie are compulsory for men. Classical Arab music is performed most Thursdays at the **Gumhuriya Theater** (Sharia el-Gumhuriya, downtown, tel: 02/390-7707).

Nile-side attractions On a hot summer night the only place to be is by or on the river. Boats to rent are moored in front of the Nile Hilton and on the opposite bank, and *feluccas* (sailboats) are best taken from beside the Meridien Hotel in Garden City. Along the Nile, there are cafeterias called "casinos" serving food, beer, and ice cream. But in the evening it can be most pleasant just to walk along the Corniche on Gezira Island, or join the Cairene families having a picnic on 6th October Bridge.

WHIRLING DERVISHES
The Mawlawiya are Egyptian members of a Turkish Sufi sect founded in the 13th century, who whirl and dance in order to lose their worldly ties and become one with God. In Cairo there is a colorful whirling performance at the Ghuriyya Cultural Center, housed in the Mausoleum of el-Ghuri (see page 80) on Wednesday and Saturday evenings, starting around 8 PM. You might need to go early to be sure of a seat.

105

A LAST COFFEE
The cafés around Midan el-Husayn are open until early in the morning and some even claim that they never close. If everything else has closed, head for this square to relax with a strong coffee and a water pipe, and watch Cairo wake up.

Lovers meet secretly in "casinos" beside the Nile to discuss their future over a cold drink

Belly dancing occupies a central place in Egyptian culture and is as much a part of its traditions as telling stories and smoking water pipes. In spite of this, some groups are calling for its abolition on grounds of indecency.

106

THE BEE

Gustave Flaubert's account of a Syrian dancer in Esna did much to encourage sexual fantasies about belly dancing, but nothing like this is on show in Egypt: "Kuchuk dances the Bee... A black veil is tied around the eyes of the child, and a fold of his blue turban is lowered over those of the old man. Kuchuk shed her clothing as she danced. Finally she was naked except for a *fichu* which she held in her hands and behind which she pretended to hide, and at the end she threw down the *fichu*. That was the Bee."

Female dancers and musicians were both a popular entertainment in ancient Egypt

A long tradition Egyptians claim that oriental dance—of which the belly or *baladi* dance is one form—began in ancient Egypt and there are tomb paintings to support the claim. So perhaps it was from Egyptian dancers that Salome learned her trade. According to the Bible story, her fame was so widespread that King Herod told her to name her price to dance for him: she demanded the head of John the Baptist.

Natural rhythm Although connected to death in Salome's story, oriental dance probably has its origins in instinctive dances that were part of primitive fertility rituals. Much of it certainly comes naturally, and if you hear music playing in a Cairene street, it won't be long before you see a child raise her arms, lean back and start to swing her hips. Egypt's greatest dancers all claim to have started like this, dancing with other children, only later learning how to refine impulses that other people often suppress. The more skillful dancers can be remarkably expressive, suggesting not just sexuality, but tenderness, vitality, and grace. Modern demands for spectacle have added large numbers of musicians to the original two- or three-member bands, while dancers now wear extravagant glittering costumes to exaggerate their curves.

Today's stars Egypt's most famous dancers enjoy the same status as movie or pop stars in the Arab world and are just as highly paid. Although much of their dancing

takes place at private parties, most of them also have contracts to dance at hotel clubs. Stars like Fifi Abduh, Lucy, and Dina have their individual styles and a devoted body of fans, although many dancers go in and out of fashion. The threat of violence from reactionary Islamist groups, the arrival of European dancers and Russian troupes of cabaret dancers, and a change of audience have forced many Egyptian dancers into retirement.

Spectacular entertainment Stories of dancers being flown off to Riyad or Amman for a night's work have made oriental dance sound exclusive—and some of it is—but the image is misleading. There is nothing in the West to compare it with, and you are just as likely to see a dancer in the poorest slums as in the president's palace. Because it cuts across social strata, you can see dancers in some very different places. Some of Cairo's big hotels have early evening shows for those foreign tourists who want to get up early the following morning, although these are often rather bland affairs. The star dancers often don't appear until the late-night shows have started, which are more popular with Arab audiences.

Cheaper clubs Many of today's stars started out in nightclubs like Palmyra and its neighbors on 26th July Street, or in the many clubs in Giza along Pyramids Road. In these cheaper, less sophisticated clubs, the show usually starts in the middle of the evening and continues until 3 AM or later, but individual dancers perform only for as long as they please the audience. The test of this is how much money admirers are prepared to throw on the stage: when the bank notes stop falling, the next act is brought on. In these clubs, foreigners, not being used to this habit, are rarely seated near the stage.

Dancers also perform at weddings, and Cairo's wealthier families frequently pay through the nose to persuade one of the stars to make a brief appearance at their reception. At other weddings, guests themselves will dance, and if you are lucky enough to be invited to one this will certainly be expected of you.

DANCE OF LIFE
Life is like a *ghaziya* (an Egyptian dancer), she dances just briefly for each.

Egyptian proverb, quoted in *Serpent of the Nile: Women and Dance in the Arab World*

Vitality and sensuality are at the heart of oriental dance

Accommodations

The main tourist areas have accommodations on offer for everyone's wallet, everything from bottom-end dives to sumptuous old palaces. The choice will be much more limited elsewhere and if, for instance, you decide to spend the night in the Delta, the oases, or Middle Egypt, you will have to put up with more basic accommodations. Most hotels are classified with star ratings from one to deluxe five stars and, while these do not conform to international ratings, it is quite obvious why most of the unclassified pensions missed their star.

Old glamour that is no more The opening of a hotel for Europeans in Cairo in 1841 by an Englishman, Samuel Shepheard, started a tradition of hostelry that has been continued until this day. By the turn of the century, Cairo boasted a handful of first-class hotels, and a couple still offer rewarding glimpses of the past. The cosmopolitan Shepheard's Hotel burned down in the riots of 1952, while the Continental Savoy now stands empty on Midan Opera. The Semiramis, once known for its weekly society dances, was pulled down and rebuilt in the 1980s as the Semiramis InterContinental. But the Gezira Palace, with two towers added, is now the Cairo Marriott Hotel, still with notable gardens, casino, and architecture, while the Mena House remains well appointed with a golf course and swimming pool overlooked by the pyramids.

Luxury palaces Most of the international chains have opened five-star hotels in Cairo. They are invariably modern, offer every facility and service, and often make you feel as though you could be anywhere in the world. But these hotels are also popular venues for wealthy Cairenes who come to stroll in the gardens, socialize on the terrace,

The old khedival hunting lodge, with excellent views over the Giza Pyramids, has become the luxurious Mena House Hotel

Accommodations

PENSION EXOTIQUE

One of the least expensive and most colorful hotels in town is the Pension Oxford (32 Sharia Talaat Harb). The Oxford has become a backpackers' institution. It is wonderfully cosmopolitan and has counted among its guests a punk Italian hairdresser, an American lady praying naked to Allah on her balcony, and a Syrian belly dancer waiting for fame, all blended in with jaded backpackers relaxing after too many months in Africa. No need to book in advance, there is always room on the floor.

The sumptuous palace built to house Empress Eugenie for the opening of the Suez Canal is now part of the Cairo Marriott Hotel

and throw expensive wedding parties on weekends. Cairo's luxury hotels are mostly clustered in four main areas: at the airport, along the river near Tahrir Square (good for the Egyptian Museum and downtown), in the quieter, more sophisticated area of Zamalek, and near the Pyramids, an hour's ride back into town. You'll get the most favorable rate if you book through the chain's central office or, even better, as part of a package tour.

Midrange and mediocre Cairo's three- and four-star hotels miss out on the ambience of the cheaper ones and never achieve the facilities and service of the five-star places. Many hotels in this range, scattered across the city, are in modern concrete buildings with bad plumbing and without character. Fortunately there are exceptions. Zamalek has some excellent modern hotels, the President Hotel among them, which have the advantage of a quiet location close to shopping and restaurants. The Victoria, Windsor, and Cosmopolitan hotels have kept much of their old-style aura and are much recommended if you don't mind sagging beds and the unstoppable hubbub of downtown as a background.

Cheap and usually cheerful Cairo is also famous for its wonderful inexpensive pensions. Most are in Mohandiseen, around Ramses Station and Midan Talaat Harb; opt for the latter area if you want some character. Some, like Pensione Roma, are in 19th-century buildings with spacious rooms and ceiling fans, while others thrive on shabbyness. The better pensions are clean, good value, and popular, so reservations are recommended.

SWIMMING POOLS

Looking to cool off in a pool? If you are staying in a hotel that doesn't have a pool, you can use the pools of hotels like the Nile Hilton, Marriott, Gezira Sheraton, and Meridien at a considerable day fee or, for less money, at the Atlas Zamalek Hotel.

Transportation

Public transportation is quite well organized in Egypt. If you can't be bothered with the crowds and waiting times for buses, you'll find taxis inexpensive and abundant, and don't forget the Metro (see page 94).

Buses The least expensive transportation in Cairo is on the battered red buses that run along fixed routes from 5:30 AM until midnight. Numbers and routes are indicated in Arabic. Apart from the main ones on Midan Abdel Mureem Riad, most bus stops are only vaguely sign-posted. Buses are usually crowded, with passengers hanging out of the doors. It is pickpocket and bottom-pincher territory and best avoided. More expensive orange and white minibuses are a more comfortable alternative. They stop only on request. River buses operating on the Nile leave hourly from Maspero across from the Television Building and go to Giza and Old Cairo, or to the Nile barrage at Qanatir.

Taxis Taxis are easy to find and reasonably inexpensive if you choose the right one. Keep an eye out for four-seater, black-and-white taxis, which you stop by holding out your hand and shouting your destination. If there is someone in it who is going your way the driver will usually take you, too. The meter doesn't actually indicate the fare: Cairenes know the going rate (usually at least twice the meter rate) Ask someone in the hotel how much you should pay or decide on a price in advance with the driver; as a tourist, you will usually pay more. Seven-seater Peugeot taxis often charge considerably more than the going rate. If you don't want the hassle, book a limousine in any five-star hotel for a higher, fixed price. It can be

a good deal if you take it for a whole or half-day excursion. For inter-city travel, shared service taxis are quick and inexpensive (see page 258).

Trains Most trains leave from Ramses Station. Buy your tickets well in advance. It is best to take express trains for longer distances, as the local trains are incredibly slow and often unreliable. Finding the right window to buy your tickets is not always easy although there is usually an English-speaking information window near the platform. You can usually pay *baksheesh* (a tip) to someone in your hotel who can do it for you.

Long-distances buses There is a good network of air-conditioned, intercity buses. Buy tickets in advance from the appropriate bus terminal. As terminals are being moved around, check beforehand with the tourist office. Buses for Alexandria and the north coast, Sharm and Sinai, Hurghada and the Red Sea Coast, Luxor, and the south, as well as the overlanders to Tripoli and Amman leave from the new Turgoman depot on Sharia el-Gisr in Bulaq. Buses for the Suez Canal and Delta leave from Midan Ulali, south of Midan Ramses. Some buses for Sinai leave from the Sinai terminal in Abbassiyya. For the western oases, services leave from a station near the west wall of the Citadel, south of Midan el-Qal'a, while Faiyum buses leave from the Ahmed Hilmi station.

Planes The fastest way to travel in the country should be to fly (see pages 258–259), but Egyptair, the national carrier, is in some disarray so some delays are standard. Privatization will eventually improve matters. Meanwhile, American Express, Thomas Cook, and other agents can buy and reconfirm tickets on all flights for you.

Amid a maze of overpasses stands the beautiful, pseudo-Moorish Ramses Train Station

The traffic in Cairo is usually chaotic, and crossing a main street can seem like a serious suicide attempt

FAST TRAINS
Some of Egypt's trains offer excellent services. The regular *turbeeni* trains to Alexandria (2 hours) are faster and more comfortable than most other options, and although the food is poor, the nightly sleeper service can be a good way to get to Luxor and Aswan. There is also a summer sleeper service to Mersa Matruh. For more information, see page 258.

Lower Nile Valley

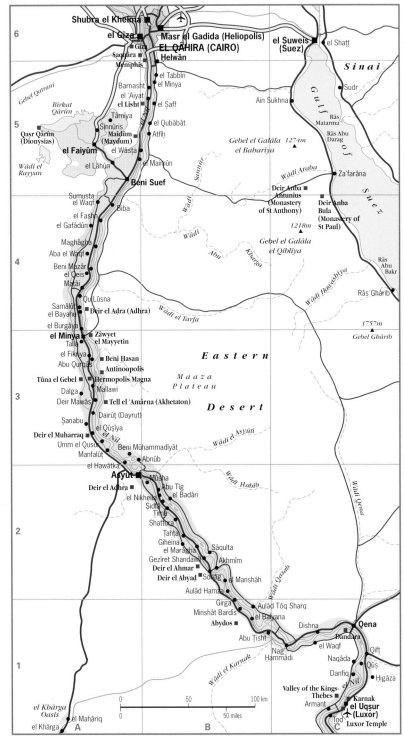

The Nile provides water for many rural communities

THE LOWER NILE VALLEY This region offered 19th-century tourists a first taste of adventure as they sailed along in their *dahabiehs* (large sailboats), heading for Luxor and Aswan. Today, it still offers an excellent introduction to the splendors of the south and some surprises of its own. Note, however, that independent travel in this area can be difficult (see warning on page 126).

THE LAND After the overcrowding and industrialization of the capital, the countryside to the south looks different, composed of a string of small villages and larger towns separated by lush farmland. The valley here is broader and less dramatic than farther south. The town of el-Faiyum, often visited as a day trip from Cairo, shares not only the Nile water, but also the appearance of the lower Nile Valley and the character of its people. Situated 60 miles southwest of Cairo, the town is easily reached by bus.

RARELY VISITED TOMBS It is easy to overlook the antiquities of the lower Nile Valley. But just as the countryside and its people are a vital link between the north and south, so some of the ruins are crucial for an understanding of Egyptian history. The Middle Kingdom tombs at Beni Hasan, for instance, and the Middle Kingdom pyramids

Relief carving of Isis, known affectionately as the "Great Mother," wearing the horns of Hathor and a solar disk

The fellaheen, *Egypt's peasantry, depend on farming for their livelihood, and agriculture remains the basis of the country's economy*

outside el-Faiyum make the shift from the Old Kingdom pyramids at Giza to the New Kingdom tombs in Luxor's Valley of the Kings all the more understandable.

BEAUTIFUL TEMPLES The lower Nile Valley also contains the ruins of two contrasting settlements. The radical pharaoh Akhenaton built his new capital, Akhetaton (modern el-Amarna), halfway between the modern towns of Minya and Asyut and worshiped the sun-god Aton there. Some 50 years after Akhenaton's death, the pharaoh Seti I built a magnificently preserved temple complex at Abydos, south of Akhetaton, to confirm the restoration of the old regime that Akhenaton had tried to overthrow.

IN JESUS' FOOTSTEPS Christian tradition claims that Joseph, Mary, and the infant Jesus traveled through Egypt to escape Herod. St. Matthew reported that an angel told Joseph, "Arise, and take the young child and his mother, and flee into Egypt." Many sites along the Nile, from churches in the Coptic quarter of Cairo to the Deir el-Adhra north of Minya, lay claim to having accommodated the family.

THE MODERN VALLEY Here, more than in the upper valley, you can see an Egypt that is not geared to tourism. The hotels and restaurants in towns and villages of this region are generally basic, if they exist at all, but in return for discomfort and for overcoming the difficulties of communicating across languages, you might find a welcome from people whose lives, for thousands of years, have been regulated by the same forces: the rise and fall of the river, the need to sow and harvest crops, and the adherence to religious calendars, now Coptic and Muslim.

CHANGING CHARACTER Like the landscape, the *fellaheen* (peasant farmers) of the lower Nile valley were once

ON THE NILE

"... and when the wind freshens, you see a fleet of little cangias coming out, like water lilies, upon the river (you don't know from where), or like fairy boats, a fleet of Efreets [spirits] coming up the Nile, doubling a cape, cutting in among each other. There are islands and headlands and creeks, just like at sea, and sometimes, when the wind blows against the current, he is no longer the solemn Nile, but a most tempestuous lake, with white horses, and turbulent little waves. But he is always beautiful."
Florence Nightingale, *Letters from Egypt* (1849–50)

characterized as gentle. One fifth of the population were Copts—many more than elsewhere—and their cohabitation with Muslims was a source of pride to Egyptians. But population growth, lack of work, and other social problems have shattered the calm. Fundamentalist Muslims have attacked Copts, government representatives, and tourists, killing many people and making a visit to the area around Asyut particularly inadvisable (see pages 126–127). Throughout the region, Christians and Muslims have built new churches and mosques, their belfries and minarets reaching higher and higher above the palm trees, trying to get the better of each other.

▶▶▶ REGION HIGHLIGHTS

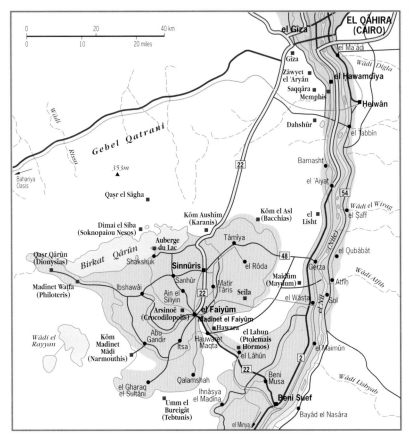

0 20 40 km
0 10 20 miles

▶▶ el-Faiyum *112A5*

El-Faiyum, 60 miles southwest of Cairo, can be reached by bus. It is surrounded by the Western Desert but it is not a true oasis, for it depends on a branch of the Nile, the Bahr Yusuf, for its water. The marshes of el-Faiyum were popular hunting and fishing grounds until the 4th century BC, when the Ptolemies drained the land and created the "Garden of Egypt." Today el-Faiyum produces cotton, clover, tomatoes, and a range of fruit and vegetables. Its chickens are considered to be the best in Egypt.

WALK ALONG THE WATERWHEELS

Following the Bahr Sinuris canal northward out of town, first on the west bank, then on the east, and passing the Governorate Club, you will reach one wheel and then beyond the weeping willows, a group of four. Farther along the canal (about half an hour's walk) are two more, completing the famous Seven Waterwheels, set in beautiful countryside.

▶▶ Madinet el-Faiyum (Faiyum City)

The 12th-Dynasty Obelisk of Senusert I stands at the entrance to the governorate capital. Tour buses stop at the Four Waterwheels, by the cafeteria in the middle of the town, but the **Seven Waterwheels▶**, north of the center, are more interesting. The **Mosque of Qaytbay▶**, the oldest in town (1499), is said to have been built for the sultan's favorite concubine. The mosque has a beautifully carved *minbar* (pulpit) inlaid with ivory and ancient columns taken from Kiman Faris. Qaytbay also built the two-arched bridge nearby, now known as the Bridge of Farewells because it leads to the cemetery. The white-domed **Mausoleum of Ali ar-Rubi▶**, the favorite local holy man, is also nearby. (Continued on page 118.)

Most visitors come to enjoy the serenity of lake and countryside, all easily accessible by public transportation. Some of the rarely visited ancient sites on the outskirts of the oasis can only be reached by four-wheel drive, but their isolation adds a sense of discovery to the visit.

Birkat Qarun (Lake Qarun), a salt lake 150 feet below sea level, is all that remains of the fabled Great Lake. Swimming is not recommended as many drainage canals pollute the *birka* (lake), but it is possible to rent boats to row across it, or to enjoy the sun on its beaches. Bird-watchers are attracted by the variety of migratory species, as are hunters who come to shoot the wintering ducks, geese, and quail. The spring of Ain el-Siliyin, en route to the lake, has been overly commercialized: spring water now comes out of metal pipes in a concrete wall.

Kom Aushim, the site of ancient Karanis, is easily accessible from the Cairo road. There is a museum (closed Monday) and the well-preserved ruins of the mud-brick Ptolemaic-Roman town (3rd century BC–5th century AD).

Dimai el-Siba and Qasr el-Sagha are difficult to reach, but are interesting for their history and their beautiful setting, overlooking the lake and the desert. The Qasr el-Sagha (Palace of Jewelers) is a small, Middle-Kingdom temple of irregularly shaped blocks, reminiscent of Inca architecture. The isolated ruins of Dimai el-Siba (Dimai of the Lions), encircled by a thick wall and with a rough-hewn temple in the middle, can also be reached by boat.

Qasr Qarun is a well-preserved and easily accessible Ptolemaic temple 27 miles northwest of the city. There are also four pyramid sites around el-Faiyum, the 12th-Dynasty **el-Lahun and Hawara Pyramids** off the Beni Suef Road, the 12th-Dynasty and ruined **el-Lisht Pyramid**, and the 3rd-Dynasty collapsed **Pyramid of Maidum**.

LEGENDS OF EL-FAIYUM
In ancient mythology the Great Lake of el-Faiyum was identified with Nun, the primeval ocean and origin of all life; the high land around Kiman Faris was seen as the primeval hill, where life first started. Diodorus records that Crocodilopolis (el-Faiyum) was built by King Menes, who united Upper and Lower Egypt, after a crocodile saved his life on the Great Lake. Modern Faiyumis claim that it took 1,000 days to build the city, and thus it was called Madinet Alf Yaum (City of a Thousand Days).

117

Lake Qarun is a favorite day-trip destination for Cairene families in need of some fresh air and some quietude

The semi-oasis of el-Faiyum has a fertile soil irrigated by a branch of the Nile, the Bahr Yusuf

GETTING AROUND
Public transportation to the ancient sites is limited and time consuming. However, before hiring a private taxi for a day excursion to Beni Hasan, Tuna el-Gebel, and Hermopolis consult the tourist office on the Corniche (off Sharia Abdel Mureem) for the advisability of making the excursion.

(Continued from page 116.) The **souk▶**, in an area on the canal called el-Qantara, is a labyrinth of small alleys with shops that, for once, are not directed toward tourism. The beautiful Faiyumi baskets are sold around the water-wheels, and the best pottery is sold at the pottery market (Tuesday morning) in Sharia el-Madaris.

▶▶ el-Minya   112A3

This provincial capital, 150 miles south of Cairo, can be reached by train from Cairo in 3–4 hours, or by bus (5 hours) from Bulaq's Turgoman terminal. There is also a direct train from Luxor, but by bus you will need to change in Asyut.

El-Minya is a pleasant, provincial town with worn-out colonial villas (once inhabited by Greek and Egyptian cotton barons), set in overgrown gardens. There is little to see in the town itself, but after sunset, the entire population seems to come out for an evening stroll along the breezy corniche (waterfront) or the busy streets between Midan el-Tahrir and Midan el-Saa. Minya has a large Christian community. Its relaxed atmosphere and good accommodations make it an ideal base for discovering the region's archeological sites, but there may be religious tension.

El-Minya's vast cemetery, the **Zawiyet el-Mayyetin (Corner of the Dead)▶**, is on the east bank of the Nile, near the village of el-Sawada. The dead were transported by *feluccas* (sailing boats) to their final resting place, but a new bridge has changed the ancient tradition. It is a spectacular sight, with thousands of domed mausoleums in the Muslim cemetery and thousands of crosses defining the Coptic tombs. On July 6, Copts camp here during the annual *moulid* (festival) of Aba Hur, whose subterranean, rock-cut church is nearby.

About 12 miles north of el-Minya, on the east bank, is the Gebel el-Teir (Bird Mountain) with the Coptic **Deir el-Adhra (Monastery of the Virgin)▶** on its summit. The monastery is still a place of pilgrimage. The 4th-century Church of the Holy Virgin, partly cut out of the rock, is said to occupy a cave where the Holy Family took shelter, and many miracles are ascribed to the picture of the Virgin that is believed to weep holy oil.

▶▶ Rock Tombs of Beni Hasan   112A3

Tombs open: daily 7–5. Admission: moderate

Only 4 of the 39 11th- and 12th-Dynasty tombs are open. These tombs of local Middle Kingdom rulers represent a transition from the Old Kingdom pyramids in Giza to the tombs in the Valley of the Kings in Luxor. Although most were unfinished, the painting on stucco is excellent, with vivid depictions of everyday life of the period.

Tomb of Baqet III (No. 15)▶▶ Baqet was the 11th-Dynasty monarch of Oryx. On the left wall there is a papyrus harvest, acrobats, women spinning and, above, a gazelle hunt in the desert. On the rear wall there is a catalog of 200 wrestling positions, and on the right wall are scenes of Baqet's daily life.

Tomb of Kheti (No. 17)▶▶ The 11th-Dynasty tomb of Kheti, son of Baqet, still has two of its six painted lotus columns. On the left and rear walls are figures in different stages of movement, like a movie in slow motion. Paintings depict papyrus harvesting, weavers, hunters, dancers, musicians, wrestlers, and a desert hunt. On the right wall, Kheti is shown overseeing various activities and receiving offerings.

Tomb of Amenemhet (No. 2)▶▶ (12th Dynasty) Proto-Doric columns support the painted ceiling. The wall to the left has the customary hunting scenes as well as Amenemhet collecting tributes. On the rear wall the voyage to Abydos is depicted and in the niches are broken statues of the man himself between his mother and wife. On the right wall are scenes of harpooning fish, musicians, wrestlers, and offerings.

Tomb of Khnumhotep (No. 3)▶▶▶ This 12th-Dynasty tomb of Amenemhet's successor has the most beautiful paintings of hunting, fowling, and fishing (rear wall). On the left wall, beneath a desert hunt, Khnumhotep receives eye paint from the Semites, meticulously depicted in their strange clothes. To the right, he sails to Abydos and inspects the work of various artisans.

DEATH ON THE NILE

In AD 30 Emperor Hadrian traveled with his lover, Antinous, through Egypt. After an oracle predicted a great calamity, the emperor's lover was drowned in the Nile. In his honor, Hadrian built the city of Antinoopolis, the ruins of which are 6 miles south of Beni Hasan.

119

Below: wrestlers on the walls of Kheti's tomb (11th Dynasty) in Beni Hasan
Bottom: unassuming entrances to the Rock Tombs of Beni Hasan

It is difficult to build a comprehensible image of religion in ancient Egypt. Most ancient litera-ture in Egypt is concerned with some aspect of religion, which means there is very little secular writing to help create a context. Egyptian reli-gion evolved gradually, and a reasonable knowledge of how it developed is an important step toward understanding the subject.

EGYPTIAN GODS

Amun-Ra: Amun and Ra, from Thebes and Heliopolis, merged to form an important state god.
Anubis: the jackal-god of funerary matters.
Bastet: a cat-headed goddess of pleasure.
Bes: a grotesquely fat dwarf, god of childbirth and children.
Hathor: the cow goddess of pleasure and protector of women.
Horus: a falcon, popularly known as the young king who avenged his father Osiris.
Isis: Osiris' sister and wife, and Horus' mother, she epitomized female qualities and was repre-sented with cow's horns and a solar disk, or with a throne on her head.
Khnum: human-headed ram, god of fertility who created men on a potter's wheel.
Maat: a woman with an ostrich feather, who symbolized justice and order.
Min: a god of fertility, usually with large phallus.
Nephthys: sister of Isis and Osiris, and sister and wife of Seth.
Nut: a naked female straddling the earth, she swallowed the sun at night and gave birth to it at dawn.
Osiris: a mummified man, with false beard, crook, and flail, associated with vegetation and regenera-tion (see pages 130–131).

In the beginning Creation myths lay at the heart of Egyptian religious belief. There were several versions, the most widely accepted of which was developed at Heliopolis. Before the world was created, the only thing that existed was the water of Chaos. Eventually some ground began to emerge above the water and on it stood the sun-god Atum (later identified with Ra). Atum created air (Shu) and moisture (Tefnut), who in turn created the earth (Geb) and the sky (Nut) and from their union came Osiris and Isis, Seth and Nephthys. The similarity between this myth and the experience of Egyptians is striking: just as the first earth rose out of the waters of Chaos, so Egyptians' fields emerged each year as the floodwaters of the Nile receded. The priests of Memphis preached that the god Ptah created heaven and earth by his command, a belief that also appears in the Old Testament account of Genesis.

Renewal through ritual Egyptians were uniquely depen-dent on hidden, natural cycles—it was of paramount importance that their river, with its hidden source, should flood with measured force and at just the right moment for the sowing of crops. So it is not surprising that their religious beliefs were intimately connected to the forces of nature and to the animals with whom they shared the valley. As their world was one of contrasts, epitomized by the fertile valley and the surrounding desert, so their pantheon divided into forces for good and evil. It was believed that good could only triumph and the well-being of the valley could only be ensured if the correct rituals were repeated. Thus the images of the gods were given fresh coverings each morning, food was offered morning and night, incense was burned at the right moment, and all other observances were kept.

The development of state gods By the end of the Old Kingdom, rituals were fairly standardized throughout the country. Feasts were observed at all the great temples. Many of them connected myths of the gods with natural cycles so, for instance, the feast of the Coming-Forth of Min (a god associated with fertility) took place at the time of harvest. The king held the post of high priest, but in his absence priests performed the daily rituals in which the public took no part, being forbidden to enter the inner sanctums of temples. As temples grew rich on gifts of land and precious objects, so their political power increased, and during a weak monarchy and in the reign of a king like Tutankhamun, it was the priests who effectively ran the country. But although gods such as Osiris maintained their popularity, others came and went and the influence of their priesthood declined with them.

Greco-Roman influences Osiris emerges as the most popular and enduring Egyptian deity, perhaps because he was seen as a victim of injustice and because he was intimately connected to the passage of the dead from this world to the next. After the conquest of the eastern Mediterranean by Alexander the Great, his successors, hoping to unite Greeks and Egyptians, encouraged the worship of a new god, Serapis, evolved from Osiris and the Greek god Dionysus. The Egyptians built sanctuaries for the god at Memphis and Alexandria, and the cult of Serapis spread to Athens, Rome, and far into Asia. When the Roman emperor, Theodosius I, declared Christianity as the religion of the empire, he unleashed a wave of Christian fundamentalism in which tombs and temples were defiled; the Serapeum at Alexandria was destroyed and the ancient religion along with it.

EGYPTIAN GODS
Ptah: mummified man with tight cap, he was seen by some as the creator of the universe.
Sekhmet: the lioness goddess of war and wife of Ptah.
Seth: god with a dog's head who murdered his brother Osiris and epitomized chaos and destruction.
Thoth: ibis-headed god of wisdom and writing.

Relief carving inside the Temple of Seti I and Ramses II, Abydos

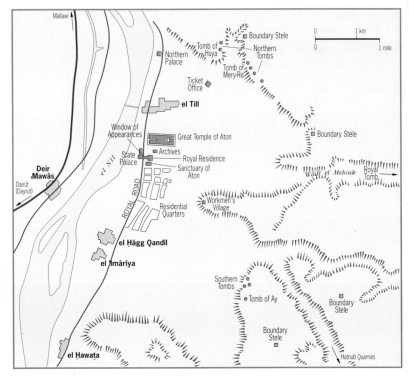

Tell el-Amarna

▶ Hermopolis Magna   *112A3*

The ruins near el-Ashmunayn, 4 miles before Tuna el-Gebel, are currently closed.

From early dynastic times Khmunu was an important cult center devoted to the moon-god Thoth and was believed to be the site of the primeval hill where the sun-god Ra emerged to create the world out of chaos. The Ptolemies, identifying Thoth with the Greek god Hermes, called the city Hermopolis. The ruins seem still to be waiting for the Creation to happen: beyond two giant baboons and a 5th-century basilica built with columns of a Ptolemaic temple, mounds of rubble, potsherds, and earth are all that remain of the temple of Thoth. But the site under the palm grove, with villagers walking through, is very picturesque.

▶ Tuna el-Gebel   *112A3*

Open: daily 7–5. Admission: moderate
Tuna el-Gebel was the necropolis of Hermopolis. On the road between the town and the site is a rock-cut boundary *stela* (inscribed stone) depicting Akhenaton and Nefertiti with their daughters, adoring the sun.

A path (right of the entrance) leads to the eerie catacombs where mummified ibises and baboons, sacred to Thoth, were buried. The most impressive building is the tomb-chapel of Petosiris (ca300 BC), the high priest of Thoth, whose exquisite coffin is in the Egyptian Museum in Cairo. Traditional Egyptian scenes of harvesting, sewing and wine-making on the vestibule walls show a Greek influence in clothing and perspective. The tomb

THE GOD THOTH
Thoth was the god of wisdom and, more specifically, the god of science and medicine. The sun-god Ra appointed him as his assistant and gave him the moon. He usually appeared as a man with the head of an ibis, because Ra gave him an ibis as a helper, or as a baboon with a large erected phallus. Baboons were identified with the sun because they shriek at the crack of dawn.

contains brightly colored scenes of the Book of the Dead and the Book of the Gates.

▶▶ Tell el-Amarna (Akhetaton) 112A3

Open: daily 7–5 (7–4 in winter). Admission: moderate/expensive
Tell el-Amarna can be reached by road from Mallawi (7 miles) and then by ferry to the villages of el-Till or el-Hagg Qandil on the east bank. From the ticket office there is basic transportation to the Northern Tombs and the palace area. A car is necessary to see the rest of the site.

Around 1349 BC Akhenaton founded his new capital, Akhetaton (Horizon of the Sun Disk), on an empty plain halfway between Memphis and Thebes. The city was abandoned soon after his death in 1336 BC, when the court returned to Thebes. Little remains of the mud-brick city, and the ruins of its palaces and temples are scattered across an arid plain, but realistic tomb paintings make it possible to imagine what the city might have looked like.

From the landing stage at el-Till a dirt track follows the Royal Road along the main axis through the center of the city. It leads to the Muslim cemetery, once the Great Temple of Aton, and then to the archives where the Amarna Letters were found. Three rectangular markers identify the Royal Residence, which was decorated with colorful scenes of birds, flowers, and fish. A walking bridge, with a window from which the royal family made public appearances, led over the Royal Road to the State Palace. Next door is the Sanctuary of Aton, and beyond it the residential quarters, mostly covered by sand. It was here in the workshop of the sculptor Tuthmosis that the bust of Nefertiti was found in 1912.

On the other side of el-Till is Nefertiti's Northern Palace, the best-preserved of Amarna's buildings. Amarna's necropolis is in the eastern cliffs. Of the Northern Tombs, the tombs of Huya (No. 1), superintendent of the Royal Harem; Mery-Re (No. 4), the high priest of Aton; and Panehesi (No. 6), vizier of Lower Egypt, are most worth a visit. There are 19 Southern Tombs, but the tombs of Mahu (No. 9), chief of police, and Ay (No. 25), scribe and confidant to Akhenaton, are the finest and best-preserved.

HYMN TO THE SUN
"At dawn you rise shining in the horizon, you shine as Aton in the sky and drive away darkness by sending forth your rays. The Two Lands awake in festivity, and men stand on their feet, for you have raised them up. They wash their bodies, they take their garments, and their arms are raised to praise your rising. The whole world does its work."
From Akhenaton's *Hymn of the Sun*

AMARNA FEES
You will need several tickets to see all of Amarna's sights, one for access to the site, another for entry to the northern tombs. If you have come without transportation, the staff can arrange a minibus to take you around, for another fee.

Self-expression seemed to be easier in Akhenaton's reign

Early in his reign, around 1349 BC, the pharaoh Akhenaton rejected the state god Amun and moved his capital north from Thebes to el-Amarna. Whatever the politics behind the move, it was a joyful liberation for his followers and this period produced Egypt's most radical art and some of its most enlightened thinking.

Right: Akhenaton's queen, Nefertiti, still embodies our ideal of beauty (see below)

THE FACE OF NEFERTITI
A 3,000-year-old bust of Nefertiti, one of the most famous images from ancient Egypt, was the prize discovery of an extraordinary dig during the winter of 1912 in the studio of Akhenaton's chief sculptor, Tuthmosis. The queen probably sat for this excellently preserved master portrait, on which all other images of her would have been based. The 20-inch-high limestone bust, showing the beautiful queen wearing makeup, a flat-topped crown, and necklace, officially belonged to James Simon, the Berlin merchant who held the license to dig. It is now on display in the Egyptian Museum in Berlin.

Akhenaton's rift It has been said that "more ink has been spilt on the Amarna period than the whole of the rest of Egyptian history." A slight exaggeration, perhaps, but there are good reasons why Akhenaton's actions— banning the worship of the state god Amun and raising Aton, the solar disk, previously a minor deity, to the status of the sole god of Egypt—have exercised the pens of theologians and Egyptologists alike. After all, to turn a well-established state religion on its head required an immense leap of the imagination, far greater, for instance, than the one that developed *mastabas* (tomb chambers) into pyramids. With Akhenaton's revolution, Egypt is seen to have been looking for a new direction. Its longing for spiritual and intellectual renewal is all the more poignant because it was so short-lived and because the reactionaries who succeeded to the throne—Tutankhamun among them—were thorough in their restoration of the old way.

God or gods? Some consider that Akhenaton's rejection of all other gods in favor of Aton was the first known instance of monotheism. The mummified remains of Yuya, Akhenaton's grandfather and a high official of common birth, were found in the Valley of the Kings in Thebes; as they don't look particularly Egyptian, one recent theory suggests that Yuya was Joseph, the youngest son of the Canaanite patriarch Jacob (and owner of a technicolor coat). If true, then perhaps it was Joseph who inspired Akhenaton to break with the past.

The new capital Akhenaton's new capital was built in a hurry, which explains its mud-brick construction. There is less for the visitor to see, but the ruins have been of great value to archeologists: because Akhenaton chose ground that had not previously been built upon and has not seen any major construction since, the ruins have afforded a privileged look at a New Kingdom community.
   From what is known, the city covered 110 square miles, facing the river and enclosed by a line of hills along its eastern edge. Its planning and decoration, its large palaces and comfortable houses, seem to have confirmed Akhenaton's emphasis on celebrating the living. The pavement from the palace at el-Amarna, painted with lush vegetation and flocks of birds (in Cairo's Egyptian Museum), and the other works that escaped the destructive hand of Akhenaton's enemies, testify to the beauty of the city.

The new art After centuries of increasingly stylized representations of Egypt's rulers, Akhenaton appears to us in an entirely different way. Here is a man we can understand: he plays with his children rather than staring into eternity, he has bodily imperfections that are shown, he eats, drinks, and clearly loves life. Identification is made even easier by the fact that his queen, Nefertiti, so closely adheres to our ideals of beauty. Much as we might like to see the beginnings of Judaism, Christianity, and Islam in Akhenaton's revolution, the artistic expression he seems to have encouraged lasted only as long as he did.

The awesome, demigod image of Akhenaton staring into eternity, sculptured in the traditional manner prior to the advent of his new art

❏ The Islamic University in Asyut, associated with el-Azhar in Cairo, has long been a stronghold for fundamentalists in the region. The struggle between Islamist groups and the security forces escalated when President Sadat tried to suppress religious extremism, a conflict that culminated in his assassination in Cairo in 1981. Egyptians returning from the Afghan war and the estimated 1 million who lost jobs in the Gulf because of the Gulf War provided fundamentalists with a new base of support. After 1992 several groups became actively involved in terrorism, most noticeably the Gamaat Islamiya, who called for the setting up of an Islamic republic and the deportation of foreigners.

Note: Tourists have been easy targets; night trains, cruise boats, and tourist buses have been attacked, with some injuries and deaths of foreigners. Following an attack in Luxor in November 1997, in which 58 foreigners and 10 Egyptians were killed, security throughout the country has been tightened. Roadblocks have made travel by road more difficult. As always, check with embassies or security services beforehand. ❏

► **Asyut** *112A2*

Asyut, the largest and least pleasant town in the Lower Nile Valley, has few sights, bad accommodations, and traffic congestion. Travel restrictions for tourists have added to the reasons to avoid it, unless you are determined to complete the Great Desert Circuit (see page 196). It lies 235 miles south of Cairo and can be reached by train from Cairo, Luxor, and el-Minya. In the 19th century, Asyut was the terminus of the Forty Days Road, and its slave market,

Pupils from Sohag attending the Coptic School at Deir el-Abyad (White Monastery)

the biggest in Egypt, offered "merchandise" from Sudan and the Libyan Desert. A few decaying *khans* (merchant hostels) survive in the *souk* as well as the Hammam el-Qadim, an early public bath. At the canal end of Sharia Gumhuriya, a small **museum**▶ displays local findings.

The large Coptic population ensures the survival of several fascinating monasteries in the area. **Deir el-Adhra (Monastery of the Virgin)**▶ (7 miles north of Asyut) is built around the caves of Dirunka, where the Holy Family is believed to have sheltered on their flight into Egypt. It is now a large commercial center, accommodating more than 50,000 pilgrims who celebrate the Moulid of the Virgin (feast day) each August. **Deir el-Muharraq (Burnt Monastery)**▶, (26 miles north of Asyut, at el-Qusiya), is believed to be the southernmost point in Egypt where the Holy Family stayed. The monastery has a thriving theological college, graduating hundreds of monks each year. For a week in the middle of June, thousands of pilgrims attend the Feast of the Consecration at the Church of the Virgin.

▶ **Sohag**   112B2

Sohag lies 290 miles south of Cairo; you can get there by train from Cairo or Luxor, and by bus from Asyut. Monasteries can be reached by private or service taxi.

Unlike Asyut, Sohag is a pleasant rural town with a large Coptic community and a university. Northwest of the town, on the edge of the desert, are two of Egypt's most celebrated monasteries. From a distance the **Deir el-Abyad (White Monastery)**▶▶ looks like a pharaonic temple. It is also called Deir Anba Shenuda, after St. Shenute, who was its abbot in the 4th century. The monastery once thrived with 2,000 monks, but only the Church of Shenuda and three or four monks remain, joined by thousands of pilgrims who attend the Moulid of Shenuda (week of July 14). The nearby **Deir el-Ahmar (Red Monastery)**▶ was founded by St. Bishoi, a disciple of Shenuda. Although it resembles the White Monastery, it is less impressive.

The White Monastery, south of Sohag

MONASTICISM IN UPPER EGYPT
Monasticism in Upper Egypt started around AD 320 after Pachom, born in Esna, founded the first community. Pachom had served in the Roman army until he converted to Christianity, and the regime of the monk, influenced by the military life, was strictly disciplined and of service to the community. Pachom's rule served as a model for monasteries in the West. Shenute (end of 4th century AD), founder of Coptic Christianity, went further and introduced strict rules to regulate every segment of the monk's daily life.

OMM SETY
In her early childhood Dorothy Eady, born in 1904 in a London suburb, had visions that in a former life she had been the mistress of Seti I. In 1933 she left for Egypt, married an Egyptian teacher and worked in Giza and later in Abydos, as a respected Egyptolo-gist. Soon divorced, she moved to the village of el-Araba el-Madfuna to be near her ancient lover, and revealed much about his temple. She had hoped to be buried in a tomb in her garden, but when she died in 1981 permission was refused. Turned away by Christian and Muslim cemeteries, she was eventually buried in the desert beyond the temple.

After Seti's death, his son Ramses II finished the decoration of his mortuary temple, but the later carvings are visibly inferior

▶▶▶ Abydos
112B1

Open: daily 7–5. Admission: moderate

The town of el-Balyana, between Sohag and Qena, can be reached by road or train from Cairo or Luxor. From el-Balyana, private and service taxis run the 6 miles to the village of el-Araba el-Madfuna near the temple of Seti I.

Few tourists take the trouble to visit this New Kingdom temple, but it remains one of the finest and most astounding monuments in Egypt. Just as Muslims nowadays hope to visit Mecca at least once in their life, so ancient Egyptians aspired to make a pilgrimage to Osiris' cult center at Abydos. Even before the Old Kingdom, when Abydos first became associated with Osiris, it was a desirable place for burial, as the ancient Egyptians believed that the afterworld began in the hills to the west of town.

The **Temple of Seti I▶▶▶** Only 29 years after the collapse of the Amarna regime (see pages 123–125), Seti I (19th Dynasty) built this lavish temple in the cult center of Abydos, hoping to reinforce his position by identifying his dynasty with Osiris and reconfirming his faith in the traditional pre-Amarna gods. The temple was built in the finest white limestone and its bas-reliefs are sublime. After Seti's death his son Ramses II continued the work, but with a less refined taste.

The pylon and the first and second forecourts have almost entirely disappeared and the temple is entered

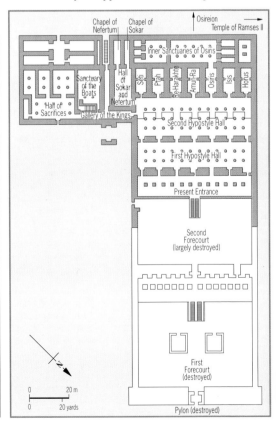

THE GREATEST TEMPLE IN EGYPT
"To pass through the great central doorway and enter into the Temple of Seti I is like entering a 'Time Machine' of science fiction. One leaves the modern world outside in the glare of the sunshine and, in the soft subdued light of the interior, enters the world of the past which for a time becomes the present...Every element in the scenes on the walls had a magical significance." Dorothy Eady (1956), quoted in *The Search for Omm Sety* by Jonathan Cott (widely available in Egypt).

Seti I wanted to forget about the Amarna interlude and led a renaissance of Old Kingdom styles in art

through the central of seven doors, leading to the seven sanctuaries. Reliefs in the First Hypostyle Hall, completed under Ramses II, are quite roughly executed. Some reliefs in the darker Second Hypostyle Hall were never finished, as Seti I died during the decoration of this part of the temple, but what is there is truly remarkable. On the right wall Seti is shown making offerings to Osiris, attended by several goddesses.

More fine bas-reliefs cover the walls of the seven sanctuaries and most have retained their original coloring. The sanctuaries are dedicated (right to left) to Horus, Isis, Osiris, Amun-Ra, Ra-Harakhte, Ptah, and Seti himself. The Sanctuary of Osiris leads to the inner sanctuaries of Osiris, where Seti performed the daily offering ritual. The Sanctuary of Seti emphasizes Seti's recognition by the gods, who lead him into the temple as the "Uniter of the Two Lands." A door near Seti's sanctuary leads into the Hall of Sokar and Nefertum, with two chapels. On the right in the Chapel of Sokar, Osiris is portrayed holding his penis, Isis hovering over him in the form of a hawk to conceive their son Horus. The other door leads to the Gallery of Kings where 76 *cartouches* (oval figures) trace Seti's descent from King Menes, omitting a few leaders like Akhenaton and Tutankhamun. Behind the temple is the Osireion or the Cenotaph of Seti I, sunk within an artificial mound. The interior, with a beautiful ceiling, is now underwater.

The Temple of Ramses II, 1,000 feet farther up, is almost completely destroyed, but must have been a magnificent edifice. Funerary monuments from the Old, Middle, and New Kingdoms are scattered across the area.

VOYAGE TO ABYDOS
Tomb paintings all over Egypt depict the voyage to Abydos, where the body of the deceased was brought by boat. One of the biggest festivals at Abydos, an annual celebration of Osiris' resurrection, which was tied in to the cycle of the moon, the seasons, and the rising of the Nile, was attended by the pharaoh and thousands of pilgrims. The festival survived until Christians sacked the temple in AD 395.

Osiris was one of the most popular and powerful figures in ancient Egyptian mythology and religion. He was a king assassinated by his jealous brother Seth and buried at Abydos by his sister-wife, Isis. His resurrection as the Lord and Judge of the Afterlife made him a figure of both fear and hope.

ISIS' LAMENT
"I am seeking after love:
Behold me existing in the city, great are its walls:
I grieve for your love for me–
Come you only, now that you have departed!
Behold your son, who caused Seth to retreat from destruction!
Hidden am I among the plants, and concealed is your son that he cannot answer you, while this great calamity remains!
Yet concerning you–
There is no likeness of your flesh left:
I follow you alone and surround the plants, each of which holds danger for your son,–
Lo, I, a woman, in front of all."
From the laments that Isis sang for her murdered husband

The story so far No complete version of Osiris' myth has survived from ancient Egypt, but in the 1st century AD the Greek historian Plutarch recorded it like this: Osiris, born a god, grew up as a man and is credited with civilizing Egypt and organizing agriculture and the cultivation of vines (he was believed to be the first person to drink wine). Osiris became king, his sister/wife Isis was his queen and everything in the valley blossomed until their brother Seth became jealous, trapped Osiris in a coffin, and threw him into the Nile. The coffin floated into the Mediterranean and was washed up on the Syrian shore, where it was encircled by a tree that eventually became a pillar in the royal palace at Byblos. When Isis eventually found Osiris' body, she took him back to the Egyptian Delta, where she and their sister Nephthys mourned him. Images in temples at Abydos, Dendara, and elsewhere show Isis as a bird, hovering over Osiris' erect penis: she was able to revive him long enough for their son Horus to be conceived.

The first mummy Seth hadn't finished with his brother and when he found the corpse, he cut it into 14 pieces and threw them into the Nile. Some 13 pieces were washed up at various places along the Nile, but his penis was eaten by fish. Wherever Isis found a part, she buried a wax copy to fool Seth (which explains why there are so many shrines to Osiris). With Horus, Anubis, and Thoth, she reassembled his body at Abydos, adding a phallus, and wrapped it in bandages to make the first mummy.

Horus' revenge and Osiris' glory When Horus reached manhood, he avenged his father's death in a heroic struggle with his uncle for control of the kingdom on earth. He then guaranteed his father's immortality by feeding one of his own eyes to Osiris. A symbol of resurrection, it was appropriate that Osiris was chosen to judge dead mortals who wanted to follow him to heaven.

Osirian rites The rituals connected to Osiris were among the most complicated and secretive in ancient Egypt, touching on the mysteries of creation and the afterlife. Because he had died and been reborn, Egyptians who could afford it had their bodies sent to Abydos, where they were mummified and had the "opening of the mouth" ceremony (whereby the *ka*, or soul, entered the deceased's body) performed in an attempt to be united with Osiris in eternity. But there were many dangers and tests to be passed before that was possible. Some of them are represented in tomb and coffin decorations, along with spells to protect the deceased.

Heavy at heart The most difficult moment of all on the journey to heaven was the trial known as "the weighing of the heart." It was a final test of worthiness and, in tomb paintings, the dead often provided reminders of gifts and offerings they had made to the gods during their lives. But there was no way to buy themselves a happy verdict. Instead, Osiris sat in judgment as their heart was put in the balance against the feather of the goddess Maat, who stood for truth.

Echoes from the past The myth of Osiris, Isis, and Horus, so central to life and death in ancient Egypt, hasn't entirely disappeared and there are many ways in which you confront their memory, most obviously in the depiction of Isis and Horus. Horus, the savior of the world, is often shown suckling the good woman Isis's breast. The parallel with Jesus and Mary might explain why some aspects of Christianity were so readily accepted along the Nile.

A PRAYER TO OSIRIS
"Glory be to you, O Osiris... king of eternity and lord of everlasting-ness, the god who passed through millions of years in your existence... As prince of the gods and of men, you have received the crook and the whip and the dignity of your divine fathers. Let your heart which is in the mountain of [the under-world] be content, for your son Horus is established upon your throne."
From the ancient Book of the Dead

Offerings being made to the dead King Osiris

112C1

▶▶▶ Dandara

Open: daily 7–6. Admission: moderate

Dandara lies 2.5 miles across the Nile from Qena, which can be reached by trains and taxis from Cairo and Luxor. From Qena there are taxis and horse carriages available to take you to the temple.

There were shrines to the cow goddess Hathor here in pre-dynastic times and throughout the Old, Middle, and New Kingdoms pilgrims were attracted by her healing powers. At the annual great festival, the statue of Hathor was taken from her sanctuary at Dandara and sailed to the temple at Idfu (Edfu) where, for two weeks, she was united with the statue of Horus. Mere mortals celebrated the divine union by copying the gods, or by getting drunk in the Festival of Drunkenness.

The present structure, built between 125 BC and AD 60, shows how the Ptolemies and Romans used their temples to emphasize their dedication to the main Egyptian gods—the Osirid trinity and the cow goddess Hathor—and also to legitimize their rule by proclaiming their divine birth and association with Horus, the deified king, as can be seen in the *mammisi* (birth houses).

The temple enclosure, surrounded by a well-preserved mud-brick wall, is entered from the monumental Roman gateway. To the right of the courtyard are the Roman Birth House, a 5th-century Coptic basilica, and the Birth House of Nectanebo I. The **Roman Birth House▶**, which was started by Augustus, has beautiful carvings on the south wall. To the left of the second birth house is a mud-brick sanatorium where sick pilgrims were treated, inspired by Hathor.

The **Temple of Hathor▶▶▶**, never completed, was covered in sand until the mid-19th century and has therefore been well preserved. The pylon and forecourt were never built, so the visit starts in front of the First

DAY EXCURSION

The easiest way to visit Abydos and Dandara is as a day-trip from Luxor. Start early, visit Abydos in the morning and Dandara in the afternoon. The option of staying overnight in Nag Hammadi is not possible with current security arrangements. A flashlight is necessary for exploring Dandara.

NEW YEAR FESTIVAL

On the eve of the New Year, at the end of the inundation (flood) season when the waters of the Nile receded, the statues of Hathor and other gods were taken in a procession to the roof of the temple where they were united with the sun, who gave them power and strength for the coming year.

The Temple of Hathor, one of Egypt's best-preserved temples

A Roman interpretation of the Hathor-headed column

Hypostyle Hall. The façade, shaped like a pylon, with six Hathor-headed columns, was built during the reign of Tiberius. The carvings show Roman emperors making offerings to the gods. The central doorway leads into the Pronaos (or First Hypostyle Hall), its 24 Hathoric columns decorated with *ankhs* (looped crosses) and scepters, symbols of life and prosperity. The ceiling preserves colorful astronomical scenes from the Egyptian zodiac, the hours of night and day, the planets and stars, and deities crossing the cosmos on their *felucca* (sailboat).

The Ptolemaic part of the temple starts with the Hall of Appearances (or Second Hypostyle Hall), where Hathor consorted with the gods before going on her journey to Idfu (Edfu). The raised reliefs on the walls show the temple foundation rites. Daily offerings were made in the Hall of Offerings, while statues of the nine deities worshiped in the temple were stored in the Hall of the Gods. Hathor's statue and ceremonial boat were kept in the closed Sanctuary, the temple's most sacred place; only the pharaoh was permitted to enter and adore the goddess. These rituals are represented on the inner walls. Behind the Sanctuary are three chapels: the middle Per-Ur Chapel was where the New Year procession started and the Per-Nu Chapel to the left was the starting point of Hathor's journey to Idfu. Return to the Hall of the Gods, turn left and then right into the Pure Place (or New Year Chapel), where all the rituals were performed before the procession went on to the roof. On the ceiling is a magnificent relief of the sky goddess Nut giving birth to the sun that shines on Hathor.

Back in the Hall of Offerings a staircase, decorated with scenes of the New Year procession, leads to the roof. In the southwest corner of the roof is the Disk Chapel, an unroofed kiosk where the statue of Hathor resided during the New Year festival. On the north side of the roof are the twin Chapels of Osiris with scenes of the Mysteries of Osiris. In the eastern suite is a plaster cast of the famous Dandara Zodiac, the original of which was taken to the Louvre in Paris.

THE EARTH MOTHER
Hathor, the cow goddess, the goddess of love, joy, and music, was one of the most ancient Egyptian gods. She was sometimes identified by the Greeks with Aphrodite. Her name, Hat-Hor, means "House of Horus," but according to mythology she first suckled Horus and later became his wife. She is represented as a cow, as a woman with a cow's head, as a woman with horns holding a sun disk, or, as in the Temple of Dandara, as a woman with cow's ears.

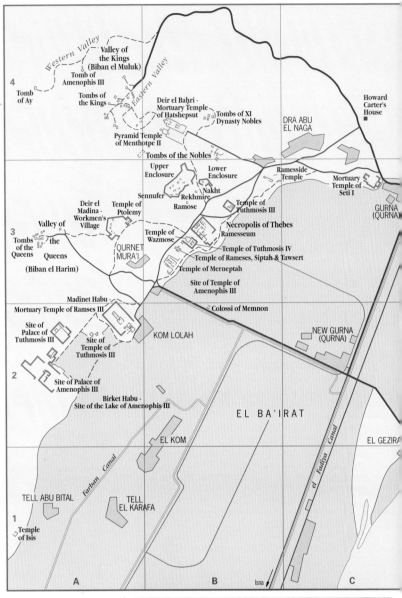

Western Valley

Valley of the Kings (Biban el Muluk)

Tomb of Amenophis III

4

Tomb of Ay

Tombs of the Kings

Eastern Valley

Deir el Bahri - Mortuary Temple of Hatshepsut

Tombs of XI Dynasty Nobles

Howard Carter's House

DRA ABU EL NAGA

Pyramid Temple of Menthotpe II

Tombs of the Nobles

Upper Enclosure

Lower Enclosure

Ramesside Temple

Mortuary Temple of Seti I

Sennufer Rekhmire Nakht

GURNA (QURNA)

Deir el Madina - Workmen's Village

Temple of Ptolemy

Ramose

Temple of Tuthmosis III

Valley of

3

Tombs of the Queens

the Queens

Temple of Wazmose

Necropolis of Thebes

Ramesseum

QURNET MURA'I

Temple of Tuthmosis IV

(Biban el Harim)

Temple of Rameses, Siptah & Tawsert

Temple of Merneptah

Site of Temple of Amenophis III

Madinet Habu - Mortuary Temple of Ramses III

Colossi of Memnon

Site of Palace of Tuthmosis III

Site of Temple of Tuthmosis III

KOM LOLAH

NEW GURNA (QURNA)

2

Site of Palace of Amenophis III

Birket Habu - Site of the Lake of Amenophis III

EL BA'IRAT

EL GEZIRA

EL KOM

Farban Canal

el Fadiya Canal

TELL ABU BITAL

TELL EL KARAFA

1

Temple of Isis

A   B   Isna   C

134

Right: crossing the Nile with animal feed

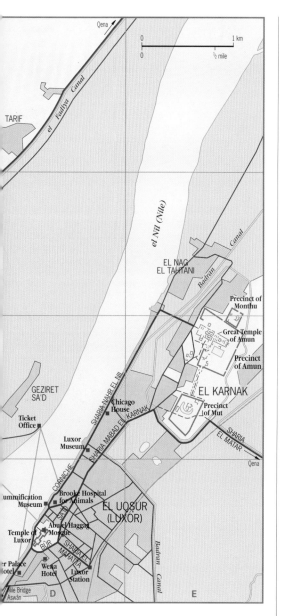

LUXOR Luxor contains the crowning achievements of Egyptian architecture. It was the capital of the New Kingdom for 500 glorious years and remained the country's spiritual center for much longer. Luxor's ruins are among the most extraordinary buildings ever constructed.

THE ANCIENT CITY Though there were settlements here from an early period, Luxor was an insignificant mud-brick village during the Old Kingdom. The kings who reunited Egypt under the Middle Kingdom came from nearby Armant but chose to be buried on the west bank of

Luxor

ESSENTIALS
(Minimum two days)
East bank (one day):
Karnak Temple, Luxor
Temple, Luxor Museum.
West bank (one day):
Valley of the Kings,
Deir al-Bahri, Tombs of
the Nobles

**BROOKE HOSPITAL
FOR ANIMALS**
In 1934 an Englishwoman, Dorothy Brooke, started an animal clinic in Cairo called the Hospital for Old War Horses. Run by a London-based charity, there are now Brooke hospitals providing free treatment to thousands of horses and donkeys in Cairo, Luxor, Edfu, Aswan, and Alexandria. They survive on voluntary donations, which can be made direct to the hospitals or via the headquarters in London (UK tel: 020-7930 0210).

the Nile at Thebes. Slowly power, both political and spiritual, shifted to the growing city until it became the capital of the kingdom.

GREAT TEMPLES Amun was a minor deity in Thebes, but he was the local god of the Middle Kingdom pharaohs. As they became more powerful, so their god's cult also gained ascendancy and, in a transformation lasting several centuries, he was united with the sun god Ra and worshiped as Amun-Ra. By the start of the New Kingdom, Amun-Ra was worshiped as the most important state god. During this period of international conquest, when Egyptian armies fought in Africa and Asia, some of the immense wealth that poured into the imperial capital of Thebes was spent building or embellishing temples. The most magnificent of these was Amun's temple at Karnak, a perfect expression of religious devotion, and its sister temple at Luxor, devoted to another aspect of the god as Amun-Min. Over successive centuries, pharaohs added to the great state temples and built their own mortuary temples on the west bank.

FAMOUS BURIALS Among Luxor's most famous monuments are the tombs of Thebes, in what are known as the Valley of the Kings and Valley of the Queens. These predominantly New Kingdom royal burial sites contained extraordinary treasures, but so far only Tutankhamun's tomb has been found intact. Their decorations are among the finest surviving examples of ancient Egyptian art. Less well-known are Deir el-Madina's workers' tombs and the

Tombs of the Nobles, decorated with less mysterious images than the royal tombs. Many show how the deceased lived on earth.

THE DECLINE OF THEBES Such was the glory of Thebes that it remained the country's spiritual center long after the end of the New Kingdom (1085 BC), when political power shifted northward to the Delta. The Nubian kings of the 25th Dynasty (747–656 BC) restored the capital to Thebes, but imagine the shock to Egypt's stability when the city was sacked by an Assyrian army in 671 BC and in 663 BC. Vulnerable and strategically insignificant, Thebes inevitably declined and when the Arabs conquered Egypt they abandoned Thebes to be buried by sand and silt.

THE RISE OF LUXOR Secular buildings in Thebes were constructed using mud bricks and these have either disintegrated under the onslaught of time and climate or been built over, but the great stone temples remain. They were used as churches and provided shelter for villagers for 200 years, and they have also been the object of a new kind of pilgrimage—tourism. Early tourists camped in or around the tombs and temples, or stayed on board their sailing boats, but for the opening of the Suez Canal in 1869 Thomas Cook arranged the first package tour. Egyptology, tourism, and the city have grown hand in hand ever since: more tombs and temples uncovered, more tourists wanting to visit them, more hotels needed to accommodate them. Luxor today is a noisy, bustling city strung along the east bank of the Nile.

After the sun sets, a gentle breeze blows away the heat of the day

137

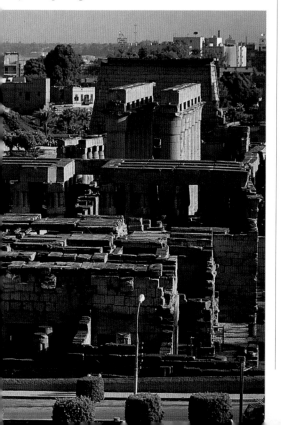

The Temple of Luxor lies right in the heart of Luxor town and seems always within sight

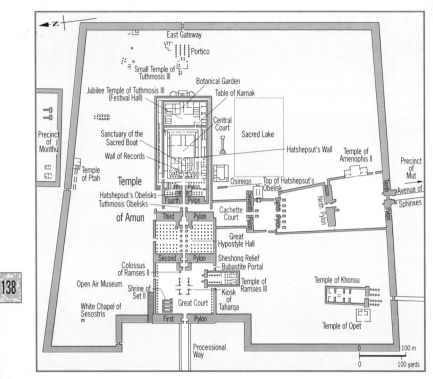

The processional avenue at Karnak

A RIDE TO KARNAK
You can take a taxi to Karnak, but it's more pleasant to go by bike or *calèche* (horse-drawn carriage). *Calèches* can be hailed in the streets, but drivers in Luxor have got haggling down to an art. Discuss the price in advance and ask your driver to spare the horse, allowing you time to enjoy the Nile breeze en route.

East Bank

►►► Karnak   135E2

Open: daily 6–6 in summer, 6–5:30 in winter.
Admission: expensive

The scale of Karnak surpasses every other pharaonic temple, with over 100 acres devoted to the gods (enough land to accommodate ten large European cathedrals). For 13 centuries successive pharaohs added their share to make this the most magnificent temple complex in the country and in the entire ancient world. It is also the most complicated design because Karnak, unlike other temples, was developed on a north–south as well as on an east–west axis. Known as "The Most Select of Places," it was not only a religious capital but also one of the most important intellectual centers in antiquity. The names of pharaohs and the different dynasties responsible for Karnak can be overwhelming; in general, the deeper you penetrate into the temple the older the monuments are.

The local god Amun started to grow in importance from the early Middle Kingdom onward and during the 12th Dynasty several temples were dedicated to him; their foundations were found under 18th-Dynasty structures in the Temple of Amun. During the 18th Dynasty, Amun was promoted to state god and Karnak soon became the most important religious center in the country. Amenophis I built a chapel around the Middle Kingdom temple, and his son Tuthmosis I erected both the fourth and fifth pylons, and a pair of obelisks. Queen Hatshepsut started building south of the older temple and added another pair of obelisks. Tuthmosis III built the seventh and eighth pylons, and the impressive Festival Hall.

Amenophis III came to power when the empire was at its zenith. Egypt's wealth was phenomenal and this was reflected in the art and architecture of the time. Amenophis started the building of the Great Hypostyle Hall and erected the third pylon. Amenophis IV (Akhenaton) added his share before turning away from Amun and founding his new capital in Amarna, but most of his buildings were destroyed. Under his son-in-law Tutankhamun, Amun was soon reinstated as the national god and Thebes regained its importance.

Seti I (19th Dynasty) instituted a period of renaissance, an early classical revival, to ease the doubts and heal the rifts caused by the Amarna revolution. Together with his son Ramses II he completed the Hypostyle Hall, which was the largest of any temple in the world. By this time the hierarchy of the priesthood at Karnak owned great wealth and wielded much power: it was inevitable that they would also seek political power. During the 20th Dynasty it was the high priest of Karnak who collected the taxes and effectively ruled the country, the pharaoh being nothing more than his puppet. The first pylon and first court were added by the later 20th–30th Dynasties.

It would take weeks to explore every relief on every wall in Karnak, but you should reserve at least two half-days to explore it—the first morning to be overwhelmed by the sheer size of it all and then an afternoon to enjoy a more detailed view in the soft warm glow of the late-day sun. The whole complex can be divided into three main areas: the most important is the Precinct of Amun (pages 142–143), with the Precinct of Mont to the north and the Precinct of Mut to the south, but the last two are rarely visited as they are badly ruined. (Continued on page 142.)

The colossal statue of Ramses II with one of his daughters stands guard at the entrance to the Second Pylon

139

Ancient Egyptians believed in the link between their own society and the universe around them: order, kept by the pharaoh and the gods, had to be maintained throughout the universe. Their temples stand as testaments to this belief.

EGYPT'S FINEST
Earlier mortuary temples can be seen at Maidum (Meidum) and Dahshur. Idfu (Edfu) is the most perfect and complete state temple to have survived. Karnak's hypostyle hall was and still is the finest and the grandest. Dandara and Philae have the best-preserved roof temples. Abydos has the finest carvings.

140

Two types of temples Egyptian temples can be divided into two groups. State or cult temples, often built on the site of earlier shrines, were intended for the worship of local or state deities, whose images resided in the temple sanctuary and were attended to by the priesthood. They would have been enlarged or rebuilt at some time in history, particularly during the New Kingdom. Mortuary temples were built as a focus for continuing rites for dead pharaohs. They were originally built onto or near the pharaoh's tomb, as at Giza and Saqqara, but as pharaohs sought greater security for their remains, mortuary temples were built at some distance from the royal tombs, which were sealed and intended never to be visited.

Approaching a temple Temple design evolved early and soon began to follow a set pattern, although pharaohs often sought to innovate or to outdo their predecessors. Temples were usually built at the border between the agricultural land and the desert, so they would be above the level of the Nile's annual flooding. Some mortuary temples also had connecting valley temples, situated at the high water point, so that boats could approach them during the annual flood. Temples were often approached along a processional way, sometimes lined with sphinxes

The processional colonnade of Amenhotep III and the pylons of Ramses II, at the Temple of Luxor

or other statuary, with the avenue usually ending at a gate in the temple wall. Except on certain holidays, this was as far as the public was allowed to go.

Interior design Enclosures often contained houses for priests, store rooms, a sacred lake, sometimes even a palace for the pharaoh, or, in Ptolemaic and Roman times, a birth house, but the temple proper consisted of a series of courts. The first was the outer or peristyle court, usually open and pillared, which led into the hypostyle hall, with pillars supporting the roof and the ceiling decorated with sky motifs. Beyond the hypostyle hall lay the sanctuary, where the deities rested in state, and beyond that, some chapels. Some temple roofs contained shrines, often concerned with the Osiris cult and the New Year celebration.

Decoration Decoration was as important as the form the building took, and from the outer pylon to the innermost sanctuary temples were often heavily adorned with painted, raised or sunk reliefs. Even the pillars were carved as Osirid figures (the kings as Osiris), or their capitals shaped as deities. The decorations often indicate the use the temple was put to and there are many images of temple processions and festival offerings.

Message in the design Temples were built on rising ground so that if you had stood at the first pylon when the doors were open—they have disappeared so you can do so now—you could have looked up through the courts, each ceiling progressively lower, each door narrower, toward the sanctuary. There was a point to this staged effect, and the themes were plain to see: nothing less than heaven and earth. Temples performed crucial symbolic functions in the struggle to preserve order in the universe, and just as the pillars of the hypostyle hall represented papyri in the primeval marshes, so the sanctuary on higher ground represented the first primeval mound that rose above the waters of Chaos and the roof represented the vault of heaven. That, after all, was the place to which the pharaoh and his people aspired.

The Hypostyle Hall with Osirid statues of Ramses II, at his temple in Abu Simbel

COLUMNS AND PILLARS
In predynastic Egypt people built with the available natural materials: mud, reeds, and trunks of palm trees. The earliest type of stone columns reproduced bundled reeds as in the entrance hall of the Step Pyramid at Saqqara. From the Old Kingdom onward there were different types of plant-shaped columns: a palm column with palm leaves tied on to a pole, or the lotus and papyrus-bundled columns. From the New Kingdom there are open papyrus columns and papyrus-bud columns. The columns in temples symbolized the plants of the primeval marshes: papyrus symbolized Lower Egypt and lotus and palms stood for Upper Egypt.

*Above: Ram-headed
sphinx, at the Temple
of Amun
Far right: The high and
massive columns of the
Great Hypostyle Hall
never fail to impress
mere mortals*

(*Continued from page 139.*) With so many additions to
Karnak by various rulers, it is hard at first to understand the
vast main **Temple of Amun▶▶▶**. The easiest place to start is
at the Processional Way, with ram-headed sphinxes, and
follow the east–west axis, walking straight through to the
Festival Hall. After that, time and energy allowing, it is
worth visiting the Open Air Museum, the Cachette Court,
and the Sacred Lake, which are off this axis.

The short Processional Way leads to the massive First
Pylon, which at 370 feet wide and 141 feet high is the
largest pylon in Egypt. It was built either during the 25th
or the 30th Dynasty, but was never finished and was left
undecorated (note the mud-brick ramp used in its
construction). Behind the pylon, the Great Court was
another later addition (22nd Dynasty), built to enclose
several earlier buildings that had previously been located
outside the temple proper. Immediately to the left is the

Shrine of Seti II, which held the sacred boats of Amun, Mut, and Khonsu during the preparations of the Opet festival. In the center of the court stands what is left of the Kiosk of Taharqa (25th Dynasty), one of the original ten open papyrus columns.

The small **Temple of Ramses III►►** (20th Dynasty), which served as another way station for the sacred *barques* (royal barges) during processions, stands to the right. The court of the temple is lined with Osirid columns, while reliefs on the walls depict scenes of the annual festival. The Bubastite Portal, a doorway between this temple and the Second Pylon, leads to the left to the fine Sheshonq relief depicting the victory of the biblical king, Shishak, over the son of Solomon. Back in the court, in front of the Second Pylon, stands the granite Colossus of Ramses II with one of his daughters. The Second Pylon was built by Horemheb (18th dynasty) using blocks from several Aton-temples built by Akhenaton.

Behind the Second Pylon lies the most breathtaking sight in Egypt, the magnificent **Great Hypostyle Hall►►►** (19th Dynasty), covering an area of 1.3 acres. It probably began as a processional way with the 12 columns with open papyrus capitals in the central nave. However, Seti I had grander plans and with his son Ramses II he added another 122 papyrus-bud columns, a roof, and walls, forming an enclosed forest in stone. Seti I decorated the left wing with fine bas-reliefs of offerings and cult scenes on the inside walls and columns, and scenes of his victories on the outside wall, while in the right wing Ramses II used a less-refined sunk relief for similar scenes.

At the eastern end of the hall is the badly ruined Third Pylon, built by Amenophis III (18th Dynasty) on top of older Middle Kingdom structures. Between the Third and the Fourth Pylon, built by Tuthmosis I (18th Dynasty), only one of the original four obelisks has survived. Beyond the Fourth Pylon stands one of two obelisks erected by Queen Hatshepsut to mark the sixth year of her reign; the tip of the second, fallen obelisk lies on the way to the Sacred Lake, near the Osireion. The columns around Hatshepsut's obelisk suggest that there was another hypostyle hall here, perhaps built by Tuthmosis III in an attempt to hide his stepmother's monuments. The Fifth Pylon was also built by Tuthmosis I and is followed immediately by a ruined Sixth Pylon by Tuthmosis III, with the Wall of Records, a list of Nubian and Asian enemies conquered by Tuthmosis. In the court beyond are two pink granite pillars, one finely carved with three lotus flowers and the other with three papyrus flowers, symbols of Upper and Lower Egypt. Toward the north of the court are two large statues of Amun and Amonet, dedicated by and looking like Tutankhamun, while a statue of Amenophis II sits against the west wall.

At the end of the court is the granite Sanctuary of the Sacred Boat, built by the

Luxor (East Bank)

144

ANOTHER STORY

"Near my room, amid thickly growing reeds, there was a small round pond full of salamanders, which was formerly the sacred basin for ablutions. My guide Temsah told me in a low voice that every night one could see, afloat on the thick, muddy water of this lake, a gold boat steered by silver women and drawn by a great blue fish. Many Arabs have tried to lay hands on it, but the enchanted boat vanished in smoke as soon as anyone came near."
Gustave Flaubert,
Karnak (1850)

The morning and evening play of light and shadow lends the Hypostyle Hall an air of even greater grandeur

SOUND AND LIGHT

If you only see one sound and light show in Egypt, this should be the one. There are two 90-minute shows per night, but check during your daytime visit for times and languages of the performances. Visitors first walk through the dramatically lit temple, while the story of Karnak is narrated. The second part is viewed from a grandstand behind the lake.

half-brother of Alexander the Great over a similar sanctuary by Tuthmosis III. In one of the rooms to the north is Hatshepsut's Wall with well-preserved reliefs.

Beyond the Central Court , the site of the original 12th-Dynasty temple of Amun, lies the **Jubilee Temple of Tuthmosis III▶▶**. The Festival Hall, unusual in its suggestion of the interior of a tent, has fine reliefs of the king celebrating his jubilee. In a chamber in the southwest corner the Table of Karnak, showing Tuthmosis making offerings to his predecessors, was found; it is now in the Louvre in Paris. Behind the hall in a small chamber with four papyrus columns, the Botanical Garden contains a splendid relief of plants and animals found in Syria.

On the north–south axis, next to the Hypostyle Hall, lies the Cachette Court where about 17,000 bronze and 800 stone statues were discovered. In front of the Seventh Pylon, built by Tuthmosis III and decorated during the 19th Dynasty, are seven statues from Middle Kingdom pharaohs. The Eighth Pylon, built by Hatshepsut, is flanked by four of the original six colossi. Between the Ninth and Tenth Pylons, built by Horemheb, is a small Temple of Amenophis II. Farther south is the partly excavated Precinct of Mut.

To the south of the Cachette Court is the Osireion, built in the Late Period, a now-cemented Sacred Lake, and a shaded café. To the north of Amun's Precinct is the Open Air Museum, with some reconstructed early buildings.

Above: calèche *on the Corniche*

Along the Corniche

Early 20th-century travelers describe the riverfront in Luxor, with colonial houses, gardens, and hotel terraces, as delightful. It is noisier today, lacking the romance of the past, but since the Corniche was restored in 1987 it makes a pleasant afternoon walk and the sun still sets magnificently behind the pink Theban Hills. See the map on page 134.

Start at the **Winter Palace Hotel**, founded in 1887 and now refurbished, though lacking the old glory. The views across the Nile to Thebes from its front terrace are beautiful, while the garden, less grand than before, is still pleasant. Turn right before **Luxor Temple** (see page 149) and walk into the garden of the **Wena Hotel**, formerly the Luxor Hotel and the oldest in town, where a bronze plaque commemorates the British physician Thomas Longmore (1864–1898).

Past the Wena, the road forks; this is the widest street leading to the station. To the left of it, Luxor's *souk* starts as a tourist bazaar before becoming a food market. Return to the Corniche and turn right at the temple past two 19th-century houses that once belonged to Europeans (one is now occupied by a political party). Below the Corniche, by the waterside, is a new shopping center and, opposite the Mina Palace Hotel, the **Mummification Museum**. In the street beside the Mina Palace is the **Brooke Hospital for Animals**, caring for Luxor's sick and abused horses and donkeys since 1963. Farther along, past the ruin of the old Savoy Hotel, the modern Etap Hotel is popular for local wedding parties.

To the right is the modern building of the **Luxor Museum** (see page 148) and farther north is Luxor Hospital, originally supported by tourist donations but now supported by the government. The walk ends at **Chicago House**, which is the home of the Oriental Institute of the University of Chicago, and which has been recording the monuments in Luxor since 1924.

Visitors rarely get to see moulids—*the celebrations of saints' days—but they are well worth tracking down as they offer some of the most distinctive, interesting, and ancient spectacles in Egypt. Festivals take place throughout the year and throughout the country.*

MOULIDS TO WATCH OUT FOR
Most *moulids* are regulated by the lunar Islamic calendar. Some of the more notable ones in Egypt are: Abu Haggag, Luxor; Moulid el-Nabi, the Prophet's birthday (all over the country, especially Cairo); el-Husayn, Cairo; Sayyid el-Badawi, Tanta; Sayyida Zaynab, Cairo.

146

Ancient traditions There is one group of historians who argue that the pagan religion of ancient Egypt wasn't abandoned when Christianity was adopted as the state religion, but rather that its beliefs and rituals were merged with the new religion. When Islam came along in the 7th century AD, another merger took place. *Moulids* seem to confirm this theory. There is nothing in Islam to encourage the elevation or remembrance of holy men, but in Egypt almost every village, and every district in the big cities, has its "saint" and their festivals are celebrated once a year, just as the local gods of ancient Egypt were fêted at their annual festivities. Some remain local events, lasting a few days and attended by no one beyond the village boundary, while others, like the *moulids* of Husayn in Cairo and Sayyid el-Badawi in Tanta, are national events, lasting more than a week and attracting millions for their blessing.

The program of a *moulid* The program of events is dictated by tradition, not by any religious obligation. The tomb of the saint is usually the focus of celebrations and prayers from different groups are said around it, increasing each day with the number of visitors, while loud speakers and lighting installations around the tomb become increasingly complex and insistent. The displays of *moulid* toys and hats, and the carts piled with nuts, boiled beans, chickpeas, or candies also multiply each day until there is a crowd of traders waiting to serve the people who come to honor the

Above and top: the moulid at Siwa of Sidi Suleyman, a local holy man who once conjured up a sandstorm to defeat a band of Sudanese raiders

Far right: the popular moulid of el-Husayn, prophet Muhammad's grandson, in Cairo

saint. Often when the crowd is at its thickest, brotherhoods of Sufis or dervishes parade through the streets before beginning their prayers and *zikrs* (ritual dances). Their chanting lasts for hours and is usually amplified through the streets in competition with the chants of rival brotherhoods intent on filling the night with noise.

A big night out The highlight of a *moulid* is the *layla kebira* or big night, the last one of the celebration. This is usually the best time to see a *moulid* if you don't mind crowds (they can be overwhelming, with more than a million people at the big *moulids*, and foreign women can feel very uncomfortable). The Sufis will be at their most energetic, their *zikrs* usually lasting till dawn.

The mawalidiya *Moulids*, like the ancient Egyptian festivals from which they are descended, are only partly to do with religion. As always when Egyptians get together, there is plenty of opportunity to do a little business or to sit and smoke with friends. The people who provide the more "social" of the services are known as *mawalidiya*. Traveling from *moulid* to *moulid* they sing, offer blessings or "medical" advice, and run food stalls, cafés, shooting ranges, swings, and often a circumcision booth.

More unusual attractions There used to be a *moulid* procession through Cairo in which a naked boy, pulled on a float, carried a huge phallus that was swung from side to side with strings. That particular attraction disappeared earlier this century, but at the *moulid* of Abu Haggag in Luxor a boat is carried around the saint's mosque—and therefore also Luxor Temple—as it was several thousand years ago. At some *moulids* there are people who enact ceremonial fights with sticks, or joust on horseback, and among the more unusual spectacles in Cairo is a *moulid* near the cemetery that includes floats of transvestites.

Not just Muslims Although most *moulids* are Muslim, some Christian and Jewish saints are also honored. The Copts celebrate the *moulid* of St. Damyanah in May and Jews from Israel and Europe come to honor Abu Khatzeira in June.

THE LANGUAGE OF LOVE
Sufis often use the language of love when singing about the mysteries of religion, as in this verse:
"She swayed as she moved; and I imagined each side, as she swung it, a twig on a sand-hill, and, above it, a moon at the full;
And my every member had, as it were, its several hearts, the one which as she glanced, was pierced by its showers of arrows."
Nicolaas H. Biegman's *Egypt: Moulids, Saints, Sufis* is an excellent introduction to *moulids*.

147

Tuthmosis III wearing the royal beard and the so-called atef-crown

148

GREAT DIOSPOLIS

"The Great Diospolis, by the Greeks called Thebes, was six leagues in circumference... The fate of her power and of her riches, celebrated by Homer, filled the universe. Her gates, and the numerous vestibules of her temples, induced this poet to bestow on her the name... the city of a hundred gates. Never did a city receive so many offerings in gold, in silver, in ivory, in colossal statues, and in obelisks of a single stone. Above all were to be admired, her four principal temples. The most ancient was surprisingly grand and sumptuous..."
Diodorus Siculus (60 BC)

►►► Luxor Museum of Ancient Egyptian Art   135D2

Open: daily 9–1, 4–10 in summer, 9–1, 4–9 in winter, 10–4 during Ramadan. Admission for museum and separate fee for the New Hall: moderate

This small, modern museum has an exquisite collection of statues and funerary objects found in temples and tombs in and around Luxor and is an absolute must. Every object is carefully chosen, well labeled, and both mounted and lit to bring out the best qualities.

On the first floor there are masterpieces from the New Kingdom, including an exquisite bust of a young Tuthmosis III (No. 61), a strange alabaster statue of the seated crocodile god Sobek holding Amenophis III (No. 107, labeled as Amenhotep III), a brightly colored wall painting of Amenophis III (No. 101) and a finely carved relief of Tuthmosis III (No. 64)—all from the 18th Dynasty.

Upstairs there is a series of sunk reliefs from Akhenaton's temple in Karnak (18th Dynasty), with the king and his wife Nefertiti worshiping the sun god Aton and detailed scenes of Egyptian laborers at work (No. 141). There are smaller relief fragments of the same temple, some representing Nefertiti praying and making offerings (Nos. 165–168), and two fascinating sandstone heads of Akhenaton, from Osirid statues, in the typically realistic Amarna style (Nos. 156 and 171).

In the glass case upstairs are a few objects from Tutankhamun's tomb (18th Dynasty): sandals (Nos. 186–187), arrows (No. 193), a fine wooden head of Hathor (No. 196), and two beautiful funerary *barques* (Nos. 199 and 200). The New Hall was specially designed to house the impressive cache of 26 statues discovered in Luxor Temple in 1989. Among the finest of the large statues are Ramses II, Queen Nefertari, Tutankhamun, and Amenophis III.

Block statue of Yamu-Nedjeh, First Herald of King Tuthmosis III

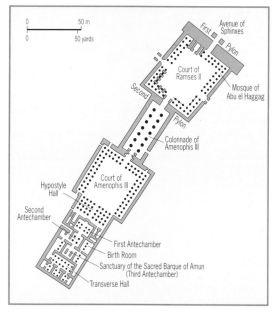

0   50 m

0   50 yards

Avenue of Sphinxes

First

Pylon

Court of Ramses II

Second

Mosque of Abu el Haggag

Pylon

Colonnade of Amenophis III

Hypostyle Hall

Court of Amenophis III

Second Antechamber

First Antechamber

Birth Room

Sanctuary of the Sacred Barque of Amun (Third Antechamber)

Transverse Hall

149

TOWN WITHIN THE TEMPLE

" ...The next day we visit Luxor. The village can be divided into two parts, separated by the two pylons: the modern part, to the left, contains nothing old, whereas on the right the houses are on, in, or attached to the ruins. The houses are built among the capitals of columns: chickens and pigeons perch and nest in great (stone) lotus leaves... dogs run barking along the walls. So stirs a mini-life amid the debris of a life that was far grander..."
Gustave Flaubert in Egypt (April 1850)

►►► Luxor Temple   135D1

Open: daily 6 AM–10 PM in summer, 6 AM–9 PM in winter, 6–5, 8–11 during Ramadan. Admission: expensive (moderate after 6:30 PM)

In ancient times ordinary people were barred from entering temples, but now the Temple of Luxor lies in the heart of town. Verdi's opera *Aida* was staged here in 1987, with thousands of extras, and for several weeks no other music was heard in Luxor's coffee houses. The Temple of Luxor is far more coherent than Karnak because it was mainly built by two kings. Amenophis III (18th Dynasty), who also built the Colossi of Memnon and the Third Pylon at Karnak, founded the temple on the site of an older sanctuary. Ramses II (19th Dynasty) added the impressive pylon with obelisks, colossi (giant figures), and a colonnaded court. Luxor Temple, dedicated to the Theban Triad of Amun-Min, Mut, and Khonsu, was known as the

When the mud-brick houses were cleared away from the temple, the mosque of Luxor's patron saint Abu el-Haggag had to stay. Its left-hand minaret is one of the oldest found in Upper Egypt

150

FLOODLIT TEMPLE
The temple is well worth a second visit in the evening when it is dramatically lit and has fewer visitors. It seems more mysterious and imposing then, more like the temple might have felt in ancient times. The depth of the reliefs is intensified by the play of light and shadow.

LUXOR'S OTHER NAMES
Ancient Egyptians knew it as Waset and, as their scribes claimed, it was "the pattern of every city" and that "mankind came into being within her." To the Greek poet Homer, Waset was the fabled "hundred-gated Thebes." When the Arabs came upon the remains of the city in the 7th century AD, they called it al-Uqsor (the Palaces), the name that it retains in Arabic and that was corrupted into Luxor.

"Harem of the South" where Mut and her son Khonsu resided, while Amun-Min stayed in Karnak. The two temples were connected by the 2-mile-long Avenue of Sphinxes and during the annual Opet (fertility) festival, Amun's statue was escorted from Karnak by a grand procession of *barques* (holy barges) to be reunited with his wife Mut at Luxor.

The temple is well preserved, especially the pylon reliefs, because it was mostly covered by sand and, until the late 19th century, by the town itself. In 1885 when excavations began, the houses were slowly cleared away, but the people of Luxor refused to allow the mosque and tomb of their patron saint, Abu el-Haggag, to be destroyed. The mosque is still there, hanging above the northeast corner of the court of Ramses II. The *moulid* of Abu el-Haggag is the largest festival in Upper Egypt. One or more boats are carried up to the mosque, a distant reminder of the Opet festivities.

The temple is best approached from the Avenue of Sphinxes, erected by Nectanebo I (30th Dynasty), which leads to the First Pylon. The pylon, built by Ramses II, was originally 79 feet high and 213 feet wide, with splendid reliefs exaggerating Ramses' victory in the Battle of Qaddesh.

Originally there were six statues of Ramses in front of the pylon, but only two seated colossi and a badly damaged standing figure remain. An exquisite obelisk, supported by dog-headed baboons, stands in front of the pylon. Its twin, given to Louis-Philippe of France, now stands in the Place de la Concorde in Paris.

The entrance passage to the Court of Ramses II was decorated by 25th-Dynasty Nubian and Ethiopian kings. The court is surrounded by a double row of papyrus-bud columns that once formed a roofed arcade. Above the northeastern corner sits the Mosque of Abu el-Haggag (see page 147), rebuilt in the 19th century but with an original 11th-century minaret. At the back of the court, on the wall to the right, is an unusual relief showing the temple with its colossi, obelisks, and banners. On the right wall of the court is a funerary procession led by 17 of Ramses' more than 100 sons. In front of the Second Pylon, two black granite colossi of Ramses are seated on bases decorated with the figures of tied-up Nubians and Hittites.

The portal leads into the main part of the temple, starting with the impressive Colonnade of Amenophis III. On either side there are high columns with calyx capitals supporting heavy architraves. The work was unfinished when Amenophis died, and Tutankhamun had the walls decorated with scenes of the Opet festival. Starting at the portal to the right, the pharaoh is seen making sacrifices before the *barques* at Karnak, followed by the floating procession and the arrival at Luxor; on the opposite wall is the happy return to Karnak after a 24-day honeymoon.

The colonnade leads into the Court of Amenophis III, with double rows of elegant papyrus columns and then a small hypostyle hall. On the back wall are reliefs showing Amenophis' coronation by the gods. Next is a columned portico whose reliefs were plastered over in the 3rd or 4th century AD by Roman legionaries using it as a chapel. The smaller second antechamber was an offering chapel, and the reliefs show the pharaoh making offerings to Amun. Beyond lies a third antechamber, which was converted by

Alexander the Great into the Sanctuary of the Sacred Barque of Amun. It once had acacia-wood doors inlaid with gold, and the walls bear reliefs of Alexander making offerings to the Theban Triad.

From the side room to the left of the sanctuary, a door leads to the Birth Room, where reliefs show Amenophis' divine birth. His pregnant mother Mutemuia gives birth, led by Isis and Khnum. Isis then gives the baby to Amun, who holds Amenophis in his arms. Khnum is molding the baby and his *ka* (soul) on his potter's wheel. It was near this room, in 1989, that an important cache of statues was found, now in the Luxor Museum. Farther south, a columned Transverse Hall leads to the private apartments of the gods, now unfortunately badly damaged.

▶▶ Mummification Museum   135D1

Open: daily 9–1, 5–10 in summer, 4–9 in winter.
Admission: expensive.
Luxor's latest attraction is opposite the Mina Palace Hotel, and cuts through the mystery of the mummy to reveal the secrets of how it was done, including the brain scoop.

Ramses II is wearing the double crown of Lower and Upper Egypt as a symbol for the united country

THE MISSING OBELISK
"The obelisk that is now in Paris... Perched on its pedestal, how bored it must be in the Place de la Concorde! How it must miss its Nile!"
Gustave Flaubert (1850)

Visitors to Luxor in recent years were shocked to find Tutankhamun's tomb closed for restoration, but it is just one of many monuments that are in danger of collapse. Rising groundwater, urban and industrial growth, pollution, and even tourists all pose a threat. There is disagreement as to what should be done to preserve Egypt's antiquities for future generations.

HOW YOU CAN HELP
Help preserve what is left of the monuments by paying attention to signs asking you not to touch them, or carve names, or use a photographic flash, and by discouraging others who are less thoughtful.

152

TWO VIEWS OF THE PROBLEM
"These monuments... do not belong solely to the countries who hold them in trust. The whole world has the right to see them endure."
Dr. V. Veronese, Director-General of UNESCO, speaking at the Abu Simbel appeal, March 8, 1960

"They [foreign Egyptologists] let us bear the burden of restoring and maintaining the monuments alone—the monuments they excavate themselves. They pick up this and that and write books about their work and they tell us that it is not their work to restore the monument."
Dr. Mohammed Ibrahim Bakr, ex-Chairman, EAO (1993)

A modern problem An 18th-century Jesuit missionary, Claude Sicard, sailed up the Nile reading a Greek account of ancient Egypt and was lucky enough to find much of it exactly as described two millennia earlier. Travelers in the 19th century were just as awe-struck as the Jesuit, but a new tone creeps into their descriptions. The monuments were wonderful, no doubt about it, but damage was being done by the modern Egyptians. The remains of ancient Egypt, some of them suggested, must be saved for the world. The argument that "if I don't take it away it will be destroyed" was the justification for the removal of statues, the cutting out of sections of walls and the transportation of shiploads of objects that became the basis of European and American museum collections. The French archeologist Auguste Mariette, who established the Egyptian Antiquities Organization (EAO) in the 1850s, tried to limit unlicensed excavation and to clear the temples and tombs. While he succeeded in containing one problem, he laid the ground for another.

The problem of preserving monuments Before the EAO cleared the temples, many Egyptians lived in and around them and while they undoubtedly caused some damage—you can see the effect of their fires on the top of many temple columns—it was nothing compared to the threats the monuments are facing now. There was great concern about damage to monuments when the second Aswan Dam was being built and a successful campaign was fought by UNESCO in the 1960s that resulted in Abu Simbel and some of Nubia's other monuments being moved above the waterline. But the dam also appears to have caused a rise in the level of groundwater north of the dam, which threatens to erode the stone monuments. The spread of industry and increases in traffic, air pollution, and urban encroachment are threatening monuments throughout Egypt. The monuments are also suffering from their own popularity as much as from neglect. For instance, tourists visiting the Valley of the Kings have been depositing gallons of sweat every day in the unprotected tombs, causing paint and plaster to peel from the walls.

Excavation or conservation? Many people know the name of Howard Carter and can retell the story of his discovery of Tutankhamun's tomb (see page 164), but not many would recognize the names of the people involved in its restoration. Conservation is not as glamorous as excavation and that is part of its problem. Egypt's own specialists lack the funds and the manpower to preserve ancient sites, and bureaucrats tend to make things worse, while the people who could help—the foreign Egyptologists—are driven by the demands of their own, increasingly cutthroat occupation. To further their careers, they need to dig, to find something important and to tell the world about it, or else get involved in documentation, publishing detailed records of images that are fading as they work. Although the technology does exist to preserve many of the monuments faced with destruction, the money is not available to pay for it in Egypt, and the will, or the interest, is lacking to pay for it in the international community.

What happens next? No one knows what will happen next, except that more tombs will be closed and more buildings will have to be propped up by scaffolding unless something is done. The threat exists not just in Luxor, or with ancient monuments—Coptic and Islamic buildings are also collapsing around the country. The only certainty is that many things included in this book will no longer exist when our children come to see them.

THE TEMPLE OF THE WORLD

"Two thousand years ago, an Egyptian scribe saw it coming. And he protested. He said, 'Do you not know that Egypt is a copy of the universe? The temple of the world? And that if it goes, the world will be full of graves and dead men?' I think what the ancient scribe was saying is that if we let all this slip through our fingers with-out caring, a bit of our humanity will die." John Romer, in the television documentary *The Rape of Tutankhamun* (1993)

The fallen head of yet another colossal statue of Ramses II, in the Ramesseum

153

THE ONE AND ONLY
Hatshepsut, daughter of Tuthmosis I, married her half-brother Tuthmosis II, who died young. As there was no direct successor, Hatshepsut proclaimed herself co-regent to the young Tuthmosis III, the son of a secondary wife. Her hunger for power didn't stop there and it wasn't long before she declared herself pharaoh. She was always depicted as a man, wearing a beard and men's clothing. After her death, when Tuthmosis III finally came to power, he erased all of her *cartouches* (oval figures) and portraits, in an unsuccessful attempt to consign her to oblivion.

The magnificent setting of the Temple of Queen Hatshepsut against the Theban Hills

West Bank

▶▶▶ Deir el-Bahri (Mortuary Temple of Hatshepsut)   *134B4*

Open: summer 7–6 daily and winter 7–5 daily.
Admission: moderate

This temple, dramatically set against the Theban Hills, often disappoints at first sight. The courts and terraces look stark and too modern, but as you go closer, imagine them filled with perfumed gardens, fountains, and myrrh trees and you'll understand the grandeur of this place. Hatshepsut (18th Dynasty), a female pharaoh, called her temple Djeser Djeseru (the Splendor of Splendors). In ancient times a promenade lined with sphinxes probably ran from the Nile to the Lower Terrace. The reliefs on the colonnades on either side of the ramp were badly damaged by Tuthmosis III and Akhenaton. The reliefs on the Northern Colonnade depict country life, with a fine picture of waterbirds caught in a net.

The lower ramp leads to the Middle Terrace. In the Birth Colonnade, to the right, Hatshepsut is shown with divine parents. At the end, the Chapel of Anubis has bright wall paintings. The Punt Colonnade, left of the ramp, has reliefs of the expedition to Punt (probably the coast of Somalia). Five ships leave the Red Sea port and upon arrival are met by the chief of Punt and his wife. The ships coming back are laden with exotic trees, myrrh, incense, and animal skins. The Chapel of Hathor has cow-eared Hathoric columns, and inside the Sanctuary of Hathor is one of the few intact images of Hatshepsut.

The second ramp leads to the Upper Terrace, which may be closed for restoration. Hewn into the mountain is the Sanctuary of Amun. To the left is the Sanctuary of Hatshepsut with fine reliefs, and to the right, the Sanctuary of the Sun.

Bike ride

buy a photo permit. Remember that it is forbidden to use a flash; take fast film instead.

The West Bank

If you want to see the main sights on Luxor's West Bank in a day, you will need to take a taxi. But if you have more time, there is nothing finer than riding a bicycle slowly from one site to another, taking in the glorious country-side and meeting people on the way. See map on page 134.

Practicalities You can rent bikes on the East and West Banks. There are places to eat on the West Bank, but a picnic under the trees at the Rames-seum is hard to beat. Most sites are open 7–5 in winter and 6 AM–7 PM in summer. Less popular tombs may close earlier but the keeper is usually around. Tickets for the sites must be purchased in advance, and can now be bought only from the ticket office at the crossroads past the Memnon Colossi. It will save time if you decide in advance what you want to see as there are separate tickets for every temple or group of tombs. To use a camera inside the tombs you have to

First day itinerary: Village of New Gurna (Qurna), on the right past the el-Fadiya Canal, designed by the Egyptian architect Hassan Fathy (30 minutes)—Colossi of Memnon (30 minutes, page 157)—Temple of Madinet Habu (1 hour, page 156)—lunch at Shahhat's café opposite the temple—Deir el-Bahri (1 hour, page 154)—walk over the hill or cycle to the Valley of the Kings (2–3 hours, pages 160–163).

Second day itinerary: Valley of the Queens (45 minutes, page 166)—Deir el-Madina (30 minutes, page 156)—Valley of the Nobles (2–3 hours, pages 165–166)—Ramesseum (lunch and 30 minutes, page 158)—Temple of Seti I (30–45 minutes, pages 158) and cycle back along the canal.

Pharaonic motifs are a common sight on houses on the West Bank

155

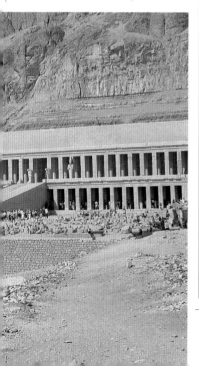

*A humble Ramses III
making offerings to the
gods, Madinet Habu*

▶▶ Deir el-Madina   134A3

Open: summer 7–6 daily and winter 7–5 daily.
Admission: moderate

Deir el-Madina was the Workmen's Village, home to the craftsmen and artists who worked in the Valley of the Kings. They recorded their daily life on *ostraca* (pottery fragments) or papyrus, from which we know that they worked in shifts of eight hours a day for ten days. In their free time they worked on their own tombs, built beneath small pyramids, taking inspiration from the royal tombs.

The ruined village is closed to visitors, but a few tombs in the necropolis are open and are worth visiting. A pyramid marks the Tomb of Sennedjem (1), well-preserved with colorful murals of funerary rituals and the owner farming his land. Peshedu is shown praying beneath a palm tree in his tomb (3). The tomb of Inherkhau (359) has a fine scene of Inherkhu and his wife listening to a harpist. To the north is a Ptolemaic temple, dedicated to Maat and Hathor. Christians turned the temple and village into a monastery, Deir el-Madina (literally the Monastery of the Town).

▶▶ Madinet Habu (Mortuary Temple   134A2
of Ramses III)

Open: summer 7–6 daily and winter 7–5 daily.
Admission: moderate

This 20th-Dynasty temple is one of the best-preserved and easiest to understand, a classical temple, with few additions. It was built on an older sacred site: according to legend, the first land that appeared above the waters of Chaos. Ramses III modeled his extravagant temple—the last great pharaonic temple—on the Ramesseum of his ancestor, Ramses II. Centuries after Ramses III's death, the Coptic town of Jeme grew up around the temple's vast mud-brick enclosure walls.

The enclosure is entered through the unusual gatehouse, which is modeled on a Syrian fortress. Inside, stairs lead to Ramses' private pleasure apartments. Inside the temple's grounds, to the right, is an older small temple, built by Hatshepsut on the site of the primeval hill.

The First Pylon of Ramses' temple is almost as high as the one at the Luxor Temple (a staircase leads to the top, with fabulous views). Like the temple's design, some reliefs were probably also copied from the Ramesseum, showing battles Ramses III never fought. His own struggle against the Sea Peoples is recorded in detail on the northern wall of the temple. Ceremonies and festivities were held in the First Court; ruins of the Royal Palace can be seen through the windows of its south wall. The Second Court was later used as a Coptic church, and Christian symbols can be seen on the pillars, but a few Osiris figures have also survived. The colors of the reliefs under the western colonnade are exceptional. Beyond are three hypostyle halls with sanctuaries and treasure rooms on the sides and, off the inner hall, three main sanctuaries dedicated (right to left) to Mut, Khonsu, and Amun; they were once covered with electrum (an alloy of gold and silver) and had a golden doorway. On the outer south wall there are fine reliefs of Ramses hunting and fishing.

▶▶ Memnon Colossi   134B2

Open at all times. Admission: free

Two colossi of Amenophis III, 64 feet high, sit peacefully amid sugarcane fields. They once guarded the gates of the mortuary temple of Amenophis III (18th Dynasty), of which nothing else remains. The right one was hit by an earthquake in 27 BC, after which it made a noise that sounded like singing at dawn, which the Greeks believed was Memnon singing for his mother Eos. Many visitors, including Roman emperors, visited it. Septimus Severus restored it in AD 199, after which it was silent.

The colossi are covered in Roman and other graffiti. On the sides are reliefs of Nile gods who are binding together the flowers of the Two Lands. Small statues of Queen Tiy and of Mutemuia, the mother of Amenophis, stand on either side of the colossi's legs.

157

The Colossi of Memnon are no longer singing for their visitors

For once Ramses II chose the wrong site for a building: his mortuary temple suffered badly from Nile floods

▶ Mortuary Temple of Seti I

134C3

Open: summer 7–6 daily, winter 7–5 daily.
Admission: moderate

The works of Seti's reign (19th Dynasty), particularly his temple in Abydos, are the finest of the New Kingdom. He built this temple for the worship of the god Amun and of Ramses I, his father, but now only the temple building remains. The columns in the hypostyle hall are decorated with fine reliefs of Seti and his son Ramses II. In the chapels and sanctuary beyond there are more superb reliefs. This temple is, surprisingly, rarely visited.

▶▶ Ramesseum

134B3

Open: summer 7–6 daily, winter 7–5 daily.
Admission: moderate

This is the mortuary temple of Ramses II, known as Ramses the Great. Although Ramses II took great care to ensure his immortality, this temple, home to his immortal spirit, was built on weak foundations and is ruined, though broken columns and fragments of pylons are now being reassembled by French archeologists.

The temple is entered from the north, which leads to the First Pylon, with scenes of Ramses II's victory over the Hittites in the Battle of Qaddesh. At the far end of the ruined First Court, steps lead down to the Second Court. To the left is the famous statue of Ozymandias, the inspiration for Shelley's poem, and one of Egypt's largest free-standing monuments, 57 feet high and weighing over 1,000 tons. The fragments are still astonishing for their size and perfect finish. The Second Pylon is partly decorated with the Battle of Qaddesh and has a top register portraying the god Min. The Second Court is lined with an Osiris colonnade. Near the stairway leading to the West Portico lies another smaller granite colossus. The Great Hypostyle Hall has 29 of its 48 columns still standing. The vestibules lead to the ruined sanctuary.

OZYMANDIAS

I met a traveller from an antique land,
Who said: Two vast and trunkless legs of stone
Stand in the desert...Near them, on the sand,
Half sunk, a shattered visage lies, whose frown,
And wrinkled lip, and sneer of cold command,
Tell that the sculptor well those passions read
Which yet survive, stamped on these lifeless things,
The hand that mocked them and the heart that fed.
And on the pedestal these words appear:
"My name is Ozymandias, king of kings:
Look on my works, ye Mighty, and despair!"
Percy Bysshe Shelley

Earlier Egyptians were often buried in tombs cut into rocks, but from the 18th Dynasty pharaohs and their families built tombs in the valleys of the Theban Hills. Their tombs, in the Valleys of the Kings and Queens, are among the most spectacular remains along the Nile.

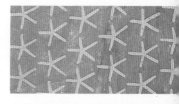

Theban tombs Pharaohs were breaking with a 1,000-year tradition when they were buried in hidden tombs, far from their mortuary temples. They were hoping to secure their remains forever, but the promise of funerary treasure brought robbers to the desolate valleys. Accordingly, tombs became more complex and included pits to trap robbers, but New Kingdom pharaohs still seldom remained in their tombs for long. As the New Kingdom collapsed, so the guardian-priests abandoned the tombs and treasure altogether and reburied the mummies in unmarked pits elsewhere. Even Tutankhamun's tomb, the best preserved of all, was broken into and then resealed by the priests of the necropolis.

Decorations Entering royal tombs at Thebes is like following the pharaohs on their journey to the underworld. The walls are decorated with passages from the Book of the Dead and the Book of the Gates, anticipating what was lying in store for the dead soul: the unworthy were assaulted by snakes or crocodiles, while the worthy had their hearts weighed for purity in front of Osiris.

The tombs today European travelers in the 18th century found local villagers making use of opened tombs as houses. The prospect of finding gold has attracted locals as well as foreigners and there are many stories of villagers uncovering tombs and trying to sell the contents. The government has tried to clear villagers out of old Gurna (see page 165), but they are loath to leave, which suggests there might be some truth in the rumors.

Top: In ancient as well as modern-day Egypt, professional mourning women beat their chests and threw sand in their faces in grief for the death

Above: Old Kingdom rulers were buried in sarcophagi, which were symbolically equated with the body of the sky goddess Nut, therefore affording the deceased the protection of the goddess

WALKS IN THE THEBAN HILLS

The hike from the Valley of the Kings to Deir el-Bahri can be done in about half an hour, but is worth doing slowly. Start at the trail near tomb No. 16 and where the path forks, turn to the left and walk along the cliff for magnificent views of the temple and the abundant, green Nile Valley. Follow the path along the wire fence and where it forks turn to the left. In the wake of the 1997 massacre at Deir el-Bahri, police now guard the hill day and night.

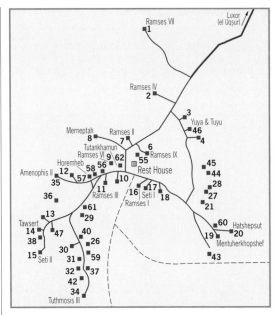

▶▶▶ Biban el-Muluk (Valley of the Kings) 134A4

Open: daily 7–6 in summer, 7–5 in winter.
Admission: expensive

From Tuthmosis I (18th Dynasty) onward, all the New Kingdom pharaohs and occasionally a high official were

Wall painting in the tomb of Ramses IV. These paintings were intended to guide the deceased through the next world to their judgment by Osiris

buried in this secluded *wadi* (dry gully), the "Place of Truth," as the ancient Egyptians called it, hidden in the barren Theban Hills. These tombs, hewn into the rock and decorated by craftsmen, were designed to preserve the royal mummies for eternity. Pharaohs usually started the work on their tombs as soon as they came to power, but many died before the decoration was finished. Every precaution was taken to protect tombs from intruders, but treasures buried with the deceased were too attractive to resist. Powerful pharaohs of the 18th and 19th Dynasties kept the tombs under close supervision, but under the weaker rulers of the 20th Dynasty looting was rife, often by craftsmen who had worked on the tombs or officials who were supposed to be supervising. By the end of the New Kingdom the priests had to rebury the mummies and some of the objects in two secret caches, which weren't discovered until the end of the 19th century.

At the end of the 18th century, other intruders arrived on the scene to disturb the pharaohs' eternity: Egyptologists and early travelers. In 1922, Howard Carter discovered the Tomb of Tutankhamun, the last of the 62 tombs that have been uncovered to date. The fine and brightly colored murals survived for thousands of years, but sadly, some have now been irreparably damaged, partly through the effects of mass tourism (see pages 152–153). A rotation system is now being introduced whereby only a small number of tombs will be open at any one time, and many of the decorations on tomb walls can now only be seen behind glass. The most radical of the plans under discussion involves closing all of the tombs and building a replica of the Valley of the Kings elsewhere.

Not all of the tombs have electric lighting, so only the ones that are lit will be described below.

Tomb of Ramses IV (No. 2)▶▶ (20th Dynasty) The bright lighting and delicate pastel colors of the murals make up for the poor quality of the carvings and an awful lot of Coptic graffiti. The ceiling of the sarcophagus chamber is adorned with a double image of Nut, while on the enormous pink granite sarcophagus, Isis and Nephthys were supposed to protect the mummy.

Tomb of Ramses IX (No. 6)▶ Ramses IX was one of the last kings of the 20th Dynasty. The walls of his tomb are covered with extracts from the Book of Caverns and images of Ramses worshiping various gods. The ceiling of the burial chamber is unusual for its Book of Night in yellow on a dark blue background.

Tomb of Merneptah (No. 8)▶ Merneptah (19th Dynasty) has been claimed as the pharaoh of the Exodus. Along the stepped corridors, descending at a sharp angle, are extracts of the Book of Gates and other texts. The lid of the outer sarcophagus was left in the antechamber by tomb robbers, while the lid of the inner sarcophagus, carved with a relief of Merneptah as Osiris, was found in the burial chamber.

ALL ABOUT MUMMIES
Dead ancient Egyptian peasants were left to the goodwill of the dry climate, but the kings were mummified as an extra insurance for eternity. The brain was pulled out through the nostrils with a metal hook, while the viscera were removed via an incision in the abdomen, to be preserved in canopic jars. The heart was normally left in place, but a stone scarab would be placed over it in the mummy bandages. The body was then washed and pickled in natron (a sodium bicarbonate compound) for over a month, after which it was dried out. Once it was ready for the final stages, all orifices were plugged and the corpse was then swaddled in bandages.

161

View over the Theban Hills toward the Tombs of the Nobles, Deir el-Madina, and the Valley of the Kings

The astronomical ceiling of the second pillared hall of Seti I's tomb (scenes from the Book of Amduat)

NEW DISCOVERY

While visiting the Valley of the Kings, you might notice work being done at a tomb opposite Tutankhamun's. This is KV5 (literally Kings' Valley 5). The tomb has been known since 1825, but was believed to be of little interest. Professor Kent Weeks of the American University in Cairo's Theban Mapping Project has revealed what is, already, the largest royal tomb—150 chambers, with more to be uncovered—believed to be for the sons of Ramses II. Work here will continue for many years.

Tomb of Ramses VI (No. 9)▶▶▶ (20th Dynasty) This tomb, originally built for Ramses V, was already popular with tourists in ancient times, as the Greeks believed it was the tomb of Memnon. The first corridors are covered in graffiti, but in general the colors have been very well preserved. This tomb may well be closed for a long time, as it has suffered immensely from recent tourists. The walls are covered with the Book of Gates, the Book of Caverns, and the Books of Day and Night. The pillared burial chamber has a magnificent ceiling decorated with Nut, the sky goddess, encircling the Book of Day on one side and the Book of Night on the other.

Tomb of Ramses III (No. 11)▶▶ (20th Dynasty) This exceptionally large tomb, the only one in the valley with depictions of everyday life, is only partly lit as the second half is ruined. In side niches off the corridor are scenes of baking and butchery, and displays of hunting equipment, furnishings, and agricultural scenes. It is called the Tomb of the Harpers because in one of these side chambers two harpists are shown playing for the gods. The corridor leads into a pillared hall decorated with texts from the Book of Gates and then descends into the ruinous burial chamber, now off limits to visitors.

Tomb of Ramses I (No. 16)▶ (19th Dynasty) As Ramses I only ruled for a couple of years, his tomb was very modest. The decoration was not carved, but painted in bright colors against a gray background. On the left wall is a fine scene of 12 goddesses representing the hours of the night.

Tomb of Seti I (No. 17)►►► (19th Dynasty) This is the most magnificent tomb in the valley, but because of damage caused by, among other things, the perspiration of visitors, it has been closed for several years. Restoration is under way but it is not certain when, if ever, it will be opened again. The exceptional carvings, painted in delicate colors, are only rivaled by the work in Seti's temple in Abydos. In the first descending corridors Seti is shown accompanied by various gods. Farther down, the walls are decorated with various scenes from the Book of Gates. In the second pillared hall, the anteroom to the burial chamber, is an important astronomical ceiling with scenes from the Book of Amduat. The sarcophagus is now in the Sir John Soane Museum in London, while Seti's mummy is on display in the Egyptian Museum in Cairo.

Tomb of Tuthmosis III (No. 34) (18th Dynasty)►► This is one of the oldest tombs, hidden high up in the valley and reached by a steep wooden staircase. The design of the tomb is most unusual with its circular burial chamber. The mummy of Tuthmosis is in Cairo, but his red granite sarcophagus remains here. A bridge crosses over a pit to reach the vestibule where 741 deities are represented as stick figures, painted in black and red only.

Tomb of Amenophis II (No. 35) (18th Dynasty)► As this is one of the deepest tombs, with decorations only in the

163

sarcophagus chamber, it is rarely visited by tourists. The walls in the burial chamber are decorated with the entire Book of Amduat on a yellow background, intended to imitate papyrus. Not only was Amenophis' mummy found in place in the sarcophagus, but in the side rooms 12 other mummies, perhaps hidden there by priests, were also discovered.

Tomb of Horemheb (No. 57) (18th Dynasty)►► With an almost identical plan to Seti I's tomb, Horemheb's tomb is only sparsely decorated, but the images are finely executed. Work was never finished in the burial chamber so it is possible to see the progressive stages of decoration. (Continued on page 165.)

Wall paintings in the tomb of Tuthmosis III. The colors used in Theban tomb paintings were made from pigments that can still be found locally

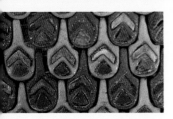

The tomb of Tutankhamun is not the most spectacular in Egypt and its contents were probably modest compared to the burial of a great pharaoh like Ramses II. But Tutankhamun's is the only pharaoh's tomb found intact and the amazing story of its discovery continues to attract visitors from around the world.

A VISION FOR THE WORLD

"Outside this great sarcophagus stood huge golden shrines, and over there were the gods of Egypt, again in gold and lapis lazuli. And over there were the royal chariots, the armor, the chairs. All the paraphernalia of a royal household. It was a treasure which nobody had ever even imagined. When old Egyptologists who studied the profession all their lives first came into this tomb, they left weeping. It was a vision for the world, you might say."
John Romer, in the television documentary *The Rape of Tutankhamun* (1993)

Howard Carter removing the consecrating oils from the mummy of Tutankhamun

The lord and the archeologist Lord Carnarvon was a wealthy, well-educated British aristocrat with an unusual hobby: excavating in Thebes. For six years he and his hired Egyptologist, Howard Carter, uncovered nothing spectacular. In 1914 they started digging in the Valley of the Kings, but it wasn't until 1922 that Carter uncovered steps cut into the rock and "a magnificent tomb with seals intact." It belonged to Tutankhamun. It took Carter almost ten years to empty the tomb, leaving the pharaoh's mummy in its inner sarcophagus.

The pharaoh's revenge Rumor that all who entered the tomb were cursed turned the discovery into one of this century's great media events: in three months of the 1926 season, 12,300 people went to visit the tomb. The first victim was Carnarvon himself. He was bitten by a mosquito in the Valley of the Kings, the bite became infected, and a few weeks later the 57-year-old lord was dead. Many other Tut-related deaths were claimed over the next couple of years.

The price of success Tutankhamun's tomb is small and not particularly interesting, but it is the most famous. The price of success has been high: every day, gallons of sweat have been left by visitors so that now the plaster is peeling from the wall and fungi attack the paintings. The tomb is often closed for repair, but restoration will only delay, not stop, the destruction.

(*Continued from page 163.*) **Tomb of Tutankhamun (No. 62)►►►** The tomb of the boy-king was intended for a high official because, however young the king was, he deserved more than this. The walls are mostly undecorated, another sign that the tomb was prepared in haste. But small as it is, this is the most important tomb to be discovered because its contents were more or less intact when Howard Carter found them. Steps lead into an ante-room with a storeroom, which was filled with grave goods, now on show in the Cairo museum. The walls in the burial chamber show the king's *barque* (royal barge) travel-ing through the underworld, Hathor with Isis and Anubis offering the *ankh* (looped cross) to the king, the funeral procession and Ay, the king's tutor, opening the mummy's mouth. The pink quartzite sarcophagus still contains the mummy, too badly decayed to be moved. (See also page 32.)

The death mask of Tutankhamun

►►► Tombs of the Nobles   134B4

Open: daily 7–6 in summer, 7–5 in winter.
Admission: moderate
Government officials and high priests were buried near and underneath the old village of Gurna. These tombs may be less elaborate and less mysterious than the royal tombs, but they depict fascinating scenes of daily life in ancient Egypt.

Tomb of Rekhmire (No. 100)►►► Rekhmire (18th dynasty) was a vizier (high official) under Tuthmosis III and Amenophis II. The entrance leads into a transverse chamber with, to the right, scenes of hunting, treading grapes, and of Rekhmire inspecting workshops and agriculture and collecting taxes. The left wing of the chamber has an interesting register of Rekhmire receiving tributes from foreign lands such as Crete, Syria, Punt, and Nubia. In the corridor, on the left wall, Rekhmire makes the voyage to Abydos (see pages 128–129) while to the right, images of a funerary banquet and procession are mixed with gardens and lakes of the afterworld.

Tomb of Sennefer (No. 96)►►► Known as the Tomb of the Vines, this is one of the most moving in this valley. Sennefer (18th Dynasty) was mayor of Thebes and over-seer of Amun's gardens under Amenophis II. The themes in his tomb are similar to those of other tombs, but the difference is in the expression of love between Sennefer and his beautiful wife Meryt. There is a sense of beauty in every picture, the coloring is magnificent, and here ancient Egypt feels very much alive.

Tomb of Menna (No. 69)►► Menna was an 18th-Dynasty 'Scribe of Royal Fields', whose enemy had his eyes scratched out so he wouldn't enjoy the afterlife. The tomb decorations, of rural scenery, are finely painted and well preserved. In the entrance he and his wife and daughter are worshiping the sun. In the right wing of the first chamber the couple is seen in front of offering tables. In the second chamber, among scenes of mourning, are beautiful hunting and fishing scenes.

OLD AND NEW GURNA (QURNA)
Walking around Old Gurna you can see that some of the houses have been built over the tombs, and many a Gurnawi will claim to have found real antiquities under his kitchen floor. In the 1940s the government, aware of the grave-robbing, tried to move villagers to a new town nearby, designed by the Egyptian architect Hassan Fathy. New Gurna, designed as a traditional mud-brick village, is now inhabited by people from outside Luxor. In a new attempt to remove people from Old Gurna, the authorities have made emergency housing, a few miles north, in New Taref, originally built for flood victims, available to them. But the Gurnawis have shown that they will not move without a fight.

BEST OF THE NOBLES' TOMBS

The Tombs of the Nobles are divided into four groups and for each group a separate ticket is required. You can easily spend three or four hours visiting the ten most important tombs: Rekhmire and Sennufer; Menna and Nakht; Ramose, Userhat and Khaemhat; and Khonsu, Userhat, and Benia. If your time is limited, to get a taste of these tombs visit Rekhmire and Sennufer, Ramose and Nakht.

Tomb of Nakht (No. 52)►►► Nakht was a scribe and an astronomer of Amun during the 18th Dynasty. The only decorated part of his tomb, the transverse chamber, has well-preserved and very bright murals of country life. On the left, Nakht is supervising the harvest, while on the rear wall, a banquet scene depicts beautiful dancers and a blind harpist entertaining the guests of the deceased. On the right side is a traditional hunting scene and another of treading grapes. In the inner chamber is a copy of the funerary statue of Nakht; the original was lost when the ship transporting it to America sank.

Tomb of Ramose (No. 55)►►► Ramose (18th Dynasty) was vizier and governor of Thebes under Amenophis III and Amenophis IV, who later became Akhenaton. His tomb is unusual in having some exquisite carvings in the classical style, especially the banquet scene left of the entrance, as well as reliefs from after the Amarna revolution in the typical Amarna style (see pages 124–125). On the rear wall, to the left, Amenophis IV is seen under a canopy with Maat, while on the right he is seen worshiping Aton. A dark tunnel leads into the burial chamber.

Tomb of Userhat (No. 56)►► The tomb of Userhat, 18th-Dynasty royal scribe, is unusual for its fine murals, mostly in pink tones. There are beautiful paintings of him hunting in the desert and fishing in the marshes.

Tomb of Khaemhat (No. 57)►► Khaemhat was another 18th-Dynasty scribe and the carvings in his tomb are as fine as those in the Tomb of Ramose. In the chapel are various seated statues of Khaemhat and his family.

Tombs of Khonsu (No. 31), Benia (No. 343), and Userhat (No. 51)► This group of tombs was opened to the public only in 1992. The scenes are traditional: hunting, the pilgrimage to Abydos, mourners, offerings, and so on, but they have been well restored.

►► Biban el-Harim (Valley of the Queens) *134A3*

Open: daily 7–6 in summer, 7–5 in winter.
Admission: moderate

The valley contains more than 70 tombs belonging to queens, princesses, and princes, mostly of the 18th, 19th, and 20th Dynasties. Queens were less important than pharaohs, as is suggested by the disappointing, sober tomb decoration: often the walls were left unfinished. Most tombs have been closed to stop further damage.

The most remarkable tomb in the valley is the **Tomb of Nefertari (No. 66)►►►**, for which only a limited number of (expensive) tickets are sold each day. Nefertari, wife of Ramses II, was buried in a beautiful tomb, which has been restored at a cost of some $6 million. The three chambers are completely decorated, but only fragments of the sarcophagus have been found.

A smallpox epidemic towards the end of Ramses III's reign killed several of his sons and they were all buried in the valley. In the **Tomb of Prince Set Her Khopshef (No. 43)►** and the **Tomb of Prince Khaemwaset (No. 44)►►**, both currently closed, Ramses III is shown introducing his sons to the gods and making offerings. The sons are taken by the hand to the gates of the underworld, guarded by strange-headed figures.

There is a third son buried in the **Tomb of Amun Her Khopshef (No. 55)►►** The boy is also led by his father,

DEATH OF A WORLD

"How pleasant it is to find oneself in beautiful country once more, in this glorious plain, all surrounded by those violet-colored hills, with rich fields bordering the blue Nile, and groves of palm trees and acacias, and tamarisks, overshadowing the ruins of a world. It is not the deathbed of a city which you come to visit here, it is the death of a world. And what a world!"
Florence Nightingale, *Letters from Egypt* (1849–1850)

who is explaining about the afterlife. In the burial chamber to the right of the sarcophagus, a glass case contains the bones of a six-month-old fetus. It is believed that the mother miscarried this child when her other sons died so suddenly.

The simple cross-shaped **Tomb of Queen Tyti (No. 52)▶**, is lavishly decorated. In the central room are scenes of guardians of the underworld. The chamber to the left contained the sarcophagus.

The tomb of Nefertari after its extensive and successful restoration

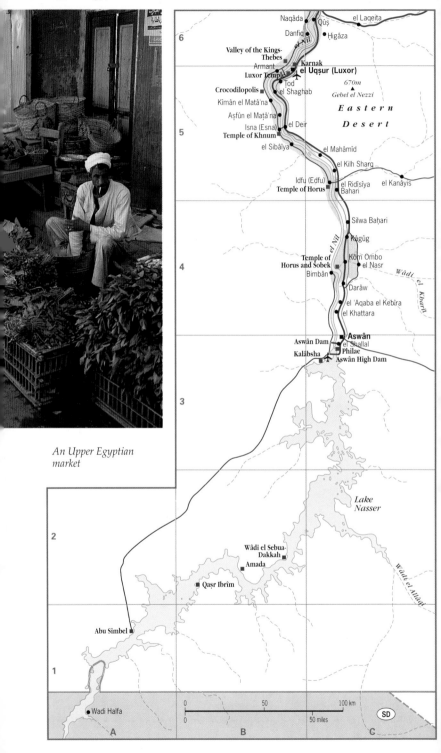

Upper Egypt and Nubia

An Upper Egyptian market

Naqâda
Qûṣ
el Laqeita
Danfiq
Higâza
el Nil
Valley of the Kings-Thebes
Karnak
Armant
el Uqṣur (Luxor)
Luxor Temple
Ṭod
670m
Gebel el Nezzi
Crocodilopolis
el Shaghab
Eastern
Desert
Kîmân el Matâ'na
Aṣfûn el Maṭâ'na
Isna (Esna)
el Deir
Temple of Khnum
el Sibâîya
el Mahâmîd
el Kilh Sharq
Idfu (Edfu)
el Ridîsîya Bahari
el Kanâyis
Temple of Horus
Silwa Baḥari
Wâdi el Kharît
Kâgûg
Temple of Horus and Sobek
Kôm Ombo
el Nasr
Bimbân
Darâw
el 'Aqaba el Kebîra
el Khattara
Aswân
Aswân Dam
el Shallal
Philae
Kalâbsha
Aswân High Dam

Lake Nasser

Wâdi el Sebua-Dakkah
Amada
Qaṣr Ibrîm

Wâdi el Allaqi

Abu Simbel

Wadi Halfa

0   50   100 km
0   50 miles

SD

UPPER EGYPT AND NUBIA It is rewarding to travel through the Upper Nile Valley, with its rich farmland, beautiful temples, and traditional villages. It is easy to think of Aswan as the end of the line, now that the High Dam has cut the Nile's flow. But although much of the land of ancient Nubia lies beneath Lake Nasser, its deeper rhythms and darker-skinned people, their culture as old as the pharaohs, are still to be found.

THE THINNING LINE The Nile becomes increasingly dramatic toward the south. The flat plains around Luxor, trimmed by limestone hills, begin to shrink, the riverbed changing from limestone to granite as you go upstream. Where the river fails to reach, the desert claims. The sands lie close around Aswan and beyond the dam, as they did through Nubia.

END OF EMPIRE Divisions between people who cultivated the Nile Valley and others who lived off herding, fishing, or trading along the river existed far back in

BEYOND THE CATARACTS
Tourism on Lake Nasser is getting a boost. In addition to specialist vacations offering fishing tours, several luxury cruise boats now operate between Aswan and Abu Simbel allowing visits to the out-of-the-way sites at Wadi el-Sebua (Sibu), Dakka, Derr, Amada, and Qasr Ibrim. Some cruises also include a night visit to Abu Simbel temples. Huge Nile crocodiles are also returning in numbers.

antiquity. Egyptians controlled Nubia and extracted its mineral wealth at various times in their history, while there were also Nubians who became pharaohs. But the two countries remained separate, with Aswan acting as the border-post between them.

A GREAT RESORT Aswan is often used as a place of transit to reach cruise boats, Philae, Abu Simbel, or even Sudan, but it rewards closer inspection. It has been spared some of the worst excesses of mass tourism by its lack of an international airport, and it has a relaxed and unhurried feel. The valley is narrow, more intimate, forcing you down to the river, whose slender stream is divided by islands and rocks. In ancient times, dissident Romans were sent to Aswan as a punishment, but a few days spent in the town now are just a pleasure.

THE LAST FLOOD In antiquity, offerings were made, prayers recited, and a watch was kept each summer on the Nilometer (measuring station) on Elephantine Island to see how fast the river was rising. The news was then relayed to the north. Villagers on Elephantine Island still talk about a booming sound that was heard if you placed your ear to the rocks at the time of the flood. But the Nilometer is abandoned, the rocks are silent, and since the Aswan dams were built the Nile's flow has been regulated throughout the year.

The Nile at Aswan, caught between the narrow banks

The job of camel driver is taught from the cradle

171

THE LOST WORLD Nubia was a harsh, arid place, but it was home to around 100,000 people, who were dependent on Egyptians to share the abundance of their harvests. The construction of the Aswan dams in the 20th century caused the flooding of the entire Nubian homeland, and many Nubian men went looking for work in Egyptian towns and cities—Nubian clerks, cooks, and watchmen are common throughout the country—but wherever they went, they maintained a separate identity.

The Egyptian architect Hassan Fathy understood that their sense of individuality was based on their architecture. "There was nothing else like it in Egypt," he wrote, "a village from some dream country." It was a dream Nubians have struggled to preserve, along with the distinctive character of their music, dance, and cuisine. It is still possible to feel something of their character in the island villages around Aswan, but without their land, the Nubians, dispersed between Sudan, Aswan, and the Upper Nile Valley, are slowly losing their identity.

MODERN NUBIA The new museum in Aswan is a good place to start building an understanding of Nubian culture, but the best source of information is with Nubians themselves. There are also remains of Nubian monuments along the shores of Lake Nasser. Some 23 temples were saved as the High Dam was being constructed. Some went to foreign museums in thanks for their help in the salvage operation, but others, most famously Abu Simbel and Philae, but also Wadi el-Sebua (Sibu), Beit el-Wali, and Kalabsha, were simply lifted above the waterline.

Painted column, the Temple of Kom Ombo

172

TWIN-TEMPLES
The Temple of Hathor in Dendera was modeled on the Temple of Horus as they were closely connected, like the temples of Luxor and Karnak. In the annual procession Horus went to Dendera to visit his wife Hathor.

Different flower- and plant-shaped columns in the Temple of Esna are highly suggestive of a garden

Upper Egypt

▶▶ Isna (Esna), Temple of Khnum   168B5

Open: daily 6 AM–6:30 PM in summer, 6–5:30 in winter.
Admission: inexpensive. The ticket office is on the quay.

Esna lies 33 miles south of Luxor and 96 miles north of Aswan. The temple is a short walk from the quay, through a narrow *souk* (market) street. Completely hidden beneath houses, it was partly excavated in 1860.

The temple, probably once as large as the Edfu temple, was rebuilt by Ptolemy VI (ca180 BC) on an earlier structure. It was dedicated to the ram-headed god Khnum, god of creation, often depicted modeling man on his potter's wheel. Only the hypostyle hall, added by the Roman emperor Claudius (1st century AD) was totally excavated; it is now approached from a staircase descending 33 feet below the current street level. Its roof is supported by 24 colorful columns with various fine capitals, like an enclosed garden with different flowers. The fine astronomical ceiling has almost disappeared under a black residue of smoke from the fires of earlier Christian occupants. The carvings on the walls portray several Roman emperors in front of Egyptian deities. In front of the temple are several blocks from an early Christian church.

In the streets around the temple, some old houses have retained fine *mashrabiya* (carved wood) screens. It was in these houses that travelers like Flaubert visited Egyptian prostitutes.

▶▶▶ Idfu (Edfu), Temple of Horus   168C5

Open: daily 6–6 in summer, 7–4 in winter.
Admission: expensive

Edfu lies 71 miles south of Luxor and 65 miles north of Aswan. The Temple of Horus is, after Karnak, the largest temple in Egypt. It is also the best preserved as it was almost completely buried in the sand until the 1860s, when Mariette started excavating the main building. Dedicated to the falcon-headed god, Horus, it was built on a site inhabited since the Old Kingdom, believed to be the site of Horus' fight with his uncle Seth for control of the world. The temple was built 237–57 BC, during the Ptolemaic period, but it faithfully maintains the traditions of pharaonic architecture and gives a clear idea of what all ancient temples must have looked like. It is also the temple we know most about as there are plenty of foundation and building texts inscribed on its walls.

The temple is now entered from the back of the court, but the visit should start at the massive pylon, built by Ptolemy IX. The reliefs on its outer walls show Neos Dionysos in front of Horus the Elder. The inside walls record the Festival of the Beautiful Meeting, when Horus joined Hathor in Dendera. In front of the First Hypostyle Hall stands one of a pair of majestic hawk statues of Horus, its twin lying headless in the sand. The back wall of the hypostyle hall has some fine reliefs of the temple foundation rituals, in which the king is shown making mud bricks. The Second Hypostyle or Festival Hall is lined with side chambers. The walls of the first

room to the left, the laboratory, are covered with fine reliefs of flowers and recipes. In the next hall, two staircases lead to the roof where Horus was revitalized by the sun. Beyond lies the strangely lit holy-of-holies, the Sanctuary where the statue of Horus was believed to be inhabited by the living god. It once contained his sacred *barque* (royal barge), of which a copy is found in the middle room behind the Sanctuary. As you leave the Sanctuary, the New Year Chapel, with a beautiful depiction of the sky goddess, Nut, is to your left. In the outer corridor around the temple is a relief of Horus' victory over Seth, depicting Seth as a hippopotamus. Outside the pylon is the Birth House.

The god Horus was often represented as a falcon or, as here at Edfu Temple, a hawk

BETWEEN LUXOR AND ASWAN

All cruise boat and *felucca* (sailing boat) trips between Aswan and Luxor include a visit to the temples in Esna, Edfu, and Kom Ombo (see pages 174–175). It is also possible to visit these three temples on the overland route if you rent a private taxi. Tell the driver you want to visit the temples and agree beforehand on a price. Current security arrangements may oblige you to travel in armed convoy.

The impressive First Pylon of the Ptolemaic Temple of Horus in Edfu

Some 200 years ago early travelers started to sail up the Nile for pleasure. Nile boats were adapted to their needs, bedrooms and salons were added, and visitors were able to admire the country from the comfort and safety of their own, well-ordered decks.

174

THE STANDARD TOUR
Cruise boat itineraries differ in the level of accommodations and service, the expertise of the Egyptologist, and the length of stay. Some cruises include visits to Dendera and Abydos. Beyond Luxor, the temples of Esna, Edfu, and Kom Ombo are visited before reaching Aswan. There are often delays at Esna due to the number of boats passing through the lock, forcing some companies to transfer passengers to a sister boat on the other side of the lock.

FELUCCAS
Boatmen have to notify the river police before they take you out overnight on their *feluccas*. Stock up in the market on food and water before you leave. The trip from Luxor to Aswan is possible if the wind is blowing upriver, but from Aswan to Luxor, the river's current will carry you down if the wind fails.

Cruising on the Nile today is more popular and more affordable than it has ever been

Early cruises Early historians like Herodotus sailed up the Nile. Movement on the river is dictated by the seasons: in autumn a strong wind from the north propels sailing boats into Africa; coming back is easier, riding with the river's flow. This seasonal timetable suited the early tourists perfectly and Egypt quickly earned a reputation as a place to spend a warm winter, as travelers like Florence Nightingale and Gustave Flaubert knew. Lady Lucie Duff Gordon was one of the first Europeans to travel far afield for their health; initially sent to winter in Egypt, she remained by the Nile and died in 1869, her seventh year in Egypt.

The rapids, known here as cataracts, were a big obstacle to boats wishing to go south of Aswan into Nubia. No amount of sails could take boats over them, so they were pulled over by the men of the "Sheikh of the Cataracts" who extracted a sizable fee for the service.

The first Cook's tour By 1869, the year of the opening of the Suez Canal, tourism was already developed in Egypt. In 1863, Lucie Duff Gordon had taken the first regular steamer service up the Nile. Thomas Cook took it all one step further. Instead of tourists having to make their own arrangements with boatmen and interpreters, Cook promised to look after them and make sure that the linens were clean, the food familiar, the temples open— and all for a reasonable sum. It was a great success, especially among people who couldn't afford to pay their way on their own. It was Cook who brought the masses to the Nile and he was the first to set up agencies to ensure that everything was ready for them when they got there.

Cruising today There are a multitude of cruise boats on the Nile today offering a wide choice of accommodations, but the itineraries they follow are invariably the same. The differences, reflected in the cost, are mostly in the standard of service and accommodations and the number of

cabins—the newer luxury boats are getting smaller. Some boats carry a small library of books on ancient and modern Egypt and all cruises provide the services of a guide to help make sense of monuments along the river.

Sailing on the Nile The nearest thing to that old-fashioned feeling of sailing up the Nile is to be had on *feluccas*. These open-topped sailing boats can be hired by the hour or day in Luxor and Aswan, but the big thrills are to be had sailing between the two, drifting slowly past villages, seeing river life, eating with the boatmen, and sleeping under the stars on the river's bank at night.

THE NEW STEAMERS
"The new passenger-steamers... will not now go till after the races—6th or 7th of next month. Fancy the Cairo races! It is growing dreadfully Cockney here, I must go to Timbuctoo..."
Lucie Duff Gordon (1863)

A modern eye of Horus keeps evil spirits away

175

The hypostyle hall of the Temple of Horus in Kom Ombo

SOMETHING OF GREECE

"The temple... Its elevation, its seclusion, the combination of sun and water flowing past as though in slow but determined search for the Mediterranean, at last suggests something of Greece... there is something in its stones of that Hellenic response to light..." Michael Haag, *Discovery Guide to Egypt* (1987)

A relief showing medical instruments

▶▶ Kom Ombo, Temple of Horus and Sobek   168C4

Open: daily 8–4. Admission: inexpensive

Kom Ombo lies 105 miles south of Luxor and 28 miles north of Aswan. As the temple stands on a promontory beside the Nile, the most spectacular approach is from the river, by boat or *felucca*, in the late afternoon when the setting sun turns the sandstone a deep golden color. The Nile has swept most of the pylon, forecourt, and birth house away, and the temple was seriously damaged during the earthquake in 1992, but what is left is well worth seeing. The temple is unusual for being dedicated to two gods: the right side is dedicated to the crocodile god Sobek, the left side to Horus the Elder or Haruris. Ptolemy VI (ca180 BC) started building the temple, but most of the work was done under Neos Dionysos (80–51 BC). The Roman emperor, Augustus (30 BC–AD 14), added the pylon, court, and outer enclosure wall.

The temple is approached passing the massive Gateway of Neos Dionysos and, to the right, the small Chapel of Hathor, its mummified crocodiles found in a cemetery nearby. Little remains of the **pylon** and the **court**, but at the back is the façade of the First Hypostyle Hall, with dual passageways leading to the twin sanctuaries. On the left wall of the façade Neos Dionysos is purified by Horus, while on the right he appears in front of Sobek. The hypostyle hall has lofty columns with floral capitals and a ceiling decorated with flying vultures. On the inner wall of the façade is a fine relief of Neos Dionysos' coronation by the gods. Inside the older Second Hypostyle Hall, reliefs show Ptolemy VII making offerings to the gods. Beyond are three vestibules, decorated by Ptolemy VI with reliefs of temple rituals, leading to the two, mostly ruined sanctuaries. Between the doors to the sanctuaries is a splendid relief of Ptolemy VI and his wife receiving a palm stalk with the Heb-Sed sign from Horus (painted blue) and Sobek (green).

Behind the sanctuaries off the inner corridor are seven decorated chapels; the middle one has a stairway leading up for a good view of the temple complex. The most interesting of the Roman reliefs in the outer corridor are on the walls at the back of the seven chapels, especially the display of medical instruments, proof that Egyptian surgeons were already sophisticated almost 2,000 years ago. Also look for the carvings of ears that heard pilgrims' prayers. The birth house in the northeast corner of the complex has almost entirely disappeared in the Nile.

Nubian and Upper Egyptian camel drivers in Daraw market

▶▶ Daraw   168C4

Daraw, 3 miles south of Kom Ombo and 25 miles from Aswan, can be reached by bus or taxi from either town.

Only one thing distinguishes Daraw from other concentrations of mud-brick compounds along the road from Kom Ombo to Aswan: it marks the end of the Forty Days Road and plays host to the main camel market (*suq el-Gimal*) between the Sudan and Cairo. The market is held every Tuesday of the year and sometimes, in winter, on Sundays as well, from 6:30 AM to 2 PM, with most of the trading completed by 11 AM. The location varies, but from the crowds and trucks loaded with camels it soon becomes clear where it is.

The camels are brought from Darfur and Kordofan in the Sudan, through the Libyan Desert to Dongola, and from there they follow the Nile into Egypt. This desert trail, one of the last surviving desert trading routes, takes about a month of walking and is appropriately called the Darb el-Arba'een (the Forty Days Road). The Sudanese camel drovers mostly come from two nomadic tribes and are often dressed in their traditional gear, daggers included. The camels, cheaper here than in Birqâsh (see page 86), are sold to local peasants or traders from Cairo. The picturesque market attracts increasing numbers of tourists, but, despite this, it remains a spectacular and exotic sight.

HORUS THE ELDER OR HARURIS
Of all the Egyptian gods Horus is the most complex and most confusing, appearing in many different forms. One of his main forms is the falcon-headed Horus the Elder or Haruris, known as the Good Doctor, and pilgrims came to his temple in Kom Ombo seeking healing. Another popular form was Horus the Younger—the son of Isis and Osiris—who fought against Seth, his father's brother and murderer.

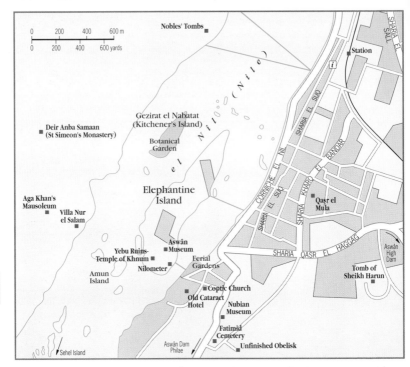

Map of Aswan showing:

0 200 400 600 m
0 200 400 600 yards

Nobles' Tombs
Station
SHARIA EL SALL
Gezirat el Nabatat (Kitchener's Island)
el Nil (Nile)
SHARIA EL SUQ
Deir Anba Samaan (St Simeon's Monastery)
Botanical Garden
CORNICHE EL NIL
el Nil
SHARIA EL SUQ
SHARIA KHARQ EL BANDAR
Aga Khan's Mausoleum
Villa Nur el Salam
Elephantine Island
Qasr el Mula
Aswân Museum
Yebu Ruins- Temple of Khnum
Nilometer
Ferial Gardens
SHARIA QASR EL HAGGAG
Aswân High Dam
Amun Island
Old Cataract Hotel
Coptic Church
Nubian Museum
Tomb of Sheikh Harun
Fatimid Cemetery
Aswân Dam Philae
Unfinished Obelisk
Sehel Island

178

Nubian women

TOURIST INFORMATION
The main tourist office (tel: 097/312811) is next to the train station. It is open Saturday–Thursday 8:30–2 and 6–8, Friday 10–2 and 6–8. It has a list of the official prices for private taxis and *feluccas* (sailboats). Shoukri Saad is particularly helpful here. The tourist police also have an office in this location (tel: 097/324393), open 24 hours.

SHOPPING
Things to buy in Aswan's *souk:* Karkadeh (dried hibiscus flowers for infusions), spices, peanuts from Sudan, colorful silk and cotton hand-woven shawls, cotton tablecloths, bright Nubian baskets, and strange charms.

►►► Aswan
168C3

Aswan, 550 miles from Cairo and 133 miles from Luxor, is Egypt's southernmost town, and it is totally different from the rest of the country. Here the green cultivated land disappears as the desert closes in on the river, which also changes from a flat and peaceful stream into a dramatic mass of water flowing between dark, dramatic granite rocks. Aswan feels more African, and the majority of its inhabitants are Nubians, darker and taller

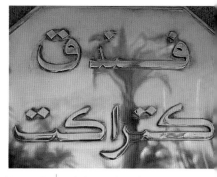

than Upper Egyptians, speaking a different language and having different customs.

Even in ancient times this was where Egypt ended and Nubia began. Yebu on Elephantine Island was the Old Kingdom border town and an important religious center, as the Nile was believed to well up from under the nearby first cataract (rapids). Two thousand years later it marked the southernmost town of the Roman Empire, and in the 19th century it was the starting point for the conquest of the Sudan.

Aswan's position made it an important market for caravans passing with gold, slaves, incense, and ivory, and today its bazaar remains the best outside Cairo, bustling with Nubian and Egyptian traders selling more exotic goods than anywhere else in Egypt. Even if it has become more tourist oriented, it is still a delight for the senses with strong smells of perfume, spice, and incense, brightly colored fabrics and everywhere the soft melodic tunes of Nubian and Sudanese musicians.

There may be less activity than in the past, and there is little to see compared to Luxor and Cairo, but Aswan is a wonderful place to rest. You can stroll around, take sailboats, walk through the gardens on Kitcheners' Island or the traditional villages on Elephantine Island, spend afternoons on the terrace of the Old Cataract Hotel, or wander around the bazaar without having the feeling of missing out on history. The town is so pleasant, its people so relaxed and friendly, that it is always hard to leave.

Aga Khan's Mausoleum▶▶ Currently the mausoleum is closed due to overcrowding, by order of the Begum. This mausoleum, beautiful in its simplicity, is where the Aga Khan III (1877–1957) chose to be buried. He was the spiritual leader of the Ismailis, a Shi'ite sect coming from

The brass plate of the Old Cataract Hotel

THE SOFITEL OLD CATARACT
For nostalgia, romance, and wonderful views stay in the Old Cataract (see page 275). Built in 1902, the hotel, which appeared in Agatha Christie's *Death on the Nile*, has been refurbished and is once again one of the nicest hotels in Egypt. If you don't stay, at least walk around, have a drink on the grand terrace, watch the sunset, or have dinner in the splendid Moorish Room.

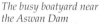
179

The busy boatyard near the Aswan Dam

The simple mausoleum of the Aga Khan has wonderful views over the Nile and the town of Aswan

NUBIAN WEDDINGS
Nubian weddings are week-long celebrations at which foreign guests are considered auspicious. They are also fun. If you are invited to one, do offer some money for the musicians. Beware of invitations by hustlers selling this as an excursion.

India, and his grandson Karim succeeded him as the Aga Khan IV. His wealth was phenomenal and so was his weight: on his diamond jubilee, in 1945, his weight in diamonds was distributed among his followers. He fell in love with Aswan because of its beauty and perfect winter climate, and he liked to spend the winter in the white villa he built on the west bank, as his wife, the Begum, still does.

Aswan Museum and Nilometer▶▶ (*Museum open Sun–Thu 8–6 (8–5 in winter), Fri 9–1. Admission: moderate includes the Ruins of Yebu*) This small museum on Elephantine Island is housed in the villa of Sir William Willcocks, the engineer who designed the old Aswan Dam. On display are local finds from predynastic to the Byzantine periods: statues, pottery, jewelry, a golden bust of Khnum, a mummified ram, and several mummies. At the back of the house are gardens where tea may be offered in return for a small *baksheesh* (tip). Beside the Nile is a Nilometer with scales in pharaonic, Greek, Roman, and Arabic numerals. The height of the river dictated the level of taxes, so this was a very important instrument until the High Dam stopped the annual inundation.

Gezirat el-Nabatat (Kitchener's Island)▶▶ (*Open daily 8–dusk. Admission: moderate*) Behind Elephantine Island lies a small, lush island that was offered to Consul-General Kitchener for his military achievements in the Sudan. He developed a passion for exotic flora and imported trees and seeds from all over the world. In the late afternoon, the shady garden, full of bird songs and sweet fragrances, makes a perfect retreat.

Deir Anba Samaan (Monastery of St. Simeon)▶▶ (*Open daily 9–5 (winter 9–4. Admission: moderate*) Start at the landing stage below the Aga Khan's mausoleum and

make the steep climb through soft sand (25 minutes) or rent a camel to the ridge. This is one of the most beautiful and romantic of Egyptian monasteries, built like a fortress in the 7th century and rebuilt in the 10th century. It was originally dedicated to Anba Hadra, a 4th-century local saint, and later to the little-known St. Simeon. Salah ed-Din destroyed it in 1173 when Nubian Christians used it as a refuge. The roofless basilica has badly damaged paintings. In a nearby chamber, St. Simeon is said to have stood reading the Bible for days on end, his beard tied up to the ceiling. The keep housed more than 300 monks. The setting is impressive: surrounded by desert, it is most spectacular around sunset.

Nobles' Tombs▶ (*Open* daily 8–5 (8–4 in winter). *Admission: moderate*) The tombs belonged to princes, priests, and governors, mostly of the Old and Middle Kingdoms. They were hewn in the rock and have simple decorations. The two finest and best-preserved tombs belonged to Sirenput I (No. 36) and Sirenput II (No. 31), with colorful scenes of the governors and their families. On top of the hill, Qubbet el-Hawa (Dome of the Wind) is the tomb of a local sheikh, with a fantastic view over the Nile, the cataract, and the desert.

Ruins of Yebu▶ (*Open* as Aswan Museum) The southern end of Elephantine Island is covered with the ruins of ancient Yebu. Sites are still being excavated and include the temples of Khnum (30th Dynasty) and his wife and a Temple of Jaweh, built in the 6th century BC by a Jewish colony.

An old Nubian man selling lemons from his garden, at the market in Aswan

If, as Herodotus wrote, Egypt is the gift of the Nile, it is a gift that constantly needs renewing. With only negligible rainfall, Egyptians are still dependent on the river for all their water needs. The Aswan Dam seemed to offer Egyptians control of the Nile and with it their destiny, but it was a controversial project from the start.

The first dam The British recognized the benefits that a dam would bring to Egypt and built the first Aswan Dam between 1899 and 1902. On completion it was the largest dam in the world and was hailed as a great engineering achievement—particularly by the British, whose engineers had carried out the project using Egyptian and Italian labor. The dam was opened by the Duke of Connaught, brother of the English King Edward VII. Lord Cromer, the British Agent in Egypt who was also present at the ceremony, later wrote that it was "by far the most popular step we have ever taken." The dam allowed an extra 10–15 percent of land to be farmed by 1911.

Early problems The original dam created a reservoir that stretched 140 miles back toward Sudan, partially submerging Nubian villages and monuments for up to eight months a year. The most famous monument to suffer was the Temple of Isis on Philae Island; photographs of the period show tourists being taken by boat, or swimming among the columns, beneath the stone roof.

Another problem with the dam was that it wasn't high enough: originally just over 98 feet high, it was raised several times and by 1933 stood at 138 feet. The biggest problem posed by the dam was its function. Although it

182

Driving in the cast-iron piles for the foundations of the dam, 1902

was desirable to control the flow of the river, it was less desirable to control the flow of silt. The Nile is fed by rain from the East African highlands and the water that flooded across the Nile Valley in Egypt deposited an important layer of silt when the waters receded. This silt fertilized the valley and farmers had to use chemicals to replace it.

Nasser and nationalism The Aswan High Dam project, which began in the mid-1960s, was swept forward by the surge of nationalism that followed the overthrow of the Egyptian monarchy and the nationalization of the Suez Canal Company, and President Nasser presented it as another step on the road to making his country strong and self-reliant. The dam was going to provide the country with sufficient water resources and would meet the country's electricity needs as well. When Nasser was refused aid for the project by western countries, he turned to the Soviet Union. Throughout its construction, the dam project was a source of national pride.

The price paid No progress without sacrifice: the benefits of the dam were considered great enough to allow the destruction of many important monuments. UNESCO and other national and international agencies became involved in saving the Nubian monuments, removing some to higher ground and others to foreign museums, but many disappeared beneath the manmade lake. The world community was less successful in saving the Nubian culture. With their villages and lands submerged, their contacts with nomadic tribes cut, and their homes relocated farther north, the Nubians lost the most obvious components of their cultural identity.

The price to pay The vast surface area of Lake Nasser is posing a number of problems, changing rainfall patterns and raising the level of underground water far to the north. This, in turn, is causing damage to monuments in places like Luxor where stonework, preserved for millennia by the arid sand, is being eaten away by salty water. But as a result of the lake, which provides a ready source of water, Egyptian politicians have launched the ambitious Toshka Canal project to irrigate parts of the Western Desert.

In addition to flooding Nubian villages and ancient monuments, the large surface area of Lake Nasser appears to be influencing the climate and ground-water levels

The Aswan High Dam Monument

*The Temple of Isis
at Philae*

OLD NUBIA
"Between these two huge
and barren expanses [of
desert], Nubia writhes like
a green sand-worm along
the course of the river.
Here and there it
disappears all together,
and the Nile runs between
black and sun-cracked
hills, with the orange drift-
sand lying like glaciers in
their valleys. Everywhere
one sees traces of
vanished races and
submerged civilisations.
Grotesque graves dot the
hills or stand up against
the skyline... everywhere
graves. And occasionally...
one sees a deserted city
up above... with the sun
shining through the empty
window squares."
Sir Arthur Conan Doyle
(1897)

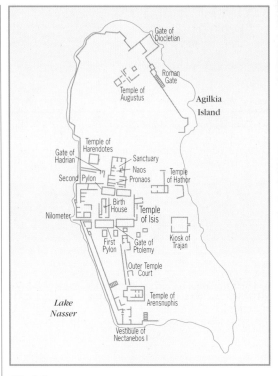

*If finished, this obelisk
would have been the
largest work of stone in
Egypt, but a flaw was
discovered and it was left
behind in the quarry*

Nubia

▶▶ Nubian Museum   178

Open: daily 9–1, 5–9 . Admission: expensive
The first museum dedicated to Nubian culture and traditions opened on a hill behind the Old Cataract Hotel. The
collection is housed in a new building constructed in
traditional Nubian style. Until now little attention has
been paid to Nubian culture or history, which was dealt a
great blow by the construction of the Aswan dams and
the creation of Lake Nasser. As the lake's waters rose,
Nubian families were forced to leave their villages and
traditional land, many of them being resettled in Kom
Ombo, Esna, and other villages in the Upper Nile Valley.
The common theme in modern Nubian art is a strong
sense of loss of freedom, of the Nubian heritage and of
their attachment to the land of their forefathers. There is a
selection of antiquities found in Nubia on display in the
Egyptian Museum in Cairo, but the Aswan museum is the
first attempt to bring this heritage into the spotlight, as
well as to illustrate living Nubian culture.

▶▶ Unfinished Obelisk   178

*Open: daily 7–6 in summer, 7–5 in winter.
Admission: moderate*
In an ancient granite quarry along the road to Philae lies a
gigantic unfinished obelisk measuring 137 feet. The
obelisk was probably intended to join the so-called
Lateran Obelisk, now in Rome, in front of the temple of
Tuthmosis III at Karnak, but it was abandoned after a flaw

was discovered in the stone. Had the work been completed, this would have been the largest piece of worked stone in history, weighing about 1,320 tons. Its loss must have been a disaster for the ancient masons, but for modern archeologists it is an invaluable source of information on ancient quarrying techniques.

Nearby in the **Fatimid Cemetery►** are some fine 10th-century mud-brick tombs where local saints, including Sayyida Zaynab, the granddaughter of the prophet Muhammad, were buried. Most of the inscriptions were moved to Cairo in the late 19th century without any record being kept of which tomb they came from.

►►► Philae, Temple of Isis 168C3

Open: daily 7–6 in summer, 7–5 in winter.
Admission: expensive

As Biga Island, identified with the burial place of Osiris, was only accessible to the priesthood, it was the neighboring island of Philae that developed into a popular cult center. The Temple of Isis was built over more than 700 years, mainly by Ptolemaic and Roman rulers who wanted to identify themselves with the Osiris and Isis cult. The temple shows a wonderful blend of Egyptian and Greco-Roman architecture. In Roman times, this was the most important pilgrimage center in Egypt. It was also the last functioning temple of ancient religion and only closed down in AD 551.

When the first Aswan Dam was built, the Temple of Isis was partly submerged for most of the year. Travelers described their boat trip around the temple as one of the highlights of their Egyptian visit, but the annual rise of the waters soon started to erode the reliefs. With the construction of the High Dam, the temple was threatened with complete and permanent submersion. In an operation led by UNESCO and the Egyptian Antiquities Organization, the island of Agilkia was reshaped into an exact replica of Philae and the Temple of Isis, the Temple of Hathor, and Trajan's Kiosk were relocated to its drier ground. The relocated Philae was reopened, with tide marks, in 1980.

The Temple of Isis at Philae, approached by boat

BOATS TO AGILKIA ISLAND
Taxis will drop you at Shallal dock, where tickets for the temple are sold and where you take a motorboat to Agilkia Island. A noticeboard near the ticket window gives the official prices for motorboats, which are cheaper if you are traveling as part of a group, as there is a minimum charge per boat.

Water marks stain the pylon from when the Temple of Isis was submerged

THE ISIS CULT

The cult of Isis, who revived her husband to conceive their son Horus, was popular throughout the Roman Empire until it was abolished by Justinian in the 6th century. As the Divine Mother, the Great Mother of All Gods and Nature, the Goddess of a Thousand Names, she was identified with the other goddesses in the Mediterranean, and soon absorbed them all. Many believe that the Virgin Mary was only given great importance in early Christianity to attract converts from the Isis cult. Early Coptic art made no distinction between them and identified Horus with Jesus.

GETTING THERE

The best way to get to Kalabsha Temple (1 hour) is by taxi, possibly as part of a half-day excursion, to include the Unfinished Obelisk (15 min) and Philae (2 hours). The taxi will drop you at a shipyard. If Lake Nasser is low, you can walk to the temple. When the water rises (usually September–December) you will need to be rowed across, which often involves serious haggling with the boatmen as the temple is rarely visited. Happily, the enchantment of arriving slowly by boat and seeing the temple in all its grandeur from the water is worth paying for.

Temple of Isis▶▶▶ Stairs from the landing lead to the Vestibule of Nectanebo I (30th Dynasty), beyond which stretches the outer court flanked by colonnades. The windows in the well-preserved West Colonnade once overlooked Biga and the columns are decorated with reliefs of Tiberius making offerings to the gods. The First Pylon was decorated by Neos Dionysos (80–51 BC). Its reliefs, showing the Ptolemy in traditional pharaonic scenes, were badly damaged by the Copts.

The gateway, built by Nectanebo I, leads into the Central Court. To the right lie the colonnaded quarters of the priests, with reliefs of the king performing rituals. To the left of the court is the Birth House of Ptolemy IV (221–205 BC) with some fine reliefs depicting the myth of Horus rising from the marshes as a falcon. Behind the Second Pylon, the small court leads to the hypostyle hall, converted into a church in the 6th century AD. Beyond, three dark vestibules lead into the Sanctuary, dimly lit by two small windows, where a pedestal that once supported Isis' sacred *barque* (royal barge) is still in place. On the top of the right-hand wall Isis suckles her son Horus, while below she suckles a young pharaoh. On the left wall the pharaoh, here a Ptolemy, stands in front of Isis, who protects Osiris with her wings.

A staircase in one of the vestibules leads to the Osirian shrine, where the Osiris myth is illustrated in beautiful reliefs—usually closed but sometimes the guard opens it for *baksheesh* (a tip). The western door of the first vestibule leads to Hadrian's Gate. An interesting relief on the right wall of its ruined vestibule depicts the source of the Nile as the Nile god Hapi, who pours water from two jars; the ancient Egyptians believed that the Nile sprung up at the first cataract, from where one branch flowed toward Africa and another toward the Mediterranean.

To the right of the Second Pylon, the small **Temple of Hathor**▶ ▶ has a beautiful relief of musicians; Hathor was the patroness of music. Farther south is the most eye-catching structure on Philae: the **Kiosk of Trajan**▶ ▶ ▶, with beautifully carved floral columns, which was intended as the formal entrance to the temple. From here there are splendid views over the lake, where the metal coffer dam used during the relocation marks the original Philae Island, now totally submerged.

Raised hieroglyphs at Isis' temple

▶ ▶ New Kalabsha 168C3

Open: daily 8–4. Admission: moderate

The Temple of Kalabsha now lies somewhat forgotten on a promontory beside Lake Nasser, in the shadow of the High Dam. The monuments were relocated here from other sites in Nubia in 1970 to save them from the rising waters of Lake Nasser. The temple is now in a military zone and became accessible only a few years ago.

The original site of Kalabsha—Talmis in ancient times—was 30 miles farther up the Nile. The **Temple of Mandulis**▶ ▶ was dedicated to the Nubian fertility god Marul, called Mandulis by the Greeks. It was built during the reign of Augustus (ca30 BC) on the site of 18th-Dynasty and Ptolemaic structures. It later became a Christian church. The once imposing causeway leads to the unadorned Pylon, which lies slightly askew of the axis of the temple. Both the court and the hypostyle hall have columns with differing floral capitals, clearly suggesting the idea of a garden. The three chambers beyond, of which the last one is the sanctuary, are decorated with reliefs of Augustus in front of the entire Egyptian pantheon. A stairway in the first chamber leads to the roof, with splendid views over Lake Nasser.

The **Kiosk of Qertassi**▶, a Ptolemaic structure with two surviving Hathor-headed columns, came from farther south. The **Temple of Bayt el-Wali**▶ ▶ came from near the original site of Kalabsha and is known by its Arabic name, which means House of the Governor. It was hewn out of a rock by the Viceroy of Qush in commemoration of Ramses II's successful military expedition in Nubia. On the southern wall of the court, reliefs show Ramses II leading the campaign against the rebellious Nubians and receiving heaps of gold, ivory, and exotic animals as a tribute after the victory. The reliefs have retained a remarkable amount of their original color.

187

SOUND AND LIGHT AT PHILAE
There are two or three shows nightly, but check with the tourist office for the latest schedules. The temple looks spectacular when floodlit at night, but it must have been even more magnificent under a bright full moon, as the 19th-century travelers described it.

When Lake Nasser is high the Kalabsha Temple can only be reached by boat

LAKE NASSER CRUISES

Foreigners are currently unable to drive to any Nubian sites except for New Kalabsha. The rest can only be reached by boat or by plane for Abu Simbel only. There are currently five cruise boats operating on Lake Nasser, visiting all the temples. The *Qasr Ibrim* and the *Eugénie*, both run by Belle Époque Travel (tel: 02/518-1857, fax: 02/353-6114), offer excellent French cuisine, stylish accommodations and pools. Staff will organize special treats such as evening cocktails and classical music by the temples.

For fishing on the lake, Aswan-based El-Bohayrat Orascom (tel/fax: 097/311011) run fishing safaris of one or more days, with everything caught being returned to the lake, except for what is needed for dinner. The Nile perch, one of the largest freshwater fish, flourishes in Lake Nasser and can be over 6½ feet long—the record catch so far weighed in at 388 lbs. The most common fish are Tiger fish, several cat fish varieties and two species of *Tilapia*. Nile crocodiles, no longer seen north of the dam, are making a comeback in the lake.

▶▶▶ Lake Nasser monuments   *168B2*

Wadi el-Sebua▶▶ *(Open* daily dawn–dusk. *Admission free)* The vast Temple of Wadi el-Sebua is dedicated to Amun, Re-Harakhte and the deified pharaoh Ramses II. It is 84 miles south of the High Dam and its name, Valley of the Lions, is suggested by the row of 16 sphinxes leading up to its entrance. Ramses II decorated this temple with massive statues of himself, as always, and members of his family. Here, in the court, he is represented as a Nubian. The statues and reliefs are the work of local Nubian craftsmen and are much cruder than those in Egypt, although the colors have been well preserved. Early Christians knocked over Ramses' colossal statue at the entrance and defaced him on many of the reliefs.

Uphill, the Ptolemaic-Roman **Temple of Dakkah**▶▶ *(Open* daily dawn–dusk. *Admission free)* is reconstructed on the site of an earlier sanctuary (originally it was built 20 miles away). The temple was founded by the Meroite King Arkamani in the 3rd century BC and later added to and adapted by several Ptolemies and Roman emperors and is dedicated to the god Thoth. This is the only Egyptian temple facing north, perhaps pointing towards Thoth's cult center, but most probably because the foreign Ptolemies did not know any better. Look for graffiti in Roman, Greek and ancient Nubian to the left of the gateway in the First Pylon. Stairs on either side of the Pylon lead to guardrooms and the roof, which commands stunning views over the temple and Lake Nasser. The main temple consists of four connecting rooms that are mostly decorated with carvings depicting the deities receiving offerings. The small room beside the first sanctuary has particularly fine reliefs of two baboons approaching a lioness. The large granite casket in the last room once contained a cult statue of Thoth. Only the hypostyle hall survives of the nearby Roman temple of **Maharraka**▶, dedicated to Isis and Serapis. The reliefs are an interesting blend of Roman and Egyptian styles.

►► Amada

In the small oasis of Amada (25 miles south of Wadi el-Sebua) stands the oldest Egyptian temple in Nubia, the **Temple of Amada►** (*Open* daily dawn–dusk. *Admission free*). It was built by Tuthmosis III and Amenophis II and is dedicated to Amun-Re and Re-Herakhte. There are some interesting Berber graffiti of animals, high on the back walls of the pillared court, that were added by Tuthmosis IV. In the right inner chapel are carvings representing the foundation ceremonies that took place for this temple, as well as depictions of the Pharaoh running the Heb-Sed race. The central chapel has fine reliefs depicting offerings made to the gods. At the back of the sanctuary is a *stela* with the story of the temple's origins. The nearby **Rock Temple of al-Derr►►** (*Open* daily dawn–dusk. *Admission free*) is another temple built by Ramses II and dedicated to the same gods. The temple has well-preserved and particularly colorful reliefs. Among them are representations of the temple's builder making offerings to the gods and glorifying his military triumphs. Only the legs remain of the four large statues of Ramses II that used to guard the entrance.

Sunrise at the Temple of Wadi el-Sebua

189

The Tomb of Pennout► (*Open* daily dawn–dusk. *Admission free*) is unusual because Egyptians generally attached great importance to being buried on home soil. Pennout, the viceroy of Northern Nubia under Ramses IV, was no exception. So, although he did not make it back, the reliefs in his rock-cut tomb express his desire to find a final resting-place in the Theban hills.

Reliefs decorate the side wall of the Roman temple of Maharraka

Qasr Ibrim►► (*Open* daily dawn–dusk. *Admission free*) Qasr (castle) Ibrim is 25 miles north of Abu Simbel and is one of the few Nubian monuments in its original position. But what was once a plateau dominating the Nile is now an outcrop that barely rises above the lake. It seems unbelievable that there was once a community living in this barren isolated spot, but it was continually inhabited from its foundation ca1000 BC up to 1812 AD, when it was manned with Bosnian troops loyal to the Ottoman sultan. The ancient city was an important healing center dedicated to Isis and pilgrims traditionally carved their footprints onto the temple floor. Remains of a 5th-century BC tavern and a 10th-century AD Christian basilica, later converted into a mosque, are still visible.

Staring at posterity: Ramses II's statues are positioned to catch the sun's first rays

GETTING THERE
Most tourists fly the 175 miles to Abu Simbel, on an Egypt Air excursion, including round-trip flights, transfers, and a guided tour, which allows 2 hours on the site. This is usually sufficient. But be warned that if the outbound flight is delayed, you are still required to check in for the incoming flight at the published time, which can reduce time at the site to as little as 45 minutes. Traveling by air-conditioned bus (4 hours each way), or shared taxi is less comfortable but allows more time on the site and is much cheaper. The best way to see the temples, if you have the time and money, is on a Lake Nasser cruise.

▶▶▶ **Abu Simbel, Temples of Ra-Harakhte and Hathor**   168A1

Open: *daily 6–5.*
Admission, which should include services of a guide: expensive
Abu Simbel lies 175 miles south of Aswan and 25 miles from Wadi Halfa and the Sudanese border. Nineteenth-century travelers, having sailed 600 miles up the Nile from Cairo, were awestruck by the sight of the newly uncovered colossi of Ramses II in front of the temple. Nowadays these giant figures are often first spotted from an airplane, dwarfed by the vastness of Lake Nasser, and the speed of organized visits leaves many visitors wondering what all the fuss is about. The two temples were built by Ramses II (19th Dynasty), the larger one flanked by four colossi of the pharaoh, the smaller one with colossi of his wife Nefertari. Originally, the rock-cut temples overlooked a bend in the Nile and no doubt succeeded in their main purpose of impressing visitors from the south with Egypt's might and power and scaring off raiding Nubians.

In 1965, as the waters of Lake Nasser threatened to overwhelm the temples, UNESCO undertook a huge operation to save them. The temples were hand-sawed into 1,050 blocks, to be rebuilt block by block on an artificial hill, 680 feet from and 200 feet higher than their original site. The reconstruction is nearly perfect, and every year on February 22 and October 22 (one day later than originally planned) the dawn rays of the sun reach to the heart of the sanctuary to revive the cult statues. But somehow the perfection feels almost too good to be true.

The **Great Temple of Ra-Harakhte**▶▶▶ The façade of the temple is dominated by two pairs of seated colossi of Ramses II, each 65 feet high, hewn into the cliff. Only the faces and torsos are finely carved; the rest of the bodies were crudely finished. The first head on the left is the most beautiful. The façade is crowned by a corvette cornice surmounted with baboons adoring the rising sun, and a niche holds a falcon-headed statue of the sun-god Ra-Harakhte, to whom the temple was dedicated, holding a scepter and a figure of Maat. The sides of the thrones, near the temple entrance, are decorated with Nile gods symbolically uniting Egypt, and below them, on one side is a row of African prisoners and on the other a row of Syrians.

Inside is the hypostyle hall, or portico leading to the sanctuary, with four columns on either side, flanked with 33-foot-high Osirid statues of Ramses. The walls are decorated with fine reliefs of Ramses' campaigns in Syria and Nubia, played up for propaganda purposes. Facing the back of the temple, to the right, are reliefs of the Battle of Qaddesh in 1300 BC (which Ramses failed to win). On the opposite wall (left) he storms a Syrian fortress, while in the center he kills a Libyan with his lance, returning from the victorious battle with black captives. The eight side chambers probably stored tributes from Nubia. In the small hall with four pillars are reliefs of Ramses and Nefertari facing the gods. Beyond lies the sanctuary, its four mutilated cult statues once covered in gold. A door outside, beside the temple entrance, leads to the innards of the futuristic structure that now supports the temple.

Temple of Hathor▶▶ Hathor was the wife of the sun god during his day's passage and mother of his rebirth at dawn. The façade here is flanked by six statues of Nefertari and Ramses, their children standing between them. The hypostyle hall contains Hathor-headed columns and reliefs of the beautiful Nefertari watching Ramses killing his enemies, and of the royal couple in front of the gods. The sanctuary contains a ruined cow statue of Hathor and is decorated with reliefs of Nefertari offering incense to Mut and Hathor, and of Ramses adoring himself and his wife.

SUNRISE AT ABU SIMBEL
"There was a morning of mornings when we lay opposite the rock-hewn Temple of Abu Simbel ... one felt rather than saw that there were four figures in the pit of gloom below it... The stronger light flooded them red from head to foot, and they became alive—as horridly and tensely yet blindly alive as pinioned men in the death-chair before the current is switched on. One felt that if by a miracle the dawn could be delayed a second longer, they would tear themselves free, and leap forth to heaven knows what sort of vengeance."
Rudyard Kipling (1913)

191

Ramses II and his wife Nefertari at the Temple of Hathor, the only time in Egypt that a woman was portrayed at a temple entrance

Oases in the Western Desert

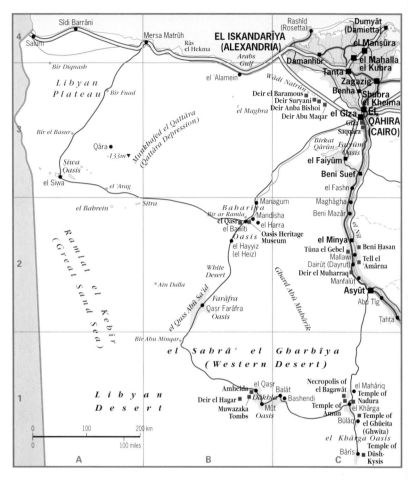

Life in the oases is still very traditional

A PLACE APART The Western Desert has traditionally been a place apart for Egyptians, the antithesis of the generous Nile Valley. But more and more of them, as well as visitors to their country, are turning to the desert and being surprised by what they find.

THE WESTERN DESERT Ancient Egyptians believed that Seth, the brother and murderer of Osiris, ruled the desert. Not surprisingly for a king-killer, he was associated with chaos and the desert was seen as a place to avoid. But they couldn't ignore it. It was too big for that—it is the eastern edge of the Sahara, the largest desert on earth. Stretching from the Nile to the Fezzan in Libya, from the Mediterranean coast to Kordofan in central Sudan, the Western Desert covers nearly 1.2 million square miles.

ISLANDS OF THE BLEST Herodotus, who visited several of the oases, called them the Islands of the Blest. But

Oases in the Western Desert

In spite of the town's rapid development, many houses in el-Kharga are still built of mud

FURTHER READING
To get the most out of a desert trip, look for the following books:
Ralph Bagnold, *Libyan Sands* (Bristol, 1935);
Ahmed Fakhry, *The Oases of Egypt: Siwa Oasis* (Cairo, 1973) and *Bahriyah and Farafra Oases* (Cairo 1974); and Cassandra Vivian, *The Western Desert: An Explorer's Handbook* (AUC, 2000) with excellent maps. Although the film *The English Patient* was shot in Tunisia, Michael Ondaatje's novel is set in Cairo, the Western Desert, and Italy.

rather than standing out like islands above the sea of sand, Egypt's oases are sunk below them in geological depressions. It is these depressions that have created the oases: being at or below sea level, they allow easy access to underground water. When, in prehistory, the climate became drier, people of the area congregated around these watering holes to survive and began to develop the first communities.

EARLY WRITERS Apart from the fabled Siwan Manuscript, the inhabitants of the desert have left few records and most of what is known about the history of their communities comes from the accounts of travelers. Nothing is recorded of the visit of Hercules, but Herodotus in 450 BC and the historians following Alexander in 331 BC all left detailed accounts, and early Arab writers, following the pilgrims' routes, contributed essential information. Although Europeans had been to the more accessible oases, it wasn't until the 19th century that European explorers really began to penetrate the Western Desert. Exploration continues now, for the desert has yet to reveal the answers to the many questions it poses.

ROMANCE OF THE DESERT The desert has a great romantic appeal. It isn't just the image of the Bedouin shaped by Hollywood and Rudolph Valentino. The stories of lost oases, hidden treasure, impossible journeys, brave deeds, and honorable behavior, increasingly rare elsewhere, are still credible in the desert. The enormity of the place and its wilderness brings out an aura of romance, whether you are lying on your back watching the brilliant night sky in

Landscape to get lost in: here, unlike the Eastern Desert, there is plenty of sand

the White Desert outside Farafra Oasis, or walking into the Great Sand Sea outside Siwa, with nothing but sand to be seen in all directions, the wind blowing away traces of your passage. It was partly because it was possible to get away from it all that religious hermits took to practicing monasticism in the desert; the remoteness of Wadi Natrun and the monasteries of the Eastern Desert seemed to bring supplicants closer to God.

THE NEW VALLEY The New Valley is the largest governorate in Egypt and includes the oases of Kharga, Dakhla, and Farafra. Some years ago the area was earmarked for considerable development in the belief that its many industries, from tourism to farming and phosphate mining, would support immigrant workers from the Nile Valley. This has not been successful in reducing the population of the Nile Valley, but it has led to improved communication and transportation between Kharga and Asyut.

HOPE FOR THE FUTURE As their cities become overpopulated and the ban on building on agricultural land stalls development, Egyptians are looking to the desert for solutions to some of their problems. The Western Desert oases are seeing an increasing number of immigrants from the Nile Valley, but that is nothing compared to some of the other projects that are being discussed by Egyptian planners. Among the most daring is the creation of the Toshka Canal, Egypt's great project for the 21st century. The canal will run north and west from Lake Nasser, a "new river" irrigating parts of the Western Desert.

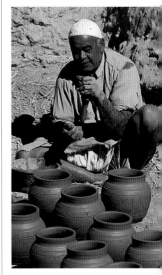

Making pots the traditional way

Drive

The Great Desert Circuit

The Western Desert is still a place of mysteries and legends, and the relatively new 600-mile road, connecting Cairo with Asyut via the four oases, offers one of the most exciting drives in Egypt. See the map on page 192.

A four-wheel drive is recommended, but if you stick to the main road a normal car will do. It is probably wise to start in Cairo and, if circumstances allow it (see page 126), to end in Asyut. The alternative is to fly back from Kharga, which is expensive, or return the same long way you came.

Above: volcanic stones give the desert its black tones

The drive starts behind the Pyramids of Giza and follows the rail line used for transporting iron to Helwan. Once past the new 6th October City, there is nothing but desert and a few rest-houses halfway. After 190 miles the road enters **Managum**, the checkpoint for Bahariya oasis, and continues on to Bahariya's capital, **el-Bawiti** (see page 197). Not long after el-Bawiti you enter the **Black Desert**, so-called because the desert is covered with black stones. After 29 miles you pass through **el-Hayyiz** (**el-Heiz**), where there are several villages and a ruined Roman camp.

After 37 miles and a signpost for Ain Della, you enter the surreal landscape of the **White Desert**►►►, and after another 12 miles, **Farafra** (see page 198) comes into sight. The 190-mile Farafra–Dakhla road, which was never finished, goes through flat, sandy desert until **Abu Minqar**, a major checkpoint 160 miles from the Libyan border, where the escarpment bordering the Dakhla oasis joins you to the right. Beyond **Dakhla** (see pages 198–199) the 122-mile road to **el-Kharga** (see page 199) is often threatened by moving sand dunes. The last 140-mile stretch to **Asyut** offers some of the most spectacular scenery in Egypt, with beautiful mountains and *wadis* (dry gullies), sand dunes, and several Roman forts.

A wind sculpture in the White Desert

Usually the only wild creatures encountered by visitors to the Western Desert are ants, beetles, mosquitoes, flies, fleas, scorpions, and, perhaps, a herd of gazelle. But happily there are many more creatures adapted to the hard desert life and they include cheetahs, oryx, hyenas, Barbary sheep, cats, and fennec foxes, as well as smaller animals like rats, hedgehogs, hares, and weasels. There are several species or varieties of snakes that hide in the sand dunes. Kharga and Dakhla are stopovers for several migrating birds and throughout the desert are birds of prey like vultures and hawks.

197

▶▶▶ Bahariya Oasis — 192B2

Beyond the checkpoint at Managum, as the road descends, there are spectacular views over the oasis, covering more than 750 square miles. Most of Bahariya's 35,000 inhabitants live in the capital **el-Bawiti▶**, which has merged with the old capital **el-Qasr▶▶**. El-Qasr, with picturesque houses and narrow streets, was built on the site of the ancient village of Qasr. Most of the monuments lie unexcavated under the houses. Of the excavated sites, several were looted or vandalized and may be closed for restoration. The most impressive building was the Roman Triumphal Arch until its stone was reused to build houses around it in the mid-19th century. Qarat Qasr Salim has two burial chambers with blackened murals and at Qarat el-Faragi (Hill of the Chicken Merchant) is a cemetery with mummies of ibises and falcons. A **Temple of Bes▶** from the Late Period was discovered in the middle of el-Qasr.

The **Oasis Heritage Museum▶**, 0.5 miles north on the road to Cairo has a display of clay figurines, made by local artist Mahmoud Eed, set in various scenes of traditional village life

The hot springs in towns like Ain Bishmu and Ain Bardir, surrounded by the gardens they irrigate, may look idyllic but visitors are warned against bathing here. A 2-mile walk out of town is the hot spring (113°F) of Bir ar-Ramla, but it is also quite exposed. Tour operators organize trips to the secluded springs of Bir Mattar, cool and refreshing, and the hot bath at the edge of the desert of Bir el-Ghaba. To the north of el-Bawiti is the village of el-Agouz, founded by families who were banned from Siwa because of their women's loose morals. A little farther is Mandisha, one of the oldest and most beautiful villages. About 3 miles farther is Qaseir Muharib with impressive ruins of a Roman Christian village.

Mr. Kadafi, the barber of Bahariya, shows his skill

▶▶ Farafra Oasis   192B2

Farafra, the most isolated and also the most beautiful of the oases, has only one inhabited village, Qasr Farafra. Many houses are decorated by a local artist, Badr, who has opened a **small museum**▶▶ in a wonderful mud-brick house he built himself. Until the 1950s, every family had its own room to shelter in the fortress of Farafra, which is still partly inhabited. Farafra has no ancient monuments, but a walk in its beautiful gardens and shady palm groves makes up for that. Local guides can lead you to Ain Dalla (Spring of Shade), 50 miles to the north of Farafra and the last water hole before the Great Sand Sea. Its refreshing clear water has saved many desert travelers from dying of thirst. However, the main attraction in the area is undoubtedly the magnificent **White Desert**▶▶▶, with fantastic chalk sculptures eroded by the wind, which change with the light from white to gold to deep purple at sunset. Many visitors camp here to see the rock formations by night, when they seem surreal.

▶▶▶ Dakhla Oasis   192B1

Driving in from the desert, visitors see the oasis of Dakhla as a feast of colors, with vibrant green fields, red earth, and a pink-colored escarpment. During the New Kingdom, **Mut**▶ was the capital of Dakhla, as it is again today. The most interesting sites are on the outskirts of the oasis, but Mut is a good base with simple accommodations. Its only sights are the **Ethnographic Museum**▶, (next to Dar el-Wafdar hotel, tel: 821311. *Open 8–2. Admission: inexpensive*), with displays of oasis life, and the hot springs near the Mut Talata Hotel, recommended for colds, rheumatism, and skin diseases.

   El-Qasr▶▶, about 20 miles west from Mut, is the medieval capital of Dakhla built over a Roman settlement. An Ayyubid mosque, a *madrasa* (theological school), and

Above and below: The mud-brick center of el-Qasr, Dakhla's medieval capital

many four-story houses have survived and it is a delight to walk around. The 1st- and 2nd-century AD **Muwazaka Tombs▶▶**, 3 miles away, are finely decorated. About 5 miles farther, **Deir el-Hagar▶** (*Admission: moderate*), a Roman temple dedicated to the Theban Triad, stands in the desert. **Amheida▶▶**, 2 miles from el-Qasr, has Dakhla's most important ruins, including a temple, cemeteries, and interesting Roman wall paintings in the central building. Balat, 22 miles east of Mut, thrived on trade with Qush and **Bashendi▶**, which has 1st-century BC tombs and good carpet-weaving.

Outposts of empire: a Roman fort at the el-Kharga Oasis

▶▶ el-Kharga   192C1

After the peace and quiet of the desert and the other oases, the modern town of el-Kharga appears like a nightmare, its inhabitants living in concrete blocks that sprawl into the desert. But the town makes a good base for exploring some fine pharaonic and Christian ruins, though it isn't a pleasant place to walk around. The Kharga Museum houses exhibits from various archeological sites in the Dakhla and Kharga oases, which trace their history from prehistoric times. The only old mud-brick houses, painted in blue and soft orange, are found in Darb el-Sandadiya, the area around the *souk* (marketplace).

North of the city are the ruined Ptolemaic Temple of Nadura and, farther down the road at Hibis, surrounded by palm trees, the **Temple of Amun▶**, one of the rare Persian monuments (6th century BC) to have survived in Egypt. It is always open and admission is moderate. Beyond, in the **Necropolis of el-Bagawat▶** (*Open daily 8–5. Admission: moderate*), Christians were buried in chapels with fine murals (3rd–7th centuries).

South of el-Kharga, the road to Baris follows the slave route that until 1884 crossed the desert from Darfur in the Sudan to Asyut; el-Kharga was the last stop en route. On the way is the 27th-Dynasty **Temple of el-Ghwita▶** (*Admission: moderate*) and a ruined Temple of Amenebis. To the south of Baris, the second-largest town, are the Roman Temple of Dush and the ruins of the ancient town of Kysis.

THE GREAT SAND SEA
The Great Sand Sea is the biggest and most dangerous dune field in the world. It runs from the southwest of Siwa oasis to the west of Farafra and Dakhla oases, and goes 500 miles south to the Gilf Kebir, with dunes reaching heights of 500 feet. Nothing lives here, and it is one of the last unexplored areas in the world. The few expeditions to come this way have found big chunks of green glass, some weighing as much as seven kilos, all over the area; although the glass was worked by prehistoric man, it isn't man-made and is thought to have been produced by a natural chemical reaction.

Oases in the Western Desert

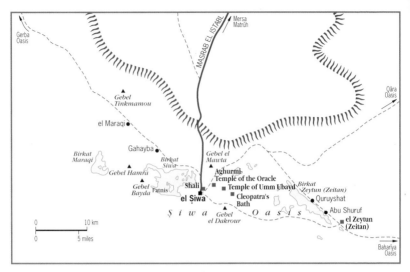

►►► Siwa Oasis

192A3

The road from Mersa Matruh (see page 222) to Siwa follows the ancient caravan route; its name, Masrab el-Istabl, translates as "the Course of the Stable." Alexander the Great took eight days to cover the 200 miles in 331 BC with a handful of companions. The Egyptian King Abbas II, with 300 camels, herds of other animals, and supplies of water, took seven days in 1907. But after King Fuad

Being unable to live outside the walls of the Shali, Siwans built upward as the community grew

LOCAL CUSTOMS
People in the oases are more conservative than in the rest of Egypt. Their lives and customs, strongly influenced by religion and their particular social code, have made the oases safe places, where crime is rare. Visitors are also expected to observe local custom and should wear decent, modest clothes. Women especially should try to keep most of their bodies covered. Locals consider it strange when a woman wanders off on her own in the gardens. One of the attractions of the oases is bathing in the hot springs, but while men can wear a bathing suit, women should bathe in a dress.

visited Siwa in 1928, a road was laid and the journey can now be done in under four hours.

Dominated by the ruins of its past, Siwa Town is undergoing rapid change. Not so long ago the main streets were covered in sand, cars were rare, and most people lived in traditional Siwan houses. The new town, where concrete houses are fast replacing mud-brick houses, is still a quiet and sleepy place where some old traditions are obviously being maintained: women are most commonly seen wearing their covering *milayah* (wrap) in the back of a donkey cart. The **House of Siwa Museum**▶▶ (near the canal. *Open* 10–noon. Closed Fri. *Admission: inexpensive*) contains a display of traditional life in the village which some fear is soon to disappear.

Founded, according to the Siwan Manuscript, in AD 1203, the **Shali**▶▶ was originally surrounded by high walls to counter Bedouin attacks. Siwans, forbidden to build outside these walls, were obliged to build extra floors on their houses to accommodate a growing population. The shortage of space was further exacerbated by the need to bring the animals in each night. In 1820, Siwa was conquered by Egyptian troops who made the area safe enough for the town council to permit building outside the walls. As at Aghurmi, Siwans built using the local *karshif* (mud), strong enough to support eight stories, but with a high salt content that dissolved in the occasional heavy rains, which accounts for the Shali's present, melted appearance. The mosque is the best-maintained building; the *muezzin* (prayer caller) here sometimes calls the faithful to prayer using his own, unamplified voice.

Although the center of the Shali has been abandoned, some houses on the edge of the old town are still habitable

SIWAN CULTURE
Siwans are unlike the people of the other oases. Descended from Berbers, intermarried with Arabs and Negroids, they speak their own dialect of Berber although they are obliged to speak Arabic for official matters. They had interesting traditions regarding sex: young workers, known as *zaggalah*, were forbidden to marry and also forbidden to live inside the town, to keep them away from women; homosexuality became accepted among them. To further safeguard their women, who continue to be completely covered when they leave their houses, Siwan men ensured that animals of different sexes were also segregated.

Oases in the Western Desert

202

SIWAN MANUSCRIPT
The history of Siwa is recorded in the Siwan Manuscript, a document based on oral traditions that date back to the mid-7th century AD. Listing blood lines, customs, history, and songs, the manuscript is a complete record of Siwan culture up to 1960, when the record was discontinued.

THE BRIGHT SPOT
"It is no longer the romantic medieval fortress which still existed up to the beginning of this century. The place is also very different from the town of Siwa which I had known 20 years ago. But in spite of all the changes which have taken place, it is still one of the most romantic and interesting of places—not only in our deserts, but in all of Egypt. It will always be a bright spot in the memory of the visitor."
Ahmed Fakhry, *Siwa Oasis* (Cairo, 1973)

SHALI PRECAUTIONS
Take care when walking in the Shali. Although many surfaces are safe, great damage was caused by a two-day storm in 1982 and occasionally a floor or path will sound hollow underfoot —it will be, and may be about to fall.

Gebel el-Mawta (Mountain of the Dead)▶ Just outside the town is the Hill of the Dead, its harsh outline sculpted by the wind and riddled with tombs from the 26th Dynasty to the Greco-Roman period. Ptolemaic corpses were prepared in the same way as mummies in the Nile Valley, which, as author Ahmed Fakhry has pointed out, suggests the oasis was completely Egyptianized at that time. Four tombs are open, the Tomb of Si-Amun being the most important. Its decoration, particularly images of the owner and his family, and of the goddess Nut in front of a sycamore tree, shows Greek influences. Some 65 feet away, the north-facing Tomb of Mesu-Isis shows signs of having been reused in the Roman period. The Ptolemaic Tomb of the Crocodile, with one decorated chamber, takes its name from a painting of a crocodile, further proof that Siwans were in touch with el-Faiyum, where the crocodile god Sobek had his center, from an early date. These three tombs were discovered in 1940, when Siwans hid on the hill to escape Italian bombers. The Tomb of Niperpathot, which was already uncovered, is largely ruined.

About 2.5 miles (a 20-minute walk) from Siwa Town lies the fortified settlement of **Aghurmi**▶▶, surrounded by palm trees. The door to the main gate is off its hinges. A path leads to the inner court, still inhabited in the early 20th century. The restored mosque has excellent views from its minaret. Below, in the court, several holes serve as reminders of the legend that there is treasure buried beneath the town. The houses are even more ruined than those in the Shali. At the back of the town, raised on the rock of Aghurmi, lies the Temple of the Oracle.

It isn't often that you can locate the exact spot on which an event took place more than 2,000 years ago, but you can at the **Temple of the Oracle**▶▶▶ at Aghurmi. The building dates from the reign of King Amasis (26th Dynasty) who is mentioned in the sanctuary. The temple, dedicated to Amun-Ra, is well preserved, although the rock on which it is built is cracking. Only the sanctuary has decorations. It was here in 331 BC that Alexander the Great, hidden from the eyes of the priests and his companions, approached one of the ancient world's most revered oracles. Alexander never repeated what he heard. He had promised to tell his mother the answers he received from the oracle when he returned to Macedonia, but he died before he saw her. Whatever was said, from then on Alexander claimed descent from Amun.

Also known as the Spring of the Sun, **Cleopatra's Bath**▶▶ is the most famous of Siwa's many springs. Cleopatra's visit is a matter of legend, but Herodotus was there, fascinated by its apparent bubbling at night, which he took to be due to a warming of the water after dark. Presumably, Alexander the Great also refreshed himself here after his desert journey. It is still a popular place for men of the oasis and visitors to swim, but the nearby road has made it too public a place for women to feel at ease.

Four miles from Siwa Town, the road runs through palm groves until it opens on to salt flats and **Birkat Siwa** (**Siwa Lake**). Foreigners started coming in large numbers to swim more privately in the spring on Fatnis Island, a hop away from the shore, but this has become just as popular with local males. The lake itself, backed by vast eroded rocks on the far side, is worth the journey.

Siwan dates, famous all over Egypt

Through the palm groves

This walk (3–4 hours) from Siwa Town through the beautiful groves and gardens of the oasis visits Siwa's original settlement and famous temples. See the map on page 200.

As you leave Siwa Town past the marketplace, houses quickly give way to gardens. The oasis is famous for its fruit trees, some 70,000 olive trees, and an estimated quarter of a million palms. Siwan custom allows anyone to eat dates from the trees, but it is an offense to carry them away.

A couple of miles on, the road forks. The right-hand path, through eucalyptus trees, leads to **Gebel el-Dakrour►►**, known in Siwan as Daran Breek. There are three hills close together, believed to be the site of lapis and emerald mines, referred to by Arab writers. A large festival is held here on the full moon of October.

You will get an excellent view of the oasis from the hill.

Returning to the fork, take the other path to follow the loop around the oasis, following a sign (occasionally obscured) to **Cleopatra's Bath** (see page 202). Continue along the road to the Temple of Amun, also known as the **Temple of Umm Ubayd►**. It was standing in the early 19th century, but an earthquake in 1811 and, more disastrously, a governor in need of building material in 1896 have left it a sad ruin. It still deserves a visit before you reach the **Temple of the Oracle►►►**, to which it was said to be connected by an underground passage.

Continue along the road to the new village of **Aghurmi**. At the crossroads, the right-hand turn leads to the abandoned village of Zeytun (Zeitan) and to the Darb Siwa, the road to Bahariya and Cairo. The left-hand road leads back to Siwa Town, passing **Ain Tamousi►►**, where Siwan brides used to bathe on the eve of their wedding, and a garden where German field marshal Erwin Rommel is said to have stopped for tea.

Oases in the Western Desert

GETTING THERE
Service taxis and the Cairo–Alexandria buses can drop you at the rest house halfway between the two cities, and from there you can sometimes get a taxi or a lift to Wadi Natrun. A surer way of getting there is to hire a taxi for the day or join an organized tour.

▶ ▶ ▶ Wadi el-Natrun   192C3

The valley of Wadi el-Natrun, lying off the desert road from Cairo to Alexandria, takes its name from the deposits of natron salts, used in pharaonic times for embalming mummies and still mined today. Monasticism began in the Eastern Desert (see pages 236 and 238–239), but the rules were developed in Wadi el-Natrun and it is from here that Coptic popes have been chosen for the last 1,500 years. The current pope, Shenuda III, enthroned in 1971, was a monk at Deir el-Suryani and lived for several years as a hermit in the desert. He has done much to revive monasticism and encourage a greater involvement of the monks in the Coptic community. Nineteenth-century visitors described the monks as dirty, anti-intellectual, even ignorant, but today many monks are highly educated and speak several languages.

The four monasteries in Wadi el-Natrun follow a similar plan. Surrounded by heavy walls, originally without an entrance as visitors and provisions were hoisted up over them, they have a keep where monks hid during the frequent Bedouin attacks in the Middle Ages. There are several churches, traditionally divided into three sections: the *haikal* (sanctuary) with the altar hidden behind a screen, the choir, and the nave. The monasteries are now easily accessible and admission is free. Visitors are welcomed with a chat and a cup of tea, for which the monks never accept money, although a donation in the offering box is much appreciated.

Deir Anba Bishoi▶▶ This monastery with 150 monks and some 22 hermits receives the most Coptic pilgrims, and it is still expanding. St. Bishoi (320–407 AD) was one of the first monks in Wadi el-Natrun, arriving at the age of 20. As an old man Bishoi is said to have had a vision of Christ, whose feet he washed and who permitted him to drink the hallowed water. He was buried in the Church of Anba Bishoi (9th century AD) together with Paul of Tamweh, who was canonized after he attempted to commit suicide seven times. Apparently Bishoi's body is still as well preserved as on the day he died and from time to time he stretches out his arm to the believers. Pope Shenuda lived in the Papal compound during his exile (1981–1985), which was ordered by President Sadat. He still returns here on retreat.

Deir el-Suryani▶▶ The monastery was founded (6th century AD) by disgruntled monks from Deir Anba Bishoi. After the monks were persuaded to return to Deir Anba Bishoi, their new monastery was taken over by Syrian monks. The 10th-century Church of el-Adhra (the Virgin) has a magnificent inlaid Door of Prophecies and striking frescoes in the semi-domes of the choir. St. Bishoi used to pray for days in his cave, which is now part of the church, his hair attached to the ceiling to keep himself upright. In 1837, Lord Curzon discovered several ancient manuscripts in the keep, which are now in the British Museum.

A new icon in 6th-century Deir el-Suryani

STAYING OVERNIGHT
If you want to stay overnight at the monasteries, it is best to arrange it beforehand through the patriarchate. Alternatively, the Burg al-Wadi Hotel in Bir Hooker is clean, or there is a more luxurious inn, 3 miles past the rest house toward Alexandria.

Monks, Deir el-Suryani

Deir el-Baramous▶▶ is the most remote and oldest monastery in Wadi el-Natrun. Baramus is Coptic for "two Romans," as the monastery is ascribed to two young sons of the emperor Valentine, buried here after they died from excessive fasting. Recent restorations in the 9th-century Church of el-Adhra have revealed medieval frescoes. About a mile out in the desert is the Cave of Pope Kyrillos VI, Shenuda's predecessor, which has become a shrine.

Deir Abu Maqar is closed to visitors, unless you have a letter of introduction from the Coptic patriarchate in Cairo. It was founded by St. Makarius, who died in 390 after he had spent 60 years as a hermit in the desert. In 1978, the monks claimed to have the head of John the Baptist, an assertion also made by Aleppo, Damascus, and Venice.

VISITING THE MONASTERIES
The monasteries (except Abu Maqar) are usually open every day. The gates are not generally unlocked before 6 AM. To find out what time the monasteries are open, or to arrange a stay (men only), tel: Deir Anba Bishoi 02/591-4448, Dier el-Suryani 01/592-9658 and Deir el-Baramous 01/592-2775.

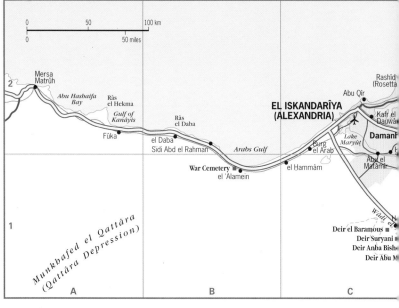

0   50   100 km

0   50 miles

Mersa Matrûh

Abu Hashaifa Bay

Râs el Hekma

Gulf of Kanâyis

Fûka

Râs el Daba

el Daba

Sidi Abd el Rahmañ

Arabs Gulf

War Cemetery

el ʿAlamein

Rashîd (Rosetta

Abu Qîr

EL ISKANDARÎYA (ALEXANDRIA)

Kafr el Dauwâ

Lake Maryût

Damanh

Burg el Arab

el Ḥammâm

Abu el Matâmir

Wâdi el

Deir el Baramous

Deir Suryani

Deir Anba Bishô

Deir Abu M

Munkhafaḍ el Qattâra (Qattâra Depression)

206

A   B   C

Above: The Alexandria Museum of Antiquities is the guardian of many precious objects
Right: The corniche at Alexandria

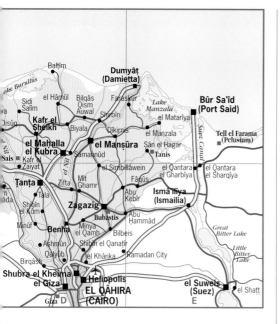

A NATURAL BARRIER After running as a single thread of water from Khartoum to Cairo, the Nile fans out into several branches and creates the luscious Delta, separating Cairo and the Nile Valley from the north coast. The Delta lacks the archeological splendors of the Nile Valley, but visitors who do no more than pass through on their way to the north coast are missing some beautiful and fascinating country.

THE NORTH COAST Egypt's Mediterranean coastline stretches 732 miles from the Israeli to the Libyan borders, a sparkling line of sand, Nile silt, and sea. Although much of the coast east of Alexandria (el-Iskandariya) is either poorly served by roads and facilities, or overlooked by industry, the old ports of Rosetta and Damietta, with their distinctive Ottoman architecture, are worth traveling to see. Some of Egypt's finest beaches lie to the west of Alexandria, but as the coastline becomes filled with low-cost vacation resorts for middle-class Egyptians, most visitors heading north of Cairo are on their way to Alexandria or, like Alexander the Great, heading west to the oasis of Siwa.

LEGENDARY ALEXANDRIA Few cities in the world lean so heavily upon legend as Alexandria. At first sight Egypt's second-largest city, with a population of over 5 million, appears to offer nothing but illusion and disillusion. Where is Alexander's city? Where is the city of the Pharos and Library, as famous for its loving as for its learning in the ancient world? Where is the more recent city conjured out of words by four great writers in the 20th century? The pictures are all distorted and your first sight, whether you approach from the sea or across the marshes to the south, is likely to be of smokestacks and too much concrete. It is easy to leave thinking that the magical city lives on only in the work of Cavafy, Forster, Durrell, and

Mahfouz. But stay awhile and slowly those other cities will reveal themselves, and you might hear what Cavafy called "the exquisite music of that strange procession," because there *are* remains from almost all of the city's many epochs. To get the most out of the city, follow Ibn Duqmaq's advice and make that pilgrimage: walk around it and piece the pictures back together.

A GREAT START When Alexander the Great conquered Egypt in 332 BC, he needed a capital to serve as a bridge between the Mediterranean and the Nile. Rhakotis, a fishing village with a natural double bay, offered the ideal solution: according to legend, Alexander himself marked the city's boundaries before leaving for Siwa. Alexander never saw the city, but after his death in 325 BC, his body was sent to Alexandria by the priests of Memphis with the warning: "Do not settle him here, but at the city he built at Rhakotis. For wherever his body must lie, that city will be uneasy, disturbed by wars and battles." But the warning was not heeded and one of those disturbances, in the 4th century AD, supposedly destroyed Alexander's tomb

Above: The intricate dome of the Abu el-Abbas Mosque
Left: The grand sweep of Alexandria's corniche from a room in the Cecil Hotel

and the rest of his city. Legends of that "lost city" within the city have left Alexandria with a haunting sense of loss. While it may no longer deserve the epithet "the pearl of the Mediterranean," it is still fascinating.

THE MODERN CITY When the American Civil War in the 1860s created a worldwide cotton shortage, Alexandria's traders monopolized the market and the city rose to prominence among the Levantine ports. The opening of new ports along the Suez Canal after 1869 took some of that business away, but Alexandria maintained its wealth and, as the summer capital for Egypt's rulers, also its social importance. The current president still prefers to spend his summers by the sea, but the city has changed. Most of the Italians, British, and Greeks have gone and Alexandria's traders are now mostly Egyptian. But in its museum, its ruined temple to the Mediterranean god Serapis, the remains of the Pharos—wonder of the ancient world—and most recently in its Levantine cafés, it is still possible to trace the development of the inspiration that came from across the water in Europe.

GETTING AROUND
Guided tours can be arranged from Cairo or at the reception desks of most Alexandrian hotels. Otherwise, one of the most pleasant ways of getting around the city is by *calèche*, an old horse-drawn carriage. Used by tourists in the center of town, they are also an essential means of transportation for people all over Egypt who need an inexpensive local taxi. Drivers and horses come in various states of fitness. Be prepared to haggle hard for the price, making it clear what you want to see and how much time you have to spend on your trip.

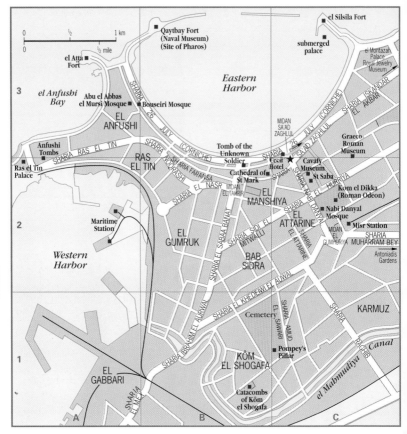

Map labels:

el Silsila Fort

Qaytbay Fort
(Naval Museum)
(Site of Pharos)

submerged
palace

el Montazah
Palace
Royal Jewelry
Museum

el Atta
Fort

*Eastern
Harbor*

SHARIA ISKANDAR
EL AKBAR

*el Anfushi
Bay*

Abu el Abbas
el Mursi Mosque   Bouseiri Mosque

EL
ANFUSHI

MIDAN
SA'AD
ZAGHLUL

Graeco-
Roman
Museum

Anfushi
Tombs

SHARIA RAS EL TIN

RAS
EL TIN

SHARIA FARANSA

Tomb of the
Unknown
Soldier

Cecil
Hotel

Cavafy
Museum

St Saba

Kom el Dikka
(Roman Odeon)

Ras el Tin
Palace

EL NASR

Cathedral of
St Mark

MIDAN
EL TAHRIR

EL
MANSHIYA

SHARIA NABI DANYAL

Nabi Danyal
Mosque

SHARIA EL SABAA BANAT

EL
ATTARINE

SHARIA SIDI EL
MITWALLI

Misr Station

Maritime
Station

EL
GUMRUK

MIDAN
EL
GUMHURIYA

SHARIA
MUHARRAM BEY

Antoniadis
Gardens

*Western
Harbor*

BAB
SIDRA

SHARIA EL ATTARINE

KARMUZ

SHARIA EL KHEDEIWI EL AWUAL

Cemetery

SHARIA
SAWARI

SHARIA EL MAHMUDIYA

SHARIA IBRAHIM EL AWUAL

Pompey's
Pillar

KÔM
EL SHOGAFA

el Mahmudiya Canal

EL
GABBARI

SHARIA
EL MEKS

Catacombs
of Kôm
el Shogafa

Scale: 0 — ½ — 1 km / 0 — ½ mile

210

▶ el-Anfushi
210A3

El-Anfushi is a fascinating old quarter at the center of the city. Originally part of the island of Pharos, it was connected to the mainland by the Heptastadion dike. Over the centuries the dike broadened into a neck of land, which later housed the Turkish town, an interesting place to walk.

Five tombs, their occupants unknown, make up the **Anfushi Tombs▶** (*Sharia Ras el-Tin. Open daily 9–4. Admission: moderate*). The walls are painted to imitate marble and alabaster, and date from the 3rd century BC. Tomb No. 2 has paintings of deities, a Greek inscription, and two sketches of boats very much like the present-day *felucca* (sailboat). Rising groundwater is threatening the tombs.

Just beyond the tombs is the 19th-century Ras el-Tin Palace, originally Muhammad Ali's summer residence. It was from here that King Farouk left Egypt after abdicating (July 26, 1952). The palace is now used to house visiting dignitaries and is closed to visitors.

▶ Antoniadis Gardens
210C2

Near Nuzha Gardens. Open: daily 8–4. Admission: inexpensive
Peaceful formal gardens surround the 19th-century villa of the Greek philanthropist Sir John Antoniadis. The villa, now another government guest residence, is officially closed to the public, but the man selling soda outside will

sometimes get you in after 2 PM. The gardens are understandably popular for an afternoon stroll, away from the noise of the city. Across the neighboring Nuzha Gardens is the zoo, less interesting than the one in Cairo.

▶▶ Cavafy Museum   210C2

4 Sharia Sharm el-Sheikh.
Open: Tue–Sun 9–2, Tue and Thu 6–8. Admission free
Alexandrian-born poet Constantine Cavafy's furniture and books, formerly housed in the Greek Consulate, have been returned to the apartment where he lived for 25 years until his death in 1933. It used to be a run-down pension; now sketches and photographs of Cavafy stare from the walls of the bedroom, salon, and three well-stocked reading rooms. If there is any of his spirit in the apartment, it is in the pictures, the books, and the view over the city where he lived and the hospital where he died of cancer (see Walk in Literary Alexandria, pages 216–217).

FISHY BUSINESS
In spite of wildlife preservation agreements, baskets of turtles are sometimes on sale in el-Anfushi's fish market —the meat is sold to eat, shells for ashtrays, and turtle blood as an aphrodisiac.

The older parts of Alexandria, like Anfushi, are full of character and crumbling buildings

Mummification survived the advent of Christianity (Greco-Roman Museum)

MUSEUM GUIDE
"...the visitor who 'goes through' it will find afterwards that it has gone through him... He should not visit the collection until he has learned or imagined something about the ancient city, and he should visit certain definite objects, and then come away—He may then find that a scrap of the past has come alive."
E. M. Forster, *Alexandria: a History and a Guide* (1922)

Sculpture in the museum's garden

▶▶▶ **Greco-Roman Museum**   *210C3*

Sharia el-Mathaf, off Sharia el-Hurriya.
Open: daily 9–4. Closed: Fri 11:30–1:30. Admission: moderate
If there is time to see just one thing in Alexandria, head for this museum, which covers an intriguing period too often overlooked in Egypt's long history. Most of its exhibits have come from Alexandria, the Delta, and from el-Faiyum. Ongoing reorganization might result in room numbers being changed, but at the moment, most exhibits are displayed chronologically, starting, to the left off the entrance hall, with Room 6. It contains two magnificent Roman busts—one in marble, the other in sycamore—of Serapis, the god of Alexandria who was a hybrid of Dionysos and Osiris, intended to unite the Greek and Egyptian cults. Along with the gigantic 2nd-century AD sculpture of the Apis bull, they came from the Serapeum, destroyed in 4th-century riots.

The Ptolemies maintained the cult of the pharaonic crocodile god Sobek. Room 9 contains the remains of a Sobek chapel from el-Faiyum, including the extraordinary mummified crocodile on a bier.

Rooms 12–17, mostly devoted to sculpture, include an imposing bust of Marcus Aurelius; marble heads of Alexander (Room 12) and of Roman emperors including Julius Caesar, Augustus, and Hadrian (Rooms 13–14); some fine Greek torsos (Room 16a); and the largest known statue from a single block of porphyry, which some believe to be Diocletian (Room 17).

The museum's most pleasing collections are the encaustic paintings—lifelike portraits painted on to mummy cases (Rooms 7, 8, and 10)—and terra-cotta *Tanagra* figurines (Room 18a), 4th–2nd century BC. Found in the tombs of children and young women, these figurines were intended as a celebration of youth and beauty and give a fascinating insight into fashions of the period.

Christian antiquities (Rooms 1–5) include an unusual mummy with a black cross in his neck (Room 1) and some beautiful textiles (Room 4), for which the Copts were renowned. When you need some air, stroll around the stone sarcophagi and architectural fragments in the garden.

The Egyptian government is building another Alexandrian Library, but you don't have to wait until it is finished to rediscover Alexander's city. If you know what to look for, you'll see fascinating traces all around you.

The ground plan Alexander's city was bisected by two principal streets: Canopic Street and the Street of the Soma. With their long vistas and cooling breezes, they survive in the modern city as Sharia el-Hurriya and Sharia Nabi Danyal. The entrance to the sparkling western harbor is also as it was, although the 15th-century sultan, Qaytbay, built his fairy-tale fort over the ruins of the ancient lighthouse and the Egyptian navy occupies the site of the Temple of Isis near the eastern point.

The palace area Stop in front of the Cecil Hotel, facing out to sea, and you are standing near the ancient palace area. Ptolemy, Caesar, and Cleopatra were here before you. The Caesareum—Cleopatra's gift of a temple for Mark Antony—was directly beneath you. Until the 19th century, two obelisks brought from Heliopolis marked the site of the temple; they now grace New York's Central Park and London's Victoria Embankment.

Alexandria's glory Alexandria's harbor bridged the gap between Egypt and Greece, but the Mouseion was an

ERATOSTHENES
Eratosthenes was born in Cyrene in 276 BC. He believed that the earth was round, and measured its circumference by measuring the sun's shadow at midday on midsummer's day in Alexandria. Knowing that in Aswan, on the same longitude, the midsummer sun cast no shadow at all, he calculated that the distance between the two was 1/50th of a complete circle. Estimating Alexandria to Aswan as 500 miles, he calculated the world's circumference as 25,000 miles and its diameter 7,850 miles, only 50 miles off.

213

essential link between the knowledge of the ancient and medieval worlds. The Mouseion stood at the center of the city, probably near the crossing of those two main streets; the ancient pillars adorning the Abd el-Razzaq Mosque, across from the Nabi Danyal Mosque, may have originally stood in the Mouseion. Within its complex of libraries, parks, and halls dedicated to the development of all knowledge, Homer was edited, Eratosthenes measured the earth's circumference, our "Julian" calendar was devised, sciences from mathematics to medicine were developed, and the city's reputation was assured.

Street stalls on Sharia Nabi Danyal, with pillars decorating the Abd el-Razzaq Mosque that came from the ancient Mouseion

▶▶▶ Kom el-Dikka (Roman Odeon) 210C2

Sharia Abd el-Muneim, Misr Station. Open: 9–4.
Closed Fri 11:30–1:30. Admission: moderate

When you walk down into the odeon at Kom el-Dikka you are walking through layers of the city's history. Polish archeologists, starting in the 1960s, have removed the ruins of a late 18th-century fort, Muslim graves, and later Roman remains to uncover what you see now. The small theater, dating from the 2nd century AD, underwent several alterations in antiquity to become this elegant, covered auditorium for musical performances. The well-preserved monochrome mosaic flooring in the vestibule would have covered this area. The beautiful bird mosaics fo a Roman villa can be seen nearby.

▶▶▶ Kom el-Shogafa Catacombs 210B1

Off Sharia Amud el-Sawari. Open: 9–4.
Closed Fri 11:30–1:30. Admission: moderate

Originally a series of 2nd-century AD private tombs, the complex was later enlarged for the community, creating the largest Roman funerary complex known in Egypt. The tomb decorations show a surprising blend of Egyptian and classical styles, so typical of Alexandria.

A spiral staircase winds around the shaft where bodies were lowered and leads to a vestibule on the first level. Beyond the vestibule is the Rotunda and the Banquet Hall, where families came to feast in memory of the dead. Through a fissure in the rock to the right of the rotunda is the Hall of Caracalla, where four painted tombs contained

The eerie depths of the catacombs of Kom el-Shogafa, a typically Alexandrian mix of Egyptian and Roman influences

the remains of young men and their horses, reputedly massacred for insulting the emperor.

The strangest part of the complex is the second-level Central Tomb, reached via the staircase in the rotunda. Limestone statues on either side of the vestibule probably represent the deceased and his wife. The entrance is guarded by two bearded serpents wearing the double crowns of Upper and Lower Egypt and, above them, a Medusa in a disk. The confusion of styles and religions becomes even more notable inside the tomb, where the three sarcophagi are decorated in classical style. Niches above the sarcophagi show bas-reliefs with Egyptian motifs: a mummy on a lion-shaped bed being administered to by Anubis, Thoth, and Horus, and a prince offering a collar to the Apis bull. On the way out, note the hybrid figures on either side of the door: the Egyptian gods Anubis and Sobek dressed as Roman legionnaires.

The third level is flooded and therefore inaccessible. Rising groundwater has left even the Central Tomb vulnerable to serious damage from occasional floods. Check at the ticket office whether there is electricity, although if your nerves are strong, frequent power cuts add to the eeriness of the place. If the prospect doesn't excite you, be on the safe side and take a flashlight.

▶▶ el-Montazah Palace and Gardens   210C3

El-Montazah. Gardens open 24 hours. Admission: inexpensive
Khedive Abbas II's turn-of-the-century, Turko-Florentine folly is now the presidential summer residence, but its 350 acres of well-tended pleasure gardens are open to the public. In summer, join Alexandrians making the 9-mile trip from downtown for a picnic. Fast-food restaurants are sprouting among the greenery, but it's still a good place for a stroll and a swim (see page 221).

▶ Nabi Danyal Mosque   210C2

Sharia Nabi Danyal
This unprepossessing mosque is tucked behind a girls' school off a busy downtown street. Some claim that in the crypt below the prayer hall (entirely rebuilt in the 19th century), beyond the two visible tombs ascribed to Sheikh Danyal el-Maridi and Lukman the Wise, lies the tomb of Alexander the Great. Archeologists dispute this, but until the foundations are excavated, or the tomb found elsewhere, the mystery will remain. For a small bribe the guardian might let you look for yourself.

President Mubarak moves to this extravagantly decorated palace when Cairo gets too hot in the summer

THE ALLURE OF ALEXANDRIA
"If a man make a pilgrimage around Alexandria in the morning, God will make for him a golden crown, set with pearls, perfumed with musk and camphor, and shining from the East to the West."
Ibn Duqmaq

MIND THE GAP
Rumors easily become legends in Alexandria as the ancient city, mostly unexplored beneath the modern one, constantly reminds Alexandrians of their heritage. Excavations had been going on around the Kom el-Shogafa for eight years when, in 1892, the ground gave way beneath a donkey to reveal the complex of catacombs. An even more bizarre occurrence took place within living memory when a bride, in her wedding procession, fell down a hole in the road. Searches proved of no use and the bride was never seen again—one more treasure lost beneath the modern city.

Above: the Cecil Hotel

Literary Alexandria

E. M. Forster, in the preface to his 1922 guide, wrote, "The 'sights' of Alexandria are in themselves not interesting, but they fascinate when we approach them through the past." In a crumbling villa at No. 19 Sharia el-Mamour, near the Mahmudiya canal beyond the Kom el-Shogafa catacombs, Lawrence Durrell lived, in his own words, "two and one half years of great, extravagant and colorful life in

wartime Alexandria." The modern city also comes alive on a walk (1½–2 hours) around places associated with Alexandria's literary figures, when its buildings resonate with the words of Constantine Cavafy (*Collected Poems*), Durrell (*The Alexandria Quartet*), and Forster himself (*Alexandria, a History and Guide*). See map on page 210.

In the **Cecil Hotel** (Midan Saad Zaghlul), Durrell's Darley first saw Justine, "...among the dusty palms, dressed in a sheath of silver drops... Nessim has stopped at the door of the ballroom which is flooded with light and music..." Across the square,

The entrance to Qaytbay Fort

the **Trianon** patisserie used to contain a discreet bar frequented by the writers and above it, on the fourth floor of what is now the Metropole Hotel, was Cavafy's office.

Turn your back to the sea and walk along Sharia Safiya Zaghlul where Cavafy used to pick up his boys. Cross the junction with Sharia el-Sultan Husayn, past Cinema Rialto, and turn right onto Sharia el-Hurriya to find

hospital leads into Sharia Sharm el-Sheikh, formerly Rue Lepsius. Here, more than anywhere else, fact and fiction mingle. At No. 4 (previously No. 10) where Cavafy lived, his third-floor apartment is now the Cavafy Museum (see page 211). In the basement of the building was a brothel, now a carpentry workshop. Balthazar, one of Durrell's characters, also lived on this street in a "worm-eaten room with the old cane chair which creaked all night..." Cavafy is reported to have said, "Where could I live better? Below, the brothel caters for the flesh. And there is the church which forgives sin. And there is the hospital where we die." It is a reminder of how geographically circumscribed was the Alexandria of the writers.

Turn left off Sharia Istanbul into Sharia Nabi Danyal along which Durrell's Darley and Pombal shared a "little dank flat". At the junction with

The terrace of Pastroudis

Pastroudis, café-patisserie and a haunt of Cavafy and of characters in *The Alexandria Quartet*, many of whom lived nearby (Justine and Nessim in a house set back from Sharia el-Hurriya). Opposite the entrance to Pastroudis, beside a crumbling 19th-century building, Sharia Zangalola leads to the Greek Orthodox Church of St. Saba, where Cavafy was mourned on his death.

Sharia St. Saba, where Durrell's Clea had her studio, runs into Sharia el-Sultan Husayn (also known as Sharia Istanbul). On this street, behind a high wrought-iron gate and advertising signs, is what is left of the Greek hospital. A left turn after the

Sharia el-Hurriya, near the café-patisserie **Venous** (its name written only in Arabic, green letters on a lime-green background), Durrell's Armenian barber Mnemjian had his shop. "We were lifted simultaneously and swung smoothly down into the ground wrapped like dead Pharaohs, only to reappear at the same instant on the ceiling, spread out like specimens. White cloths had been spread over us by a small black boy while in a great Victorian moustache-cup the barber thwacked up his dense and sweet-smelling lather...." A similar experience can be had in several of Alexandria's barber shops: the old barber in the Cecil Hotel, like Mnemjian, also served as "the Memory man, the archives of the city."

MAKING AN IMPRESSION
Midan el-Tahrir (Liberation Square), formerly Place Muhammad Ali, suffered badly in the 1882 national-ist uprising. After the British fleet bombarded the city, killing as many as 2,000 people, rioters destroyed almost all the buildings in the square except the Anglican church and Muhammad Ali's statue. The square was later rebuilt along even grander, neo-classical lines and many of those buildings, suffering from neglect and alteration, are still standing.

Pompey's Pillar, cut from a single block of stone, fascinated early travelers in Egypt

▶▶ **Midan el-Tahrir (Liberation Square)**   *210B2*

This was once the center of European Alexandria, known as Frank Square, and though it has lost most of its impor-tance, it still carries reminders of its former grandeur. The equestrian statue of Muhammad Ali, who was responsi-ble for Alexandria's 19th-century reconstruction, is now rather marooned in the middle of the square. The Bourse, Alexandria's Cotton Exchange, stood on the site of the parking lot across from the Banque du Caire until it was burned down in the food riots of 1977. The Anglican Church of St. Mark, with its memorials to the British regi-ments who fought in Egypt in 1882, looks abandoned in its quiet garden. The crowded bus stop on Midan Orabi was once the pleasant French Gardens. For a sense of how grand these late 19th-century buildings must have been, beyond Midan Orabi look for the Okelle Monferrato department store. A passageway cuts through the build-ing into an arcade with one of the city's most atmospheric cafés, where men play dominoes and enjoy excellent water pipes. Across the square are the Law Courts, and just to the south is the Passage Menasce. Beyond it lies Alexandria's largest food market.

▶▶ **Pompey's Pillar**   *210C1*

Sharia Amud el-Sawari. Open: daily 9–4. Admission: inexpensive
Alexandria's most prominent antiquity, Pompey's Pillar, was named in error by the Crusaders: it was raised in honor of Diocletian in the 4th century AD and probably supported a statue of the emperor. The column, of pink Aswan granite topped with a Corinthian capital, is 88 feet high and 29 feet thick. Nearby are two Ptolemaic granite sphinxes found in the vicinity; in front of these are the scant remains of the Serapeum, the temple of Serapis, one of ancient Alexandria's most important buildings. The Serapeum and the library Cleopatra established along-side it were destroyed so completely by 4th-century Christians that there is little now to interest the casual

Built on the site of the
ancient Pharos,
Qaytbay's majestic
fort still commands
the busy harbor

visitor. But climb up to the pillar for the view beyond the crumbling tenements of the living city.

▶▶▶ Qaytbay Fort   210B3

End of eastern harbor. Museum open: daily 9–4.
Admission: fort, inexpensive; museum, moderate
In the morning, as the sun rises over the Mediterranean, this extraordinary 15th-century fort looks as if it is made out of butter. Sultan Qaytbay built the fort with the remains of the legendary Pharos lighthouse, which once stood on the site. The lighthouse, built in 279 BC by Sostratus under Ptolemy II, was reputed to be over 400 feet high, with more than 300 rooms for the mechanics and attendants; it remains a mystery how the lantern worked. In the 14th century earthquakes brought the 1,500-year-old lighthouse to the ground. But the Pharos still serves as a symbol of ancient Alexandria's desire to combine aesthetic beauty and scientific knowledge. Underwater excavations have identified parts of it that fell into the sea, and there is even talk of a new Pharos being built, with a hotel and restaurant complex. Nowadays the fort houses the Naval Museum. There are magnificent views over the Corniche and the sea from the ramparts.

▶ Royal Jewelry Museum   210C3

21 Sharia Ahmad Yahia, Zizinia.
Open: daily 9–4. Closed: Fri 11:30–1:30. Admission: moderate
Princess Fatma el-Zahraa's imposing palace contains a sparkling collection of jewelry, covering a period from the rise of Muhammad Ali to the abdication of King Farouk. The Egyptian royal family was noted for its extravagant tastes and it is not surprising to see rare jewelry—including a platinum crown inset with 2,159 diamonds—as well as gold and silver chessboards, ashtrays, *kohl* (eye make-up) pots, and water pipes encrusted with diamonds. Apart from all that glitter, the museum is worth visiting for its ornate interior decoration.

219

Part of the glittering display in the Royal Jewelry Museum

Alexandria is famous for its food and for its eating places and, although they may have lost some of their old atmosphere, the many café-pâtisseries around the city are still good places to join the Alexandrians at play and watch the city reveal something of its character.

CAFÉ FARE

You can taste some of the influences that have shaped Alexandria in the fare on offer in its cafés, which resemble English tea rooms more than anything else: English cream cakes, Swiss-style chocolates, French pâtisserie, Italianesque ice cream, and, of course, delicious oriental candies.

220

Alexandrian spirit Alexandrians, considered more liberal than other Egyptians, are known for their fondness for good living, and while cafés elsewhere in Egypt are often exclusively for men, you'll often be served by female waitresses in Alexandria's café-pâtisseries. Around you will be elderly Levantine gentlemen reading the news from Greece or a well-thumbed volume of poetry, a well-dressed lady and her friends sipping *cappuccinos*, and couples making romantic plans for their future from behind the whipped cream topping of a black forest cake. Although many places have replaced wood and old mirrors with plastic and aluminum, you can still catch a hint of their former glory beneath the glittering chandeliers in Athineos, or surrounded by the surviving art-nouveau paneling in Trianon.

Different moods There are different places for different times of day. While enjoying the *prix fixe* breakfast at Trianon, near Ramleh Station, watch Alexandrians rush to work. The terrace of Pastroudis, the favorite hang-out of Lawrence Durrell's characters, is particularly enjoyable on a sunny morning. Farther down Sharia el-Hurriya, Confiserie Venous sits at the crossroads of ancient Alexandria near the reputed site of Alexander the Great's tomb—an excellent place for afternoon tea entombed by pyramids of sweets. Athineos, another old Greek café, has lost much of its charm, but at the end of a busy day it is welcomingly empty for a tea or an ouzo. Later, on a hot summer's evening, sit in Baudrot's garden and watch young couples hold hands under the trellis of vines.

Pastroudis is still famous for its European-style pâtisserie

Every summer, several million Egyptians escape the dazzling heat of the Nile Valley and descend on Alexandria to catch the sea breeze. Alexandria has sun and the azure Mediterranean, but to enjoy them to the full you will need to choose your beach with care.

Crowds and pollution From May to September, it is hard to find an empty patch of sand on Alexandria's beaches, a problem that gets worse on weekends with the arrival of additional thousands of Cairene and Alexandrian families. The most popular beaches are along the Corniche between the Cecil Hotel and el-Montazah. Easy to reach by public transportation, they are also within 150 feet of some of the 47 pipes draining untreated sewage into the sea. Once alerted to this fact, many visitors to Alexandria prefer to look at the Mediterranean from a distance.

Peach of a beach The beach experience in Alexandria is unlike anything you can experience in the West. Egyptians prefer to picnic under canvas shades rather than expose their bodies to the sun, and on most beaches women remain fully dressed, some even veiled. Stray sunbathing foreigners often receive the same treatment as veiled women on the other side of the Mediterranean—they are a welcome source of entertainment. Foreign women in bathing suits, however, may be harassed or thrown off the beach.

In spite of alluring names, public beaches like Chatby, Cleopatra, Stanley, Glym, Sidi Bishr, and Miyami are best avoided unless you want to make a sociological study of crowd behavior. Swimming is more pleasant and umbrellas are available on the cleaner, fee-charging beaches of el-Montazah and, beyond it, Ma'mura. Agami, the most fashionable resort on the north coast and the choice of wealthy Cairenes, has some of the best and cleanest beaches within striking distance of the city and although most of them are private, they will often admit foreigners for a fee.

Khedive Abbas's bridge decorates one of the city's best beaches, at Montazah

THE UNTHINKABLE
Be very careful on empty beaches along the Mediterranean coast: according to a 1997 report, some 17.2 million mines and unexploded shells, mostly from World War II, are still lying along the shoreline and in the desert. Shifting sands uncover them occasionally, resulting in loss of life.

Lest we forget: hardware left over from World War II

A TURNING POINT
Winston Churchill wrote of the battle at el-Alamein, "Before Alamein we never had a victory. After Alamein we never had a defeat."

WILD AT HEART
Sir Ronald Storrs, civil servant, Alexandria, 1905: "… I went for long walks alone by the canals or along the eastern shores without meeting a soul; sometimes bathing, some-times riding, once combin-ing both in an experimental gallop naked to see what it was like, and proving it to be better adapted for bronze or marble than for human contours." (Orientations)

West of Alexandria

▶▶ el-Alamein   206B1

El-Alamein, 65 miles west of Alexandria, was the site of a series of famous battles during World War II. On July 1, 1942, the German commander Erwin Rommel and his Afrika Korps arrived in the area, forcing a British with-drawal through the Suez Canal. In October the same year, the new British general Montgomery launched a counter-offensive that drove the German army westward out of Egypt. Around 11,000 soldiers were killed and some are buried in the British, Italian, and German war cemeteries. These are open to visitors, as is the Military Museum in the center of el-Alamein town, which displays artifacts from the battle (*Open* daily 8–6. *Admission: inexpensive*).

West of el-Alamein, the coast is infinitely beautiful and the empty desert sand dunes roll gracefully into the transparent, azure waters of the Mediterranean (but see warning on page 221).

▶ Mersa Matruh   206A2

Mersa Matruh, 180 miles west of Alexandria, is an increasingly popular beach resort. It used to be a quiet fishing village and trading post, but with the reopening of the border with Libya it is turning into a boom town. The town itself is of little interest unless you are en route to Siwa oasis and Libya, or you want to stretch out on a magnificent beach.

The beaches in town, as in Alexandria, are not really recommended for foreign women unless they are prepared to follow the local custom of swimming fully clothed, even on the private beach of the Beau Site Hotel, which welcomes nonresidents for a fee. Of the public beaches, those around the bay tend to be covered with litter, so head for Rommel's Beach, where the Desert Fox is said to have taken a swim. A nearby cave has been turned into the small Rommel Museum with his maps and other objects of war. Farther west is Cleopatra's Bath, where another unfounded legend has it that the famous queen enjoyed herself with Mark Antony. The best beaches lie even farther west, out of town: Ubbayad Beach and Agiba Cove are among the most isolated and desir-able, lapped by magnificent turquoise water (but see panel on page 221).

Drive

Rosetta

This drive eastward through countryside and along an increasingly industrial coastline to the town of Rosetta (Rashid) is 87 miles round-trip. Rosetta, renowned for the inscribed stone that led to the deciphering of hieroglyphics, is remarkable for its well-preserved Ottoman buildings. See the map on pages 206–207.

The Rosetta road follows Alexandria's corniche past **el-Montazah**►► (see page 215) and Ma'mura, through groves of date palms, orange, and guava trees, then past some of the Middle East's largest factories—paper mills and fertilizer plants. For much of the trip, the road follows a canal and train line (infrequent trains from Alexandria to Rosetta are only for people with time to waste).

Among the reeds on lakes **Abu Qir** and **Idku**►, you might see people fishing from rowboats, using the same techniques shown on ancient Egyptian tomb paintings. Beyond the lakes, Tabia, el-Ma'diya, and Manshiyet el-Aman are concrete towns busy with donkey carts and vintage cars. Relief is on hand when you reach the sign "Welcome to Rashid."

The road into **Rosetta**►► leads along the Nile, and past warehouses

The Abu Mandar Mosque

from the 18th century, when this was Egypt's principal port. Leave the car by the two cannon in the main square to

The Rosetta Stone

223

explore on foot (see page 224).

From the square, follow the Nile 3 miles farther north to reach Sultan Qaytbay's 15th-century **Citadel**►►. Note the way ancient stones, some with cartouches and hieroglyphs, were reused. In 1799, Captain Bourchard, serving with Napoleon's army, discovered the Rosetta Stone near here (see page 224). A copy of the stone is inside the fort, beside the modern mosque. Climb the ramparts for a view of the **Abu Mandar Mosque**► and, 3,373 miles from its source at Lake Victoria, the gaping mouth of the Nile.

Retracing the route to Alexandria, stop at Abu Qir, 14 miles before the city, and eat at the **Zephirion** restaurant, looking out over the water where Nelson sank Napoleon's fleet in 1798.

The Delta contains some of the most lush farmland in the world

SAINTLY BEHAVIOR
Among the Crusaders who attacked Damietta in 1218 was St. Francis of Assisi, who valiantly crossed the battlefield to inform Salah ed-Din's nephew, the Sultan el-Kamil, that he had come to convert them all to Christianity. El-Kamil replied by introducing him to the Christians in his entourage, offering him the usual hospitality, and sending him back to his side of the lines.

CARVED IN STONE
In the 2nd century BC, a declaration from the priests of Memphis was inscribed on a basalt slab in the three scripts current in northern Egypt—hieroglyphics, Egyptian demotic, and Greek. The stone was recovered by a French officer at a time when scholars were trying to decipher hieroglyphs. The Rosetta Stone was handed over to the British after the defeat of Napoleon's expedition and the original was dispatched to the British Museum, but a copy was also sent to France, where, in 1822, Jean-Francois Champollion used it to read hieroglyphs for the first time since antiquity.

The Delta

The Delta Unlike the well-preserved temples and tombs in the Nile Valley, the Delta's monuments have all but vanished due to the changing course of the Nile, heavy Mediterranean rainfall, and dense cultivation of the land. What remains is of most interest to scholars and specialists and few tourists do more than catch a glimpse of the Delta from the window of a train between Cairo and Alexandria. Even then, some of its attractions are obvious: the immense, flat landscape of carefully divided fields of cotton and rice, the ponderous buffaloes turning waterwheels, and *feluccas* (sailboats) cutting through the green.

The Delta has other attractions and is particularly famous for its *moulids* (see pages 146–147). Much more than merely Islamic festivals, *moulids* echo pharaonic celebrations and have outlived the ancient Egyptian towns in which they were first celebrated. The Moulid of Sayyid el-Badawi in Tanta is especially popular, attended by up to 2 million people from all over the country. In winter, the northern lakes and marshes are a popular refuge for water birds, herons, and storks, and also for people hunting them.

▶ **Dumyat (Damietta)** 207E2
Damietta, at the end of the eastern branch of the Nile, is a busy port and industrial zone. In the Middle Ages Damietta was a prosperous trading town, but it was vulnerable to seaborne attack and was twice sacked by the Crusaders. The Ottomans brought life back to the town and built Delta-style mansions, but like Rosetta, Damietta declined in importance when Muhammad Ali restored the fortunes of Alexandria. The main tourist attraction these days is the excellent bird-watching on Lake Manzala.

▶▶ **Rashid (Rosetta)** 206C2
Rosetta is a sleepy town at the end of the western branch of the Nile (see page 223). Apart from its fine Delta-style mansions, some of which can still be visited, its real claim to fame is the Rosetta Stone, which is now in the British Museum in London. The **Arab Killy House**▶▶ (*Sharia el-Geish. Open* daily 9–4) is remarkable for its black and red brickwork, typical of Delta architecture. This 18th-century house, once the town governor's residence, is now Rosetta's museum. The **Mosque of Zaghlul**▶, at the end of Sharia el-Suq, is the most famous of Rosetta's 128 mosques. Built in the 17th century, its roof has fallen in but pillars still support the lintels and a forest of columns stand reflected in a pool of stagnant water. The **Bayt el-Amasyali**▶▶ (*Sharia el-Geish. Open* daily 8–2) is one of the finest early 19th-century townhouses in Egypt, with beautiful painted ceilings and exceptional inlay work; it gives a fascinating glimpse into the life of the leading members of the town.

▶ Tanta   207D1

Tanta, in the center of the Delta, is Egypt's fifth-largest city. The Ottoman-style mosque and tomb of Sayyid el-Badawi, founder of the Ahmadiya Sufi order, is visited by pilgrims from all over the Arab world.

Sais, northwest of Tanta, was Egypt's capital during the 26th Dynasty, but unlike Luxor, it is now only a few muddy holes.

▶▶ Zagazig   207D1

Zagazig itself is an agreeable and bustling regional center, but the main reason to visit is to get to the nearby ancient sites. **Bubastis▶**, 2 miles south of Zagazig, was one of the most ancient cities in Egypt, dedicated to the cat goddess Bastet. Her temple is in ruins, so we must trust Herodotus' claim that of all the temples in Egypt, this was the most pleasant to look at. Many fine bronze statues of Bastet were found in a nearby cat cemetery.

Tanis▶, 37 miles northeast of Zagazig, is by far the most interesting archeological site in the Delta. Tanis was long thought to be Pi-Ramses, birthplace of the Ramessid Dynasty and of Ramses II; it is mentioned in the Bible as having been built by Moses and the Israelites and as the departure point for the Exodus from Egypt. Recent excavations, however, are suggesting that Pi-Ramses might be near Qantara in Sinai. The **Great Temple of Amun▶** is in ruins but there remain many fragments of colossal statuary. The most significant finds—at the time as important as Tutankhamun's tomb—were the six, almost intact royal tombs from the 11th and 22nd Dynasties, discovered in 1939. The splendid collection of funerary equipment and jewelry is often overlooked in the Egyptian Museum in Cairo.

225

Fishermen fixing their nets at Rosetta

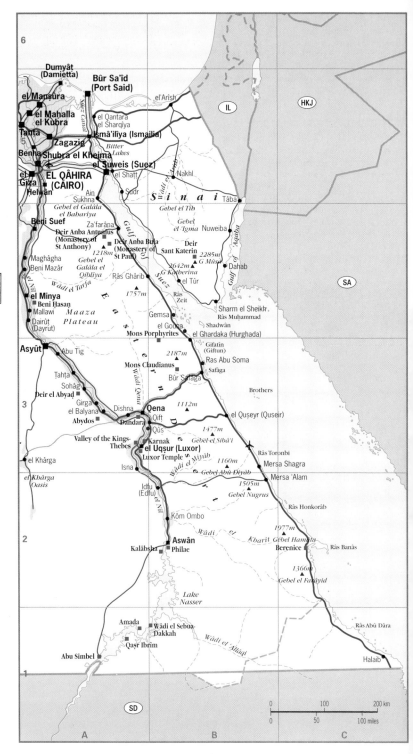

CANAL ZONE AND RED SEA COAST The Suez Canal and Red Sea coast are different in character from the rest of Egypt. There are no great archeological sites to visit and most traces of previous habitation have disappeared beneath water or sand. But along the canal, beneath the surface of the Red Sea, and among the mountains of the Eastern Desert there are surprising and beautiful things to be found.

A LIFELINE Since its grand opening in 1869, the Suez Canal has been a lifeline in global transportation. Cutting through the isthmus of Suez, linking the Mediterranean and Red Seas, it was fought over several times during the 20th century. It was nationalized in 1956, and remains one of Egypt's largest earners of foreign currency. It also remains an object of inspiration and although the days of P&O passengers throwing their topees (hats) overboard at Suez have long passed, the canal still represents the divide between east and west.

CANAL TOWNS Suez, at the northern end of the Red Sea, was a thriving port before the canal was opened, an important stage along the overland route from Europe to the East via Alexandria and Cairo. Isma'iliya and Port

Left: the Suez Canal

Canal Zone and Red Sea Coast

A TALE OF TWO TOWNS
William Russell, the London *Times* correspondent traveling in Egypt in the 1860s, wrote of Isma'iliya: "You would be tempted, as you hear the click of billiard-balls and the rattle of the dominoes, and look in through the gauze blinds and see the smoking crowds, to imagine that you were in some country quarter of La Belle France."

A less flattering view of Port Said was written by Major C. S. Jarvis in *Oriental Spotlight* (London, 1937): "In 1860 it did not exist, but by 1890 it had achieved the distinction of being called the wickedest town in the East, and vice and evil were rampant on its streets."

Said—both created by the canal—immediately eclipsed Suez, which has since regained some of its importance. Isma'iliya quickly developed an air of cosmopolitan gentility that somehow it has held onto, while Port Said, the main trading port and base of the Suez Canal Authority, earned a different sort of reputation as "the wickedest town in the East." It now has tax-free status in an attempt to lure cruise ships and freighters to its port, while Isma'iliya, with a large slice of world trade sailing past its doors, has become an alternative weekend resort for people wanting to escape Egypt's cities.

THE RED SEA Early travelers expected to find a sea whose water was red, but instead they found the blue, black, or turquoise waters; the sea seems more likely to have earned its name from the color of the mountains behind it, which glow red beneath a lowered sun. Gustave Flaubert described swimming in the sea as one of the most voluptuous pleasures of his life—like "lying on a thousand liquid breasts that were caressing my entire body"—and its waters continue to exert a powerful attraction over visitors to the region. But throughout history it has been the Red Sea's importance as a trading route that has brought people to its shores.

Above: A shoal of black-spotted grunt. The teeming waters of the Red Sea provide some of the best diving sites in the world. Right: St. Paul's Monastery on the edge of the Red Sea Mountains

NATURAL RESOURCES Egypt has 775 miles of coastline between Suez and the Sudanese border. In antiquity, several ports made trading contacts possible between the Nile Valley, Somalia, and the Yemen. Some of those ports, such as Quseir and Safaga, are once again important trading posts for Egypt, especially since oil and gas reserves were found offshore in the Red Sea. But the largest changes to Egypt's Red Sea coast have been to its tourism facilities. Twenty years ago, these were scarce and unsophisticated, but Hurghada has developed quickly and is now an important resort with a busy international airport and an extensive range of resort hotels. As Hurghada grows, the search for new areas to develop has created a building boom south of Safaga and Quseir, toward the Sudan border and north into Sinai. A new international airport is under construction at Mersa Alam.

EASTERN DESERT Unusually, in this region you have to look to the desert to find signs of previous lives and of contemporary ones as well. The Bedouin moving their camels or goats in search of pastures, the miners digging for gold or valued stone, trading caravans passing through the *wadis* (dry gullies), hermits seeking religious enlightenment in solitude—now, as thousands of years ago, the traces of their lives are scant. Surrounding them are the beautiful, barren mountains of the Eastern Desert, with the highest peaks in Egypt outside Sinai and many of the last survivors of the country's wild animals.

229

QANTARA
Before the Suez Canal existed, pilgrims, armies, and caravans used to cross the Isthmus of Suez at Qantara (meaning "bridge" in Arabic), between Isma'iliya and Suez. The pontoon bridges have long gone, but there are still ferries going from the west bank of the canal to the east bank on Sinai.

DARIUS'S CANAL
The canal dug by Darius in 500 BC connected the Red Sea with the Nile at Zagazig. It was later improved by the Ptolemies and the Romans. The Arab conqueror of Egypt, Amr, had it restored to export corn to Arabia. But 100 years later it was abandoned, and many invaders thought about restoring it until Napoleon proposed a canal from the Red Sea to the Mediterranean.

The distinctive dome of the Suez Canal Building, Port Said

▶▶ Isma'iliya 226A5

Isma'iliya, by far the most pleasant of the canal cities, lies 80 miles from Cairo and can be reached by train (3–5 hours) or by bus (3 hours) from the Koulali bus station. It is cut in two by a railway line. The European-style garden city, south of the track, with its tree-lined boulevards and restored colonial villas, looks very much as it must have in the 1930s. The other side of the track is less idyllic, with run-down apartment buildings built between slums, but this is where the majority of Ismailians live.

Near the intersection of Muhammad Ali Quay with Sharia Orabi, the **House of de Lesseps▶** (see page 232), containing his books and his belongings, is sometimes open for visitors (check with the tourist office). The small **museum▶** (*Open* daily 9–4. Closed Fri 11–2. *Admission: inexpensive*), built like a Ptolemaic temple, houses a collection of Greco-Roman and pharaonic objects and an exhibit about the building of Darius's canal between the Nile and the Red Sea. Beside the museum is the Garden of Steles and across from it is the shady Fountain Park. The city lies on the shore of Lake Timsah (Crocodile Lake), whose fine beaches are mostly owned by beach clubs. It is possible to use the beach of the PLM Azur Hotel (the admission fee usually includes lunch); from here you can watch freighters slowly passing. Outside town, the suburb of Nimrah Sitta offers beautiful colonial villas and excellent views over the canal.

▶ Bur Sa'id (Port Said) 226A5

Port Said lies 50 miles north of Isma'iliya. It can be reached by bus or service taxi from Isma'iliya and Suez, by train (5 hours) from Cairo, or by Superjet bus from the Abdel Muneem Riyadh Terminal; there are also buses from Alexandria (6 hours).

Port Said is now a duty-free port and is trying hard to forget its old reputation as a city of smugglers and prostitutes. The original wooden buildings on Sharia Gumhuriya vaguely suggest the colonial past, but the city is looking toward the future by attracting Egyptian vacationers to its new resorts and modern shopping centers.

The port's most famous landmark is the Suez Canal Building on Sharia Filastin with its three shiny green domes. The **Military Museum** on Sharia 23rd July (*Open* daily 9–2, Fri 10–1:30. *Admission: inexpensive*) has paintings and dioramas of the Egypt-Israel wars. The pleasant **Port Said National Museum▶** on Sharia Filastin (*Open* daily 9–4. Closed Fri 11–1. *Admission: inexpensive*) has a small collection of pharaonic objects, Coptic textiles, and Islamic art, as well as objects from the 1869 canal opening, including the khedive's (viceroy's) carriage. A ferry leaves from the quay (opposite the tourist office on Sharia Filastin) to Port Fuad (15 minutes), which officially lies in Asia. This suburb, founded in 1927, has some interesting 1930s villas surrounded by lush, well-kept gardens, and makes for a pleasant afternoon stroll.

▶ el-Suweis (Suez) 226A5

Suez is 83 miles from Cairo and can be reached by express train (3 hours) or by bus from Koulali Terminal. Buses and service taxis come and go to Alexandria, Luxor, Hurghada (6 hours), and Sinai.

A typical building in old Port Said

Suez, at the southern end of the canal, suffered more than other canal cities in the 1967 and 1973 wars with Israel, and three-quarters of the city was totally destroyed. It has been rebuilt, with money from the Gulf states, as an important industrial center for fertilizers, cement, and petrochemicals. In the Middle Ages this was the port of Qulzum, a walled city important in the spice trade and as a stopover point on the pilgrimage to Mecca. For all its interesting history, there is little to attract the visitor beyond its seafront atmosphere and a few crumbling colonial houses, which are overwhelmed by neighboring modern blocks. Sharia el-Gheish runs to the customs and docks at Bur Tawfiq (Port Tawfiq). The Ahmad Hamdi tunnel, 7 miles to the north of Suez, runs under the Suez Canal to Sinai.

ON YOUR BIKE
It is delightful to walk or ride a bike around the old town of Isma'iliya. Bikes can be rented from the PLM Azur or in the alleys off Muhammad Ali Quay, and information is available at the tourist office on Muhammad Ali Quay (closed Friday 8–2).

It is hard today to imagine the fuss that was made over the idea of building the Suez Canal, but at the time of its construction it was considered the greatest engineering feat and proof of the progress possible in the Industrial Revolution.

SOME CANAL STATISTICS

An estimated 20,000 Egyptians worked on the construction (thousands of them died in the process); 97 million cubic yards of earth were removed along the 103-mile-long canal. Work started on April 25, 1859 and the canal was officially opened on November 17, 1869. The distance between London and Bombay using the old route, via South Africa, is 11,000 miles; via the Suez Canal it is 5,800 miles.

Antecedents A waterway connecting the Mediterranean and Red Sea was completed in the reign of Darius (ca500 BC). It was a series of canals: one from the Red Sea to the Great Bitter Lake, and one from there to the Nile. Extended under the Ptolemies and Romans, it was still in use in the 8th century, when the Arabs closed it.

The impossible project The merits of a canal had been discussed for hundreds of years, but in the 1790s Napoleon's engineers reported that the project was impossible: the two seas were at different levels. Only they weren't, and in the 1840s, when the French consul and engineer Ferdinand de Lesseps discovered the mistake, there was a boom in trade and transit between the two seas as European powers consolidated their eastern empires. The canal was a project of its time.

Pros and cons The canal project was caught up in Anglo-French rivalry. Britain, needing to guarantee fast passage to its colonies, had backed a British-built railroad from Alexandria to Suez. After great difficulties, it wasn't the French government but the Egyptians and the independent Suez Canal Company, founded by de Lesseps, that financed construction.

Posterity De Lesseps assured Said, the Egyptian ruler, that his name would be "blessed from century to century" but that has not been the case. Said died before work was completed and is remembered in the name of the port. Ismail, who opened the canal, had Isma'iliya named after him. And de Lesseps' commemorative statue, which stood beside the canal in Port Said, was blown up in 1952.

A dredger at work on the canal, 1869

Red Sea Coast

▶ **el-Ghardaka (Hurghada)**   *226B3*

El-Ghardaka, 255 miles south of Suez, can be reached by air, bus (6–8 hours) from the Arbaeen terminal in Suez, or by service taxi. The trip from Cairo takes 8–12 hours by bus (Bulaq's Turgoman Terminal) or service taxi and 1 hour by Egypt Air flight.

The small fishing village of el-Ghardaka has developed, in less than ten years, into one of Egypt's most popular resort towns. The town itself has little more to offer than guaranteed sunshine most of the year, good diving facilities, and a wide range of accommodations. The modern town is ugly and completely dependent on tourism. Tourists fly in directly from Europe to sunbathe and dive, and most of them stay by the pool and forget about ancient Egypt. The majority of the hotels are resorts with restaurants, bars, and shopping centers within the grounds, so there is no cause for adventure.

There is a public beach, but as it is usually covered in litter, most tourists opt for one of the private hotel beaches. Unlike in Sinai where the coral reefs are near the shore, it is necessary to take a boat to explore the coral islands, which are truly magnificent. In most hotels it is possible to book a day-excursion to Gifatin Island (Giftun Island), with fish for lunch and plenty of time to snorkel. More experienced divers can explore Gubal Island, the Careless Reef, Shadwan Island—popular with reef sharks—and, farther away, the spectacular Brother Islands. For the less adventurous there are excursions on glass-bottomed boats—from Shedwan, Three Corners Hotel, and some other hotels—to see the marine life around the smaller reefs. In town, the New Aquarium▶ on Sharia el-Bahr (*Open 9–11. Admission: inexpensive*) has a small selection of fishes in its dark tanks. The Oceanographic Museum, 6 miles north of town, has a quirky collection of dusty, stuffed fishes in very unnatural colors.

The road to Hurghada

FERRY TO SINAI
To avoid a long bus ride, it is usually possible to take a ferry from Hurghada to Sharm el Sheikh. Boats leave daily and take 5–6 hours. Reservations should be made in advance through your hotel or for the high-speed service call Travco (02/446024). Take food, plenty of water, and a good protective sun cream.

233

Hurghada's facilities, sailing and diving opportunities, and clear water have helped it to develop into a major resort

Unlike the Western Desert, the desert to the east, between the Nile and the Red Sea, is a mountainous region that stretches to the Sudanese border. Rich in minerals, the beautiful but harsh Red Sea Mountains are still home to hermits, miners, and tribes of Bedouin.

OLD MINERS
The 1st century AD Jewish historian Josephus recorded that after the Romans sacked Jerusalem, Jewish captives over the age of 17 were sent to the Egyptian mines. Regimes before and after the Romans adopted the same policy to provide labor for the mines. The earlier Greek writer Agatharchides explained that while the strongest men worked deep in the gold mines, "the old men and children carried the ore to the crushers, where it was broken up by men and then further ground by women. It was then washed on sloping tables, the quartz being all washed away and the gold remaining behind."

Composed mainly of granite, porphyry, and breccia, the Red Sea Mountains rise to a maximum height of 7,175 feet

Ancient remains Long before St. Anthony came looking for solitude (see pages 236–237), people searched for gold, copper, and precious stone. There is little to see from the ancient Egyptians, but at Mons Porphyrites there are the remains of Rome's largest porphyry mine. The broken huts and ruined temple are from Hadrian's reign. Farther to the south, at Mons Claudianus, there are the remains of a walled miners' camp, with the temple on its highest ground. From these mines, stone was carried 90 miles and more to the Nile, and from there throughout the Roman empire, where it was used in the great imperial buildings.

Bedouin tribes The mountains are divided between two main Bedouin tribes. The Ma'aza, to the north of the Qift-Quseir road, are descended from Arab nomads. The Ababda, to the south, used to graze their herds far into Sudanese territory and are of African descent. Like Bedouin elsewhere in Egypt, these tribes are being settled by the government in Cairo.

Last of the wildlife When the Red Sea Mountains were covered in forests, they were also home to a great variety of wildlife. As their cover and food supply disappeared, the animals became vulnerable. Earlier this century, great numbers of gazelle, ibex, and Barbary sheep were hunted, many shot en masse with machine guns. Some of King Farouk's "trophies" are now lining the walls of Cairo's Manyal Palace museum.

Modern miners Mining companies have been prospecting in the mountains, hoping to use modern techniques to further exploit the ancient mines, but so far Egyptian bureaucracy has proved more impenetrable than the rock.

234

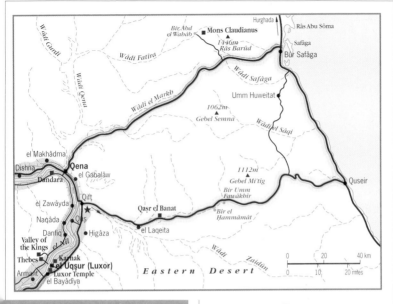

Drive

In the Red Sea Mountains

The drive from Qift to Quseir can be done as a day trip from Hurghada or Luxor, returning along the faster Qena-Port Safaga Road. Take enough water and food for the day. First ask the tourism police if the road is open.

The well-paved road from Qift to Quseir (134 miles) crosses the Eastern Desert through the Red Sea Mountains. After a series of wells were dug in the reign of Ramses IV (1164–1157 BC), trade flowed along the route between the Nile and the Red Sea. It has been in almost continuous use since then. The romance of caravans is gone, but there are some fascinating and rarely visited sights and beautiful mountain scenery along the way.

Qift was known as the place where Isis heard of her husband Osiris' murder. The road leaves to the east, away from the Nile, following the ancient route suggested by Greek and Coptic inscriptions at **Qasr el-Banat** (the Maidens' Palace), some 5 miles past el-Laqeita. The road winds upward and after 46 miles enters the **Wadi Hammamat**, a beautiful route through the mountains. The Wadi was prized for its breccia stone and gold. At several places its walls contain ancient inscriptions and its hilltops preserve the remains of ancient and Arab watchtowers.

Bir Umm Fawakhir, 77 miles from Qift, is an ancient well with hieroglyphic inscriptions. Farther east, a long wire fence encloses **el-Sid**, a British gold mine abandoned after the Suez crisis of 1956, its equipment still untouched. The guardian may be persuaded to let you in. The remainder of the road to **Quseir** is lined with old gold and newer phosphate mines.

ROAD TO THE MONASTERIES
There is no public transportation to the monasteries, so it is best to book an organized tour with Misr Travel or hire a taxi for the day from Hurghada or Suez (about 100 miles). It is possible to ask any bus driver, from Cairo or Suez to Hurghada, to drop you at the turnoff for St. Paul's, 16 miles south of Za'farana. It is an 8-mile walk to the monastery, though you may get a lift. For St. Anthony's, service taxis from Beni Suef to Za'farana can stop at the turnoff for this monastery, 20 miles south of Za'farana; you can then walk 9 miles uphill, or pray for a lift.

WALK ACROSS THE MOUNTAINS
It is possible to get a lift between the two monasteries (over 50 miles by road), but experienced walkers may prefer to do the three-day hike across the mountains, as St. Anthony did when he visited St. Paul. A map of the region is available at St. Anthony's monastery, but take plenty of advice before you start as it can be dangerous. Beware of getting lost or running out of water.

In the past few years Coptic monasteries have seen an increase in the number of men wanting to become monks

►► **Deir Anba Antunius (Monastery of St. Anthony)** *226A4*

Open: daily 9–5. Closed during Christmas and Lent

The monastery was founded by followers of St. Anthony shortly after his death in AD 356, and it is often mentioned as the oldest monastery in the world. Set dramatically beneath a barren ridge of cliffs, the compound, which is surrounded by 39-foot-high walls, contains houses, gardens, churches, and palm trees and looks very much like an Egyptian village. Until the beginning of the 20th century, it took three or four days to get here by camel. Nowadays busloads of Copts and tourists arrive here on a tour or a pilgrimage. Some monks do a small tour of the monastery in several languages.

The oldest structure is the newly-restored **Church of St. Anthony►►**, with paintings and murals from the early 13th to 16th centuries, some only recently discovered. To the northwest of the church is the more recent Church of the Holy Virgin. On top of a four-story keep is the 16th-century Church of St. Michael. Near the south wall is the Spring of St. Anthony, believed to be the place where Moses' sister took a bath during the Exodus; it used to be the only water source in the compound. A path from the west side of the monastery makes the steep climb to St. Anthony's Cave (see page 238), with magnificent views over the Red Sea.

►► **Deir Anba Bula (Monastery of St. Paul)** *226A4*

Open: daily 9–5. Closed during Christmas and Lent

The Monastery of St. Paul is smaller than its neighbor, more dilapidated, and truly in the middle of nowhere, not even on a caravan route. St. Paul (AD 228–348) was the earliest hermit, but it is said that when, at the age of 113, he was visited in his cave by St. Anthony (then aged 90), he acknowledged St. Anthony as his superior.

Because of the monastery's remoteness, there are fewer visitors here and the monks are friendlier. Saint Paul's Cave is in the Church of St. Paul; the sarcophagus nearby is said to contain his remains. On top of the four-story keep, where the monks hid from invading Bedouins, is the Church of the Virgin, adjacent to the Church of St. Mercurius. In the 17th-century Church of St. Michael there is an icon of the Virgin, believed to have been painted by St. Luke in AD 40.

The twin towers of St. Anthony's Monastery, built at the foot of the hill where the saint went into retreat

▶ El Gouna   240B1

El Gouna, Egypt's latest luxury resort, has its own airstrip (with private flights from Cairo's Imbaba airfield), in addition to a string of new international hotels. Villa developments have attracted wealthy Cairenes, a golf course is under construction, while the brewery (Sakkara) and winery (Obelisque) are producing some of Egypt's better drinks. The big hotels arrange for guests to be picked up from Hurghada airport (about 14 miles south of the resort.).

▶ Bur Safaga (Port Safaga)   226B3

Port Safaga, 36 miles south of Hurghada on the junction of the road to Qena, is a commercial port that exports phosphates and imports U.S. grain. It has also developed as a new resort with several excellent hotels.

▶ Quseir   226B3

Until the 10th century Quseir, 90 miles south of Hurghada, was the largest trading port on the Red Sea. In ancient times boats left from here on expeditions to the Land of Punt (either Yemen or Somalia), and until the 19th century it was the most popular port for pilgrims going to Mecca. Quseir lost its importance with the opening of the Suez Canal, but the small fort of Sultan Selim still dominates the town.

SOUTH OF HURGHADA
In the 1980s, you needed a military permit to get much farther south than Hurghada. In 1990, the only people going down there were serious divers in search of fresh sites. Now the coast is being developed all the way to Berenice, with a string of tourist resorts under construction in places such as Ras Abu Soma and Marsa Shagra. To serve these resorts a new international airport is being built at Mersa Alam, some 20 miles south of Quseir.

Monasticism is one of Egypt's many gifts to civilization. The idea of coming closer to God by retreating from the world was a natural one to the inheritors of pharaonic Egypt.

ST. ANTHONY

St. Anthony (AD 251–356) became a hermit at 18 when he heard Matthew's gospel: "If thou wilt be perfect, go and sell what thou hast, and give to the poor, and thou shalt have treasure in heaven." He started off in his own garden, then joined a caravan into the Eastern Desert and found his isolated cave in Mount Qalah, where he lived until the age of 105. His life was the inspiration for monasticism, which quickly spread to England, Ireland, and Northern Europe where it soon had many followers.

St. Anthony, one of the founders of Christian monasticism

238

Beginnings of monasticism The beginnings of monasticism are bound up with the beginnings of Christianity in Egypt. Tradition says that the Holy Family hid from Herod in Egypt, but of more importance to the growth of the Church was the arrival of St. Mark, who founded the Patriarchate of Alexandria in AD 61. The translation of the scriptures into Coptic in the 3rd century AD gave the new religion a popular touch at the same time as Roman emperors were persecuting Christians with increasing severity, culminating in the outrages committed under Diocletian. During the persecutions of his predecessor Decius, two of the Coptic Church's most revered saints left their very different homes and sought refuge in the Red Sea Mountains. Both St. Paul and St. Anthony renounced the pleasures of the world and retreated to caves in the hope of drawing closer to their God.

Martyrs or monks While tens of thousands of Christians were being slaughtered, "so many," according to a contemporary writer, "that the exhausted executioners had to be periodically relieved," huge numbers of others were also seeking sanctuary away from the Nile Valley. For Egyptians, to whom the river and its rhythms were life itself, leaving the valley for the desert was indeed like giving up life. Strangely, after Diocletian's rage had been replaced by Constantine's vision and Christianity was declared the favored religion of the Roman empire, even greater numbers of Egyptians abandoned the valley in favor of a life of religious seclusion.

Monastic orders St. Anthony is said to have forbidden his many followers to stay near the cave into which he had retreated, so they camped at the foot of the hill, forming a community that became a permanent settlement and the basis of today's Monastery of St. Anthony. The next step in monasticism was taken back in the Nile Valley when, around AD 320, the soldier-convert St. Pachom decided that these communities should be run along military lines. His ideas, which included the taking of vows, the wearing of habits, and the regulating of every hour of the monks' days, were observed by the dozen communities he founded. They also formed the basis of monasticism throughout the Christian Church, and 19th-century Europeans, rediscovering his beliefs, nodded in admiration as they read, for instance, of his insistence that a healthy body leads to a healthy mind.

Hermits Visit a monastery in Egypt these days and the chances are that one of the monks will have recently ended a period of complete retreat, sometimes for a matter of days, sometimes for 20 or more years. For monks, the status of being a hermit is one that they must work toward, first spending up to ten years in a monastery, then securing the permission of monastic superiors and even the pope. A new hermit must then find a suitable place to hide, usually a cave, where other monks can bring the weekly supply of food. But even out in the wilderness, the hermit's life is governed by rules that dictate how many hours a day he may spend in prayer, rest, or physical activity.

St. Paul the ascetic and the lions with which he is associated

Monastic revival Nineteenth-century travelers mourned the decline of Egyptian monasteries, but since Shenuda III was made pope in 1971, the Coptic Church has had a leader who himself spent many years in retreat. Neglected, understaffed, and underfunded for so long, the monasteries are again attracting the interest of the Coptic community, who are restoring the old buildings and paying attention to the farmland that provides food to support the community and thus reversing monastic fortunes. This in turn has led to a huge increase in new monks and in visitors to their monasteries.

OSTRICH EGGS
Some people insist that the ostrich eggs in the Coptic church are a symbol of resurrection. Others, less poetic, point out that they were often placed above oil lamps to discourage rats from climbing down. What is certain is that they were used in this way in ancient Egyptian temples.

Coptic monks with embroidered cowls

Sinai

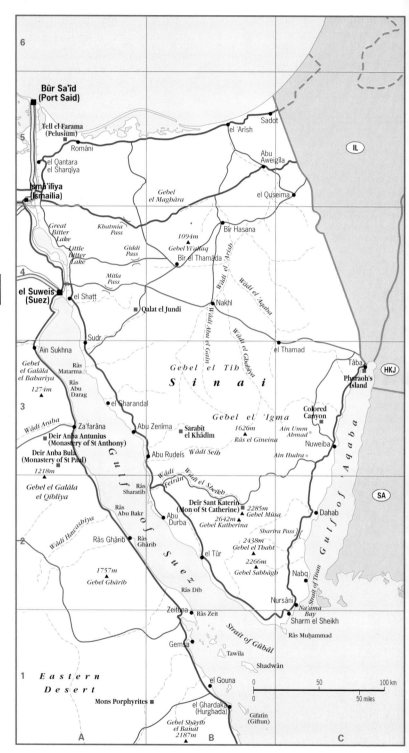

SINAI Sinai is unlike the rest of Egypt. A varied and beautiful desert, a land of miracles and holy places, its importance in connecting Africa and Asia has often made it the scene of bitter fighting. Since its return to Egypt in 1982 under the Camp David agreement, the peninsula's tourist potential has been realized, first as a beach and diving center and now for its cultural attractions.

THE LAND OF SIN Sinai's first settlers were nomads from the east, who predated the Nile civilization and worshiped a moon goddess called Sin. Five thousand years ago, as the Egyptian empire expanded, expeditions from the Nile came to the area looking for copper. They found it around Mafkah, east of modern-day Abu Rudeis. For nearly two millennia Egyptians extracted copper, manganese, and turquoise from Sinai, and the ruins of their temples and settlements tell the tale of their hard lives on the peninsula.

Sinai

MINE ALERT
According to a 1997 report from the National Security Commission, 5.5 million mines remain buried in Sinai, a deadly legacy from the wars with Israel.
If concerned, check first with the tourist office that the area you wish to visit is safe.

WEST AND EAST Sinai's position, standing firmly between two continents, rather than its mineral wealth has dominated its history and also the course of its main routes. The northern route, following the Mediterranean coast, was known as the Horus Road of War and its name suggests its function. Egyptians, Syrians, Canaanites, and Israelites marched across it to fight for land and power. The Romans, who conquered them all, improved the route to allow easy access between their Syrian and Egyptian provinces and called it the Via Maris, reflecting a more peaceful period, although the Holy Family would have fled along it to escape the vengeance of King Herod. Muslims going to Mecca defined a more southern passage, the Darb el-Hajj (Pilgrims' Road), from Suez to Eilat, its route lined with the ruins of Arab and Crusader castles. These are still the peninsula's two main roads and, not for the first time, there is already an increase in traffic now that political stability is coming to the region.

DESERT HIDEOUTS Sinai's climate is harsh, discouraging settlement, but the mountains at its heart provided Jews and then Christians with a sanctuary in which to hide. Particularly in the south, there was an abundance of wildlife and, if you knew where to look for it, of water as well. The Israelites settled around palm-filled *wadis* (dry gullies) such as Wadi Feiran—according to the Bible, Moses received the Ten Commandments on a nearby mountain—and Christians escaping Roman persecution established settlements there. By the 5th century AD, the community was important enough to be made a

bishopric, though continuous attacks from nomadic tribes made it necessary to enclose the settlement, creating the Monastery of St. Catherine.

NATURAL BEAUTY Bird watchers gather along Sinai's coasts to observe the migration of flocks between the continents in spring and autumn. The underwater wonders off Sinai's coasts are famed throughout the world and its coral reefs, particularly along the eastern coast from Ras Muhammad, are often described in superlatives by experienced divers. Its central mountain ranges, their jagged peaks rising over 8,000 feet, look like forbidding places but, as persecuted Israelites and Christians found, among the rocks there are beautiful *wadis* and canyons, abundant with water and vegetation. Here the more traditional of the desert's Bedouin live surrounded by wildlife, from lizards and scorpions to the last of Egypt's endangered wild animals.

A PLACE OF TRADITIONS Bedouin tribes used to control the peninsula and only the strongest of rulers in Cairo, Jerusalem, or Damascus were able to claim sovereignty over them. But Israeli and now Egyptian control, and the reduction in Bedouin numbers, has led to the majority of Sinai's Bedouin being found around el-Arish on the northern coast, with the 1,000-strong southern group in the Wadi el-Aradi. While their tribes are a shadow of the hordes who fought alongside Lawrence of Arabia, and those that remain are increasingly subjected to outside influences, Sinai's Bedouin are still the guardians of ancient traditions.

Sinai's mountains look forbiddingly barren but they contain large reserves of water and sustain the Bedouin communities

RELIGIOUS TOURISM
Nineteenth-century travelers scoured Sinai in the hope of finding evidence to support the Bible. By proving that Moses did exist and really did wander in the desert, they hoped to add credence to the Bible's other stories, especially its account of the creation, which had been called into question by Charles Darwin and his theory of evolution. Recent discoveries in northern Sinai are likely to revive religious tourism in the region.

*Sinai style: going
"Bedouin" at Shark Bay*

CAMEL TREKS
Nuweiba is a good place to
organize three- or four-day
treks to the interior of
Sinai, where the scenery is
wild and wonderful. The
cost of the trip includes a
Bedouin guide, who will
also cook for you. Gazelles
can be seen in the dunes
of Wadi Ghazala, the
scenery in the Colored
Canyon is magnificent,
tradition claims the oasis
of Ain Khudra as the site
where Miriam caught
leprosy, and the cool
stream of Ain Umm
Ahmad offers welcome
refreshment in the
summer.

► el-Arish 240B5

El-Arish, in northern Sinai, may be the peninsula's largest
town, but its construction is increasingly spoiling its
magnificent beaches. The Romans called it Rhinocolorum
because prisoners exiled here had their noses cut off. Once
just a Bedouin settlement under the palm groves, el-Arish
has become a resort, especially popular with middle-class
Egyptian families. Bedouins sell rugs, jewelry, and traditional dresses in the Thursday market. For another insight
into the increasingly threatened traditional life of the
Bedouin, visit the **Sinai Heritage Museum** on the coast
road. (*Open Sat–Thu 9:30–2. Admission: inexpensive*).

►► Dahab 240C2

Dahab means "gold" in Arabic, the color of its superb
beaches. Back in the 1970s, there was little more than sand
and Bedouin here, but Dahab now has something of a
unique character in Egypt—a reputation as a place to
hang-out and a scene familiar to anyone who has been to
Goa or Ko Samui. There are large-scale resort hotels, but
because the majority of visitors are independent travelers,
Dahab has a very different character to Sharm or
Hurghada and is relatively low-rise and low-key. A word
of warning, though, in spite of the relaxed atmosphere,
drugs offenses are dealt with harshly by the police (Egypt
tends to execute its drug dealers) and topless bathing is
frowned upon by the authorities. The best snorkeling and
diving sites are just outside town. The most famous and
most dangerous is the Blue Hole, a 220-foot-deep shaft,
which is farther north. The Lagoon and Napoleon Reef
are near the resort village.

► Nuweiba 240C3

Nuweiba lacks some of the charm of Dahab. It is changing
fast, and is beginning to suffer as its port business
increases. As in Dahab there are two main tourist areas:
Nuweiba itself is popular with well-off Egyptians and
European and Israeli tourists, while Tarabeen, the
Bedouin village, attracts a younger public. Check out the
good diving around the offshore reefs. Two ferries a day
leave Nuweiba for Aqaba in Jordan.

As much as anyone else in Egypt, the Bedouin provide a direct line back to another age, before the spread of nationalism and the arrival of the combustion engine. Although they are increasingly settled and their culture is being quickly eroded, they still value many of their nomadic traditions.

Mixed ancestry Bedouin in Sinai and elsewhere in Egypt claim descent from the Arab tribes of the Hejaz; others, particularly in the Western Desert and the mountains of the Eastern Desert, were living there long before Arabs arrived.

Romance of the nomad As nomads living in a harsh environment, Bedouins were constantly searching for pasture until tribes established feeding grounds to which they would return each year. Not having settlements, they placed strong emphasis on family and tribal structures. Their nomadic life forced them to reject anything that could not be carried, a habit that continues to be admired by people whose lives are ruled by their possessions.

Desert life Because they spent part of each year in the desert, Bedouin were forced to master their environment to support and protect themselves. Skills such as finding water, tracking animals, and navigating by stars became second nature. While the Bedouin of Sinai have been able to use their skills and earn a living by guiding tourists, the future seems less comfortable for Bedouin elsewhere.

Settling the nomads Nomads who lived in places that other people (particularly those of the Nile Valley) found hostile were difficult to control. But the helicopter and the four-wheel-drive car have tamed their wilderness, and the development of nationalism has forced them to conform to the will of central authority. Increasingly, Bedouin are being settled, often in unsuitable camps or villages where there is little prospect of work. Under these circumstances, Bedouin culture is bound to die out, even among the few groups who continue to be seminomadic.

THE COMING OF CARS.
Bedouin girls, singing of their love, refer now to young men driving cars rather than riding horses or camels, as in: "Welcome driver of the jeep I'll make you tea with milk if not shameful" and: "Toyotas when they first appeared brought life's light then disappeared." Lila Abu-Lughod, *Veiled Sentiments: Honor and Poetry in a Bedouin Society*

245

Sinai's Bedouins have been settled but they still raise goats and camels as they did when they were semi-nomadic

Sinai

St. Catherine's Monastery

This Transfiguration of Christ is one of the earliest mosaics of the Eastern Church

▶▶▶ Deir Sant Katerin (Monastery of St. Catherine)   240B2

Open: Mon–Thu and Sat 9–12. Closed Fri, Sun and Orthodox holidays. Dress modestly

The Greek Orthodox Monastery of St. Catherine is set dramatically in the Wadi Deir, in the shadow of two mountains: Gebel Musa (Mt. Sinai), where tradition says Moses received the Ten Commandments, and Gebel el-Deir. St. Catherine's, a place of pilgrimage since long before the 4th century, is considered to be the oldest continuously inhabited monastery in the world.

In AD 337, the Byzantine empress Helena ordered the building of a chapel on the site of what was believed to be the Burning Bush, to which the 6th-century emperor, Justinian, added a fortress monastery to protect the monks and pilgrims from raiders. The monastery was only later dedicated to St. Catherine, a beautiful 4th-century Alexandrian who converted to Christianity and was martyred for accusing the Roman emperor, Maximus, of idolatry. According to tradition, five centuries later priests found her previously lost body glowing on top of Gebel Katerina (Mt. St. Catherine), apparently transported there by angels.

The lush gardens of olive and apricot trees surrounding the fortified walls contain a cemetery and Charnel House, where bones of the dead monks are stored. The present entrance and the south and west walls are original (6th-century), but the north and east walls were rebuilt after an earthquake in the 14th century.

The **Church of the Transfiguration▶▶▶** (now called the Church of St. Catherine) dominates the enclosure. Built in AD 542 by Justinian in memory of his wife, it is, along with the Chapel of the Burning Bush, the oldest structure on the site. The entrance is through the narthex (vestibule), added in the 10th or 11th century, where some of the world's rarest icons are displayed. From here, exquisite 6th-century cedarwood doors lead to a high nave. The original 12 granite pillars represent months of the year, each bearing an icon of the saints to be worshiped that month. The wooden bracing beams of the 18th-century ceiling are original (6th-century) and finely carved with animals and cherubs. Between the nave and choir, a gilded iconostasis has 17th-century icons of Mary, Jesus, John the Baptist, and St. Catherine. Behind it, under the marble canopy, are what are believed to be the relics of St. Catherine: her left hand and her skull.

In the sanctuary is one of the masterpieces of Byzantine art, the 6th-century mosaic of the Transfiguration of Christ, portraying Christ in the middle, with Elias and St. John to his left, St. Peter at his feet, and to his right Moses and St. James. Above the arch are medallions of the Virgin and John the Baptist,

and beside the windows are biblical scenes of Moses receiving the Holy Commandments (right) and Moses taking off his sandals in front of the Burning Bush (left).

Visitors with special permission can visit the Chapel of the Burning Bush, but must remove their shoes before visiting the earliest level of the monastery. Strangely enough, the altar was built over the roots of the bush, while the thorny bush itself was transplanted at the back of the church where everyone can see it flourishing. The monastery has more treasures, but a letter of introduction from the Greek patriarchate in Cairo is needed to gain admittance. There is a priceless collection of around 2,000 icons and nearly 100 are exhibited in the Icon Gallery. They are all worth seeing, but the oldest 12 icons (6th and 7th centuries), made in the melted wax technique on wood, are particularly striking. The Library has the most important collection of religious manuscripts after the Vatican, with some 5,000 books and 3,000 manuscripts. To the left of the Church of St. Catherine is Moses' Well, where Moses is said to have met his wife Zipporah. Opposite is a mosque that was originally a 6th-century hospice for pilgrims.

Icon of St. Catherine: the monastery holds one of the most important collections of icons in the world

CODEX SINAITICUS
Even with a letter of introduction the monks are hesitant to show their valuable manuscripts. This is not surprising since a 19th-century German scholar borrowed one of their rarest manuscripts, the 4th-century Codex Sinaiticus, and never returned it. It came into the possession of the Czar of Russia and the Communist regime later sold it to the British Museum.

Walk

Up Gebel Musa (Mount of Moses)

Christians, Jews, and Muslims believe that Gebel Musa—Mt. Sinai of the Bible—is where Moses received the Ten Commandments. The climb takes about 2 hours and is best done early in the morning, in order to see the sun light up this wild and rugged landscape.

Gebel Musa is an important pilgrimage spot, so you will not be alone. If you don't mind roughing it, you can climb up before sundown, spend an extraordinary night near the summit and be woken up by psalms sung by pilgrims (and maybe also someone's ghetto blaster). Luggage can be left in the monastery, but take warm clothes, a sleeping bag (you can rent blankets at the monastery, but nights can be very cold), and some food and drink, as the Bedouin who makes tea on top of the mountain sometimes takes a day off. A more comfortable alternative is to stay at the monastery and join the pilgrims in the early morning.

The monastery is built at an altitude of 4,900 feet, which makes walking up the 7,497-foot mountain less of a climb. There are two ways to the top. The Sikket Sayyidna Musa (Path of our Lord Moses), a 3,750-step "stairway to Heaven," starts south of the monastery. It is the shortest but steepest route, best saved for the descent. The easier route, a camel path built in the last century, starts behind the monastery and winds slowly around the mountain, allowing plenty of photo opportunities. Along the way, Bedouins with camels wait for the feeble to collapse. The two routes meet just before the top for the last few hundred steps. The simple chapel on the summit, near the cave where Moses is said to have stayed for 40 days, has been closed due to vandalism. You can get trail maps and notes from the monastery's Visitor Center. It's important to obey the rules and not to take any souvenirs.

Many pilgrims and visitors climb Gebel Musa to watch the sun rise over the spectacular range

▶▶ Sharm el Sheikh 240C1

Sharm el Sheikh, and especially Na'ama Bay, a few miles north, has become one of Egypt's most popular resorts. The town was developed by the Israelis when they occupied Sinai in the 1967 war, at first merely for strategic reasons and later as a tourist resort. When it was returned in the 1980s, Egyptians set up some camps and diving centers. Since the opening of the airport and the first five-star hotel—the Fayrouz Hilton—both Sharm and neighboring Na'ama Bay have changed dramatically. Four- and five-star hotels now line the bay, which has become a major package-tour destination, as well as a place for wealthy Cairenes to enjoy their leisure time. Backpackers now head straight for Dahab (see page 244). There are no alcohol restrictions at Sharm el-Sheikh and the nightlife is very active.

Sharm's only "sight" is Ras Kennedy, a rock formation resembling the face of President John F. Kennedy. In Na'ama Bay, most waterfront hotels and restaurants lie along the promenade. The beach shelves gently, so is safe for children, but the best reefs for snorkeling lie to the north of Na'ama Bay. Half an hour's walk beyond the pontoon pier are the amazing Near Gardens, full of brightly colored fish and strangely shaped corals. Another 30 minutes along the coast brings you to the Far Gardens, just as spectacular and often deserted.

▶ Taba 240C3

Taba is a developing beach resort, with several new hotels popular with Israelis. It was returned to Egypt in 1989 after ten years of negotiations. The Crusader castle on **Geziret el-Faraun (Pharaoh's Island)▶**, outside town, was built around 1115 by King Baldwin I of Jerusalem to protect pilgrims on their way to St. Catherine's monastery. A museum is planned to commemorate the 20th anniversary of the October War. Taba is one of the border crossings into Israel, and from there it is now possible to cross to Aqaba in Jordan.

There are other things to do in Sharm el Sheikh apart from diving

CAMEL TREKS
The manager of the Pigeon Hotel (Na'ama Bay) organizes a week-long camel trip to St. Catherine's, crossing some spectacular and wildly beautiful scenery. The guide is, of course, a Bedouin, who cooks and tells stories about desert life in the past.

Sinai and the Red Sea coast share the honors with Australia's Great Barrier Reef for having the best scuba diving in the world. As "scuba-tourism" rapidly develops, the challenge for Egypt is to ensure that its underwater wonders are still there for the next generation to enjoy.

CORRIDOR OF MARVELS
"The Red Sea is a corridor of marvels... The happiest hours of my diving experience have been there."
Jacques Cousteau

Dive sites are often reached after treks across rough ground

CORAL CARE
Significant damage continues to be inflicted on the coral and under-water environment by boats dropping anchor on the reefs, divers taking trophies, refuse and building rubble being thrown into the water, and other acts of environmental vandalism. Egypt has no shortage of regulatory bodies, including the Environmental Affairs Agency and Coastal Protection Research Institute, but they have been ineffective. You can help by not touching the corals or leaving litter of any sort.

The underwater landscape The Red Sea is warm enough and in some places shallow enough to encourage the growth of corals. Corals are minute polyps, anemone-like creatures, which group together in colonies and feed off other small organisms that live in their environment. When corals die, the next generation grows up on top of them. Over a long period of time, they accumulate into myriad extraordinarily beautiful formations. Lagoon or fringe reefs are the most common formations, running along the coast, just under the surface, with a steep shelf or cliff on their sea side. Patch or pillar corals grow up directly off the seabed in a tower or spike, often reaching to just below the surface of the sea.

Creatures of the deep Corals and the organisms they feed off are part of a mini-ecosystem supporting more than 100 species of brilliant, warm-water fish. The most common inhabitants are yellow anemone fish and damsel fish and a host of other animal-named fish, like goat-, parrot-, turkey-, scorpion-, and butterfly-fish. The big fish, usually found at greater depths, include various types of shark, barracuda, stingrays, and whales.

How to see them Especially around Sharm el Sheikh, some coral reefs are accessible to the energetic snorkeler, but the real thrills are to be had farther from the shore. For the safety of the diver *and* the coral, most scuba centers will want to see a diving proficiency certificate from a recognized association before allowing you to rent equipment. If you aren't already trained, or want to improve your skills, there are excellent courses at diving centers all along the Sinai and Red Sea coasts. Many are attached to hotels, and sometimes their fees are included as part of a package with rooms and flights. Instructors should belong to an internationally recognized body, the largest of which is the Professional Association of Diving Instructors (PADI). A doctor's certificate, that confirms fitness to dive, is usually required to enroll in a five-day course leading to the basic PADI certificate.

Dive options Diving equipment and a boat on your own are expensive to rent, but joining a club and diving as part of a group brings the price down considerably. At Sharm el Sheikh it is possible to visit some fine reefs without renting a boat, but the best reefs and most exciting dives will involve some transportation. A boat is also a must for divers on the Red Sea Coast around Hurghada in Sinai. Diving clubs offer day trips to popular reefs, but their accessibility means there can be crowds underwater as well as above it. Farther afield, some of the dives within easy reach of Sinai's eastern coast can present a formidable challenge: the Blue Hole is the most notorious,

TROPHY HUNTING
Photographs are the best souvenirs of your dive, and if you don't have an underwater camera you can rent one from the diving clubs or photographic shops in the resorts.

a 220-foot shaft that has claimed the lives of several experienced divers. The ultimate dive experiences are probably to be had on "live-aboard" boats—in effect, Red Sea dive-cruises that spend several days or a week around the farther-flung, less-visited reefs.

Conspicuous against its background, a clown fish nestles among the protective forest of anemone tentacles

Diving clubs There is a choice of diving clubs in Sharm el Sheikh, neighboring Na'ama Bay, Dahab, Nuweiba, Taba, and on the Red Sea coast. Their rates, group sizes, and departure times in the morning (some leave very early) will be a deciding factor. The Sinai Divers, Camel Dive, Subex, and Aquamarine clubs are the longest-established.

The diving year Like the world above, the underwater world has its seasons. Among the highlights are: manta rays in the northern Red Sea (March–May), spawning season around Ras Muhammad (July–August), and the appearance of Napoleon wrasse (September).

Most people visit Sinai for its beaches and world-class water sports, but the interior of the peninsula has much to offer. St. Catherine's monastery has attracted pilgrims and tourists for centuries, but new discoveries are also drawing attention. As a change from Egypt's manmade treasures, the desert is also a place of remarkable natural beauty.

252

Newly discovered antiquities Egyptologists are still debating the implications of the latest archeological discoveries in Sinai. A large fort, uncovered some 15 miles east of the Suez Canal, marks the starting point of the Horus Road of War, along which Egyptian armies marched into Palestine. Some claim the fort was built by Seti I, others that it is the city of Pi-Ramses. If it is the latter, then it may be the Old Testament city built by the children of Israel, from which Moses led the Exodus to the promised land. On the road to el-Arish, the mounds at Tell el-Faramah contain the remains of ancient Pelusium, where the Persians surrendered to Alexander the Great in 332 BC.

Medieval ruins Many Arab ruins await rediscovery in Sinai, particularly along the pilgrims' route south to Sharm el Sheikh or due east from Suez to Taba. The latest discoveries include buildings near el-Tur, an important medieval port, and the Mamluk citadel and two circular towers east of Taba, thought to date to the reign of el-Ghuri, the last sultan before the Turkish invasion.

Eternal treasures Although they are hard to visit without Bedouin guides, and are sometimes hard to visit with them, the wadis (dry gullies) of southern Sinai are worth seeking out. Treks of several days, preferably by foot or camel, will take you through desert mountains to brilliantly colored valleys and cool, clear pools.

In Bedouin society the camel is still perceived as a measure of wealth

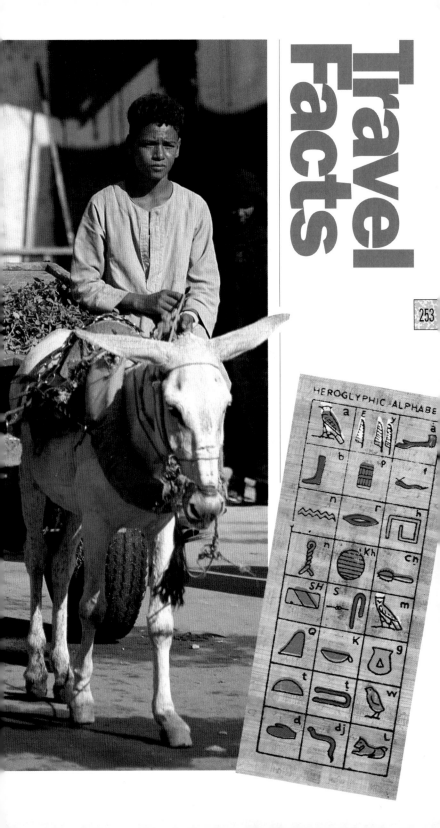

HEROGLYPHIC ALPHABE

Arriving

By air There are direct scheduled flights from New York and Los Angeles, and all European capitals, to Cairo. Some international scheduled flights also land in Alexandria, Luxor, and Aswan. Charter flights operate to Luxor, Sharm el Sheikh, and Hurghada. Egypt Air flights arrive in Cairo's Terminal 1 (the old airport), while most European airlines arrive in the more efficient Terminal 2 (the new international airport). In Cairo, the easiest way to get into town is to take a limousine with a fixed price or to haggle with a taxi driver for a less expensive ride. Buses No. 949 (24 hours a day from Terminal 2) and No. 400 and minibus No. 27 (from Terminal 1) leave regularly for central Cairo. In Luxor and Aswan, you will need to take a taxi and to discuss the price in advance. If you need help, ask for the tourist police.

Signposting in Cairo has improved over the past few years

By bus There are regular buses from Tel Aviv, Jerusalem, and Eilat in Israel to Sinai and Cairo, crossing the border at Rafah or Taba, where Israeli departure tax and an Egyptian entry fee have to be paid. Frequent buses also connect Cairo with Tripoli and Benghazi (Libya), but few tourists venture that way.

By car Most people avoid entering by car as the bureaucracy can be painful. You should be allowed to bring a car into Egypt for three months if you can show an *international triptyque* or a *carnet de passage de douane* issued by the automobile club in the country where the car is registered. An extension of three months can be given to the driver in person by the **Automobile Club of Egypt**, 10 Sharia Qasr en-Nil, Cairo.

By sea Since Adriatica Lines stopped running regular ferries from Venice to Alexandria, cheaper but more erratic ferries from Istanbul to Alexandria via Piraeus are the only option. Tickets can be purchased only in Istanbul, Athens, or Piraeus. Daily ferries also run between Aqaba (Jordan) and Nuweiba (Sinai).

Customs regulations

Visitors are allowed to bring in 200 cigarettes and 1 liter of alcohol. In Luxor and Cairo airports there are duty-free shops after customs where you can buy another

254

4 liters, or else within 24 hours of your arrival you can buy three more bottles and cigarettes from the Egypt Free Store at the end of Sharia Gama'a el-Duwal el-Arabiya in Mohandeseen. There is another shop in the Cairo Sheraton in Dokki and in the center of Luxor (take your passport). Video cameras, computers, and other electronic equipment should be declared on a D-form upon arrival. In case of theft always get a police report, otherwise the equipment will be considered sold and a duty of 100 percent will have to be paid. The export of antiquities or any item over 100 years old, if you do not have a license, is forbidden.

Departing
Confirm your flight with the airline if necessary, and allow at least an hour to get from downtown Cairo to the airport. There is no departure tax.

Passports and visas
All visitors to Egypt must hold a passport valid for at least six months after the day of arrival. In case of loss, photocopy the data page; keep one copy with you separate from your passport and leave one copy with friends at home.

Most foreign tourists are no longer required to register their passports with the Ministry of the Interior. Most visitors to Egypt need a tourist visa. Egyptian consulates abroad issue visas, but it is cheaper and easier to buy one upon arrival at Cairo, Luxor, and Hurghada airports or at the Alexandria port. However, you **cannot** obtain a general visa at the land crossings. You can enter Sinai without a visa if your stay for less than 1 week. Both the single-visit and multiple-entry tourist visas are valid for one month from the time of arrival and visa extensions can be applied for at the passport offices at the Mugamma on Cairo's Midan Tahrir; on Sharia Khaled ibn el-Walid near the Isis Hotel, Luxor; 28 Sharia Talaat Harb in Alexandria, and in the port of Sharm al-Sheikh. Take your passport, two photographs, money, and bank receipts proving that you exchanged $180 worth of foreign currency for every additional month you wish to stay. Overstaying your visa for a few days is usually okay, but after two weeks a fine has to be paid.

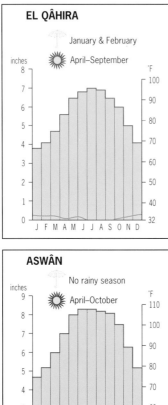

EL QÂHIRA

☂ January & February
☀ April–September

ASWÂN

☂ No rainy season
☀ April–October

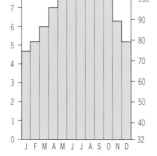

EL ISKANDARÎYA

☂ November–February
☀ May–September

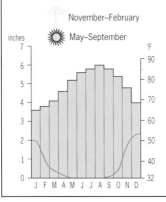

Essential facts

Climate
Temperatures in Egypt differ greatly between night and day. The climate is less extreme on the Mediterranean coast, where it is always cooler than in the rest of the country. March and April can bring the *khamaseen*, a strong, hot wind that carries dust and sand from the Sahara. Cairo is extremely hot from June to September, but at night it becomes more bearable. It can be quite cold in the winter months, often with rain around Christmas. The air becomes drier and hotter toward the south, but although Upper Egypt is hot even in winter, the nights can be surprisingly cold. Aswan has a perfect climate in winter with daytime temperatures around 77°F.

When to go The tourist season is from November to February, but Cairo and even Luxor are chilly then, and hotels may be overbooked. The best time to visit is May, or in October to November when the long, hot summer has ended.

Money matters
The Egyptian **pound** (LE, *Guineh* in Arabic) is divided into 100 piastres (PT, *Irsh* in Arabic). There are notes for 25 and 50 piastres and 1, 5, 10, 20, 50, and 100 pounds. It is possible to buy Egyptian currency abroad.

Banks are generally open from Monday to Thursday and Saturday 8:30–1 and sometimes on Sunday 10–noon. Banks in the airport and in the Marriott and Nile Hilton hotels in Cairo are open 24 hours. Travelers' checks are accepted in banks and hotels, and more and more places accept major credit cards. Many five-star hotels and major banks have automatic cash machines. Independent exchange offices are quicker than banks and often offer a better rate. Always keep the bank receipts as you need them to apply for a visa extension, to buy an airline ticket, or to pay the bill in a five-star hotel in Egyptian pounds.

National holidays

Banks, offices, and often stores close for public holidays as well as for religious holidays. These include:
April 25 (Sinai Day)
May 1 (Labor Day)
June 18 (Evacuation Day)
July 23 (Revolution Day)
October 6 (Armed Forces Day)

The Islamic calendar is lunar-based, and compared to the Western calendar the Islamic holidays come about 11 days earlier each year. There are 12 Islamic months and *Ras as-Sana* (Islamic New Year) on the first day of *Muharram* is a holiday. The *Moulid el-Nabi* (Prophet Muhammad's birthday) is celebrated all over the country, while every neighborhood, town, and city celebrates the *moulid* (feast day) of its local saint (see pages146–147). The most important Islamic holiday is the holy month of Ramadan when Muslims don't eat, drink, smoke or have sex from sunrise until sunset. Non-Muslims don't have to observe the fast but should show some respect and refrain from eating, drinking, and especially smoking in public. Many restaurants and cafés will be closed until the evening and it may be difficult for visitors to travel during this month. Everything slows down in a big way, or at least closes much earlier in the afternoon, but the joy and

The concept of time is not necessarily a Western one

the air of festivity at the end of a long day has some kind of magic, which compensates for the frustration. Stores and offices close for the few days of the *Aid el-Fitr* marking the end of Ramadan, and the *Aid el-Adha* when sheep are slaughtered in memory of Abraham's sacrifice.

The main Coptic holidays are Easter (variable) and Coptic Christmas on January 7. Shamm el-Naseem (spring festival) is a public holiday celebrated by both Copts and Muslims the day after Coptic Easter. Friday is a day off for most Egyptians.

Time differences

Egypt is 2 hours ahead of GMT. New York and Montreal are 7 hours behind Egypt, and Sydney is 7 hours ahead. But there is another time difference called the IBM of Egypt: *"Insha'allah, Bokra, Ma'alesh." Insha'allah* (God willing) suggests that it may happen, then again it may not; *Bokra* means tomorrow, in two weeks, or maybe never; *Ma'alesh* is what you hear all the time, meaning "never mind, don't worry, it wasn't that important anyway."

Getting around

Public transportation

Buses Intercity buses are inexpensive
and often more comfortable and
faster than the train, especially for
short distances. For longer distances it
may often be preferable to take a night
bus. The bus services in Cairo are
being reorganized at the time of
writing (see pages 110–111). There are
three main bus operators. The Upper
Egypt Bus Company operates buses to
the Nile Valley, el-Faiyum, Western
Desert Oases, and Red Sea coast. The
East Delta Bus Company runs buses
to the beach resorts in Sinai,
St. Catherine, and the canal towns.
Alexandria, Mersa Matruh, and the
Delta are served by the West Delta
Company. The Arab Union Transport
Company runs more expensive but
brand-new Superjet buses, with air-
conditioning, food, video, toilets, and
hostesses on board. They run between
Cairo, Alexandria, Luxor, Aswan,
and Hurghada. Tickets should be

*Egypt has an excellent network of
internal flights*

bought in advance at the appropriate
terminals (see pages 110–111).
Air-conditioned buses are newer,
more comfortable, and somewhat
more expensive than the old
non-air-conditioned buses, but be
warned, the air conditioning doesn't
always work.

Domestic flights The national airline,
Egyptair, operates frequent daily
flights between Cairo, Luxor,
Hurghada, New Valley, Alexandria,

Abu Simbel and Aswan, and less
often Marsa Matrouh. There are
several flights a day between Aswan
and Abu Simbel; the round-trip ticket
is usually sold as a package including
bus transfer from Abu Simbel airport
to the antiquity site (see pages
190–191). Air Sinai flies daily from
Cairo to Hurghada, Sinai and Tel
Aviv. The private airline Orascom
(tel: 02/301-5632) operates regular
flights from Cairo and Luxor to
el-Couna.

Always book as far as possible in
advance as flights get quickly overbooked, especially in winter. All
domestic flights leave Cairo from
Terminal 1, in the old airport.
Domestic flights are often delayed
and there is no entertainment in the
airports, so always bring something
to read.

Ferries The ferry between Hurghada
and Sharm el-Sheikh makes for a
pleasant alternative to the overland
trip via Suez. Lately the service has
been running frequently and almost
daily, but check locally as the schedules change often.

Trains For short rides, trains are often
unreliable and much slower than
buses, but there are some comfortable
trains between major cities.

Several fast turbo-trains per day run
between Cairo and Alexandria
(2 hours), and overnight sleepers to
Luxor (9 hours) and Aswan (12 hours).
Tickets should be booked in advance
at Ramses station (tel: 02/574-9474) or
through a travel agent.

There are also cheaper first- and
second-class air-conditioned trains,
without sleepers, to Alexandria,
Luxor, and Aswan, for which advance
bookings should also be made at the
train stations. The crowded non-
air-conditioned trains need not be
booked beforehand. A new railroad
has opened from Safâga on the Red
Sea to the New Valley.

Service taxis The collective service
taxis called "Beejou" are a faster
alternative than the bus, although the
driving is more dangerous. They go
just about anywhere. The fare is
usually not higher than the bus, and

The village trains give you time to enjoy the view

on the main routes there are departures all day until late at night. The taxis are usually Peugeots seating two passengers and the driver in the front, three in the middle, and two or three in the back. The drivers often drive like sheer maniacs, as fast as they can, so that they can pick up their next set of passengers. Accidents happen with alarming regularity and once you've taken a Beejou it will come as no surprise at all that they are known as "Flying Coffins." They can be dangerous at night and on the Cairo–Alexandria route, so be warned. There is usually a terminal for service taxis in every town and city. You can't book: just turn up and listen to the drivers shouting out their destinations. Sometimes they try to overcharge tourists; it can be worth checking to see what Egyptians are paying.

Driving

Car rental

International car rental companies like Hertz, Budget, and Avis are represented in the airport and in major hotels at most tourist centers. You can either book in advance from abroad, or arrange a car with a local company. Local company rates are sometimes lower than international agencies. Car rental and gas are cheap, but you have to be between 25 and 70 years old and have an International Driver's License. Most companies now accept credit cards though some of the smaller local

Everyday Cairo traffic

agencies may be reluctant to accept them. Make sure the compulsory third-party insurance, insisted on by the government, is included for damage to someone else's car.

As the traffic is hellish in Cairo and other urban areas, and sometimes even more hazardous outside the cities, most tourists prefer to rent a car with a driver, which may also be cheaper. Limo 1 in Cairo (tel: 02/340-5320) and other limousine agencies provide an air-conditioned Mercedes with a driver for as little as an hour or as

much as a few days, as required.

For a somewhat lower cost, a taxi driver will often be pleased to change his daily routine for a small adventure; make sure his car is up to it as well.

Driving tips Officially traffic drives on the right in Egypt, but when it comes to it, drivers will do whatever they can to get around: driving down one-way streets the wrong way, backing up main overpasses if they miss the exit, and zigzagging at speed through the traffic. As well as cars there are donkey carts, motorbikes, an occasional flock of sheep, people jumping off buses, and many, many pedestrians. It soon becomes clear that there are no fixed rules and that anarchy reigns. If you enjoy those sort of games, Cairo is for you; if not stick to taxis and close your eyes until you arrive at your destination.

It may seem incredible but there are relatively few road accidents in towns. The real danger is out on the country roads and "highways." Many roads are in bad condition. Many have deep potholes and drivers veer into the other lane without warning to avoid them. Children often play on roads, cattle wander across them, and trucks suddenly stop in the middle of nowhere. Avoid driving at night as Egyptians drive without lights, but will turn them on full beam if they see another car approaching. On country roads you may drive into an unmarked roadblock, in the dark, or a broken-down truck or just some soldiers playing a game of cards on the tarmac. The official speed limit outside towns is 90kph (56mph).

Gas and car breakdowns Cairo and large towns are well provided with gas stations (*mahattat benzeen*), but they are rare in the desert and countryside. When you find a station, check how far away the next one is and fill your tank up full. Most gas stations do oil changes and some maintenance. In larger towns there may be a good range of spare parts, while in more remote places mechanics may adopt a more creative approach. Desert driving is hard on vehicles; stick to the track and carry plenty of extra water, gas, and tools.

Hitchhiking Hitching is virtually non-existent in Egypt. You may get a ride on a truck or a van in areas where there is no public transportation, but you will almost always be expected to pay something, as most locals do. Women on their own should never, ever, even consider hitching.

Student and youth travel Youth hostels in Egypt may be inexpensive but they cannot be recommended. They close for most of the day, are out of the center and, worst of all, they are often filthy. You will need a membership card at some hostels: for more information, check with Hostelling International, 7 Sharia Dr. Abdel Hamid Said, downtown Cairo (tel: 02/575-8099). Museums and sights offer a 50 percent discount and there are reductions on rail and airline tickets if you have an official student card. An ISIC Student Card can be issued at the Egyptian Scientific Centre, 23 Sharia el-Manyel, above the National Bank on Roda Island (tel: 02/363-7251). Bring proof that you are a student and two photos.

Public transportation is inexpensive

Communications

Bookstores

Several stores specialize in foreign language books.
Cairo: American University Bookstore, Hill House on the main campus, Midan el-Tahrir (tel: 357-5377)Les Livres de France, Immobilia Building, 36 Qasr en-Nil (tel: 393-5512) L'Orientaliste (rare editions and prints), 15 Qasr en-Nil (tel: 575-3418) Lehnert and Landrock:, 44 Sharia Sherif, downtown (tel: 393-5324) Zamalek Bookstore, 19 Sharia Shagaret el-Durr, Zamalek (tel: 341-9197). Alexandria: Dar el-Mustaqbal, 32 Sharia Safiya Zaghlul (tel: 483-2452). Luxor: Aboudi Bookshop, Tourist Bazaar next to the New Winter Palace, Corniche el-Nil (tel: 373390).

Language guide

Egyptians speak Arabic, but English is taught in schools and someone is usually happy to practice with you. Try out some Arabic and you will be surprised by the enthusiastic response, often "Oh, you speak Arabic very well, better than me!" Egyptians love language and they constantly play with words. The following is a phonetic transliteration from the Arabic script.

Basics

Yes	aywa or na'am
No	la
Thank you	shukran
You're welcome	'afwan
Please	min fadlak (to a man), min fadlik (to a woman)
God willing	insha'allah
Good	kwayyis
Bad	mish kwayyis

Greetings

Welcome	ahlan wa-sahlan
(*response*)	ahlan bik (to men), ahlan biki (to women)
Hello	(to Muslims) as-salaamu aleikum
(*response*)	wa aleikum as-salaam
Good-bye	ma'a salaama
Hello	(to Copts) saeeda
Good morning	sabaah el-kheer
(*response*)	sabaah en-nur
Good evening	masaa el-kheer
(*response*)	masaa en-nur

Numbers

0	sifr
1	wahid
2	itnayn
3	talaata
4	arbah
5	khamsa
6	sitta
7	sabah
8	tamanya
9	tesah
10	ashara
11	hidaashar
12	itnaashar
13	talataashar
14	arbahtaashar
15	khamastaashar
16	sittaashar
17	sabahtaashar
18	tamantaashar
19	tisahtaashar
20	ashreen
21	wahid wa-ashreen
30	talaateen
40	arba'een
50	khamseen
100	miyya
1000	alf

Calendar

Sunday	youm il-hadd
Monday	youm il-itnayn
Tuesday	youm it-talaat
Wednesday	youm il-arbah
Thursday	youm il-khamees
Friday	youm il-gumah
Saturday	youm is-sabt
Today	innaharda
Tomorrow	bukra
Yesterday	imbaarih
Later	bahdeen

Directions

Where is the Hotel...?
feyn funduq il- ...?
Where is the bus station?
feyn mahattat il-autobees?
Where is the restaurant?
feyn il-matam?
Where is the toilet?
feyn it-twalet?
Right, left, straight ahead
yimeen, shimaal, alatoul

Questions and remarks

Is there? There is...:	fi? fi...
How much?	be-kaam?
It is too expensive	da ghaali awi
What's your name?	ismak eh? (to a man) or ismik eh? (to a woman)
My name is...:	ismi...
I don't understand	ana mish faahem (man), fahma (woman)
Go away	imshee
Impossible	mish mumkin

Media

The main foreign newspapers are available, with a few days' delay, from kiosks outside Groppi on Midan Talaat Harb, on 26th July Street in Zamalek (Cairo) and in five-star hotels. The daily *Egyptian Gazette* is published in English, as are the weekly *Middle East Times* and *Al-Ahram Weekly*. The weekly *Cairo Times* and monthly magazine *Egypt Today* have both good listings of what is going on and interesting features. There is daily television news in English at 8 PM on Channel 2; the new Nile TV also broadcasts in English.

Post offices

Most airmail letters to Europe take around a week to arrive; mail to North America or Australia takes longer. Since about 15 percent of all letters get lost, you can increase your luck by sending mail from a main post office or a five-star hotel, which should also sell stamps, or by EMS (Express Mail Service). Make the letter look as uninteresting as possible: avoid inserting photographs or other things that may appeal to someone on the way. Post offices are open from Saturday to Thursday, 8:30–3. The central post office on Midan el-Ataba in Cairo is open 24 hours.

Telephone and fax

Local calls can be made from hotels, kiosks, and phone booths. International calls can be made from Telephone and Telegraph (TT) offices, open 24 hours, most of which will

Egyptians love to read the newspapers

also send faxes (cheaper than from most hotels). Look for the orange direct-dial phones, which take phone cards (sold in post offices) and avoid the old system whereby you have to pay for a minimum of three minutes to open the line. The main TT offices in Cairo are on Midan el-Tahrir and at 8 Sharia Adly. AT&T, BT Direct and other direct call services are cheaper for international calls.

Emergencies

Crime and police

Cairo is safer than most European
capitals, but tourists are considered
wealthy, and some Egyptians cannot
resist the temptation. Always take
special care of your passport, money,
and plane tickets. In most hotels you
can deposit valuables at the reception

Tourist police are usually helpful

desk for safety, but always ask for a
receipt. The tourist police are usually
more helpful to foreigners than are
the ordinary police.

Drugs It is illegal to bring drugs into
the country. There is a serious fine for
possession of drugs and mandatory
sentences of life imprisonment or even
hanging for anyone convicted of
dealing or smuggling.

Emergency phone numbers in Cairo
Ambulance:123
Fire Brigade: 02/361-0257
Police: 122
Tourist Police: 126

Embassies and consulates

A complete list of embassies and
consulates can be found in the Cairo
Practical Guide. A few countries are

also represented in Port Said and
Alexandria. Addresses in Cairo
include:
Australia: World Trade Center (11th
Floor), 1191 Corniche el-Nil, Bulaq
(tel: 02/575-0444)
Canada: 6 Sharia Muhammad Fahmy
el-Sayyid, Garden City
(tel: 02/354-3110)
Ireland: 3 Borg Abu el-Feda (north of
Zamalek Bridge), Zamalek
(tel: 02/340-8264)
U.K.: 7 Sharia Ahmad Ragab, Garden
City (tel: 02/354-0850)
U.S.A.: 5 Sharia Amerika Latina,
Garden City (tel: 02/355-7371)

Egyptian embassies abroad
Australia: 1 Darwin Avenue,
Yarralumla, Canberra
(tel: 062/734437)
Canada: 454 Laurier Avenue East,
Ottawa, Ontario K1N 6R3 (tel:
613/234-4958)
U.K.: 26 South Street, London W1Y
6DD (tel: 020-7499 2401)
U.S.A.: 2300 Decatur Plaza NW,
Washington DC 20008
(tel: 202/232-5400)

Lost property

Report loss or theft to the tourist
police, open 24 hours in most cities. If
a passport is lost, report to the tourist
police first and then contact your
consulate or embassy as soon as possible. For traveler's checks or credit
cards, notify the issuing company.

Health
Vaccinations No vaccination certifi-
cates are required to enter Egypt
unless you are coming from an
infected area. The World Health
Organization issues regular health
bulletins for travelers, which you can
obtain from your doctor. They may
recommend polio, tetanus, yellow
fever, cholera, typhoid, and hepatitis
A inoculations. Malaria occurs in the
Delta, and may become a bigger problem, so check with your doctor in
advance when you know what part of
the country you will be visiting.

Precautions Although the heavily
chlorinated tap water is safe to drink, it
is advisable to stick to mineral water.
Dehydration is a risk, so drink at least

3 liters of fluids a day. Make sure the food you eat has been properly washed and that the place where it was prepared is clean. For the first few days, avoid eating seafood, rare meat, and raw food, including salads, and fruits that have not been peeled by yourself. As the sun is hot year-round, it is advisable to use a high-factor sun protection cream and to wear a hat and sunglasses. Avoid iced drinks during the heat of the day and wait until after sunset to have alcoholic drinks. Take antiseptic cream for cuts as flies can spread infections, and insect repellent as mosquitoes can make life a misery and may carry malaria. Mosquito coils and plug-in machines with tablets are available in most pharmacies.

Common health complaints In Egypt, the major health risk is diarrhea, caused by eating contaminated fruit or vegetables, or drinking contaminated water. Stay away from ice (though some is made with bottled water), uncooked food and unpasteurized milk and milk products, and drink only bottled water or water that has been boiled for at least 20 minutes. Eat fruit only if you have peeled it yourself. Mild cases may respond to Imodium (known generally as loperamide), Pepto-Bismol (not as strong) or paregoric, another anti-diarrheal agent. All are available over the counter.

In severe cases, rehydrate yourself with a sugar-salt solution (½ teaspoon salt and 4 tablespoons sugar per quart of water), and refrain from eating.

Hospitals In emergencies, these private hospitals are recommended (a cash deposit may be requested): the **Anglo-American Hospital** beside the Cairo Tower, Gezira (tel: 02/341-8630) and **As-Salaam International Hospital**, Corniche el-Nil, Maadi (tel: 524-0250/0077).

Pharmacies Pharmacists usually speak English and are happy to recommend remedies for minor complaints. They stock a wide range of medicines, which are cheap and available over the counter. Check expiration dates. Some pharmacies, like the ones on **26th July Street** and **Sharia Brazil** in Zamalek (Cairo), have more expensive imported medicines. Also in Cairo, try **Ataba**, 17 Midan el-Ataba (24 hours) or **Isaaf**, 3 26th July Street, Bulaq (24 hours).

Providing water is an act of charity in a hot country

Other information

Camping

Egypt is not an obvious place for camping, as campsites, mainly found along the coast and in the oases, often lack proper facilities and shade. The camps attached to hotels are slightly better and at least provide showers and toilets in the hotel. Before camping on a beach check with the local police and be aware that many isolated beaches are still mined (see page 221). Camping in the desert is less problematic but if you camp somewhere near water, the land is sure to belong to someone, so again ask for permission to avoid getting into trouble later.

Children

Egyptians just love children and wherever you decide to go, your children will be welcome, too. You may find a restaurant comes to a standstill as all the waiters are cooing over your blue-eyed darling, and people will stop you in the street to kiss the baby. Five-star and some four-star hotels provide high-chairs and cribs, and they can usually arrange for babysitters. You may find that their attitude toward safety is different from yours, so explain clearly what you expect. You will need to take particular care of your child's hygiene, as children are even more prone to stomach bugs and other infections, and do bring a sun block (hard to find in Egypt) as the strong sun is dangerous for their skin. Disposable diapers and powdered milk can be found in most pharmacies, and baby food is sold in the bigger cities.

Children will enjoy walking in the bazaar, playing hide-and-seek in

Don't worry about the children—Egyptians will keep them entertained

temples, riding in a horse cart or on a camel, or sailing along the Nile in a felucca. In Cairo there are a few special attractions for children:

Cairo Puppet (Arayis) Theater, Midan el-Ataba in Ezbekiya Gardens, downtown (tel: 02/591-0954); open October–May, daily performances at 6:30 PM, and also at 11 AM Friday and Saturday.

Cairo Zoo, Giza; open daily 8:30–4:30 PM (avoid Fridays when it is very crowded); small admission fee.

Dr. Ragab's Pharaonic Village, Jacob Island, Corniche el-Nil, 1 mile south of Giza Bridge; open daily 9–5 (winter), 9–9 (summer); admission fee for children over age 6 and adults. tel: 02/571-8675.

Sinbad Amusement Park, near the airport; open daily 5 PM–2 AM in summer, 2–11 PM in winter, on Fridays open from 10 AM; admission fee for children and adults.

Clothing
Bring a few warm woolens, as well as lighter cotton clothes in fall, spring, and winter, as the temperature drops considerably once the sun has gone. In summer you will need light cotton clothes and a sweater for some cooler nights. However hot it gets, try to dress modestly and avoid shorts, sleeveless T-shirts, and transparent clothes. Take walking shoes for walking around the sights. A sun hat and sunglasses are essential.

Electricity
Electrical current is 220 volts AC and sockets take the standard European two-pin plug.

Opening times
In general, shops and department stores are open from 9–1 and 5–9. Stores in tourist centers may open later and stay open all day until 10 PM. Some stores close on Fridays, but most close on Sundays. Museums are usually open daily from 9–4 and most of them close for Friday prayers from 11–1. During Ramadan the timetable changes again: most museums will close around 3 PM and shops will close around 3 but reopen from 8–10 PM or later. For banks see Money matters, pages 256–257.

CONVERSION CHARTS

FROM	TO	MULTIPLY BY
Inches	Centimeters	2.54
Centimeters	Inches	0.3937
Feet	Meters	0.3048
Meters	Feet	3.2810
Yards	Meters	0.9144
Meters	Yards	1.0940
Miles	Kilometers	1.6090
Kilometers	Miles	0.6214
Acres	Hectares	0.4047
Hectares	Acres	2.4710
Gallons	Liters	4.5460
Liters	Gallons	0.2200
Ounces	Grams	28.35
Grams	Ounces	0.0353
Pounds	Grams	453.6
Grams	Pounds	0.0022
Pounds	Kilograms	0.4536
Kilograms	Pounds	2.205
Tons	Tonnes	0.9057
Tonnes	Tons	1.104

MEN'S SUITS							
US	36	38	40	42	44	46	48
UK	36	38	40	42	44	46	48
International	46	48	50	52	54	56	58

DRESS SIZES						
US	6	8	10	12	14	16
UK	8	10	12	14	16	18
France	36	38	40	42	44	46
Italy	38	40	42	44	46	48
International	34	36	38	40	42	44

MEN'S SHIRTS						
US	14	14.5	15	15.5	16	16.5	17
UK	14	14.5	15	15.5	16	16.5	17
International	36	37	38	39/40	41	42	43

MEN'S SHOES						
US	8	8.5	9.5	10.5	11.5	12
UK	7	7.5	8.5	9.5	10.5	11
International	41	42	43	44	45	46

WOMEN'S SHOES						
US	6	6.5	7	7.5	8	8.5
UK	4.5	5	5.5	6	6.5	7
International	38	38	39	39	40	41

267

Photography

Egypt is a photographer's paradise and the light is magical. As it is usually bright outside, slow film speeds like 100 ASA or 64 ASA are recommended. Photography in most museums and sights is allowed but you will need to buy a special ticket, and even then it is forbidden to use a flash so you will need at least 400 ASA film, which is hard to find in Egypt. Brand-name films are widely available in the tourist areas, but anything more specialized will need to be brought from abroad. Check the sell-by date as it may be old, sun-bleached stock. Film can now be processed in one or two hours in most tourist centers, but if you are a perfectionist it's better to wait until you get home, as films may get scratched or fogged.

It is forbidden to photograph bridges, airports, train stations, government buildings, dams, or anything that Egyptians consider important to their security. Ask permission first or they may confiscate your film. Always ask people before taking their picture as some, especially villagers, religious people, and women, may find it offensive.

Places of worship

Cairo and Alexandria both have several Catholic, Greek Orthodox, Protestant, and Coptic churches, as well as Jewish synagogues. The following places in Cairo have services in English; times are listed in *Egypt Today* magazine.

Come prepared to take plenty of photographs …

St. Andrew's United Church (Protestant/International): 38 26th July Street, Bulaq (tel: 02/360-3527)
St. Joseph's Roman Catholic Church: 2 Sharia Bank Misr, downtown (tel: 02/393-6677)
All Saints' Cathedral (Anglican/Episcopal): 5 Sharia Michel Lutfallah (near the Marriott Hotel), Zamalek (tel: 02/341-8391)
Jewish Synagogue: Sharia Adly, downtown (check here for information on services)

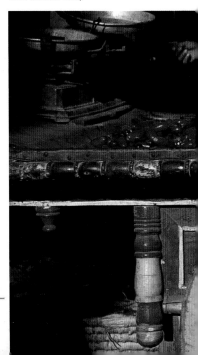

Tipping or Baksheesh

In Egypt you are a *khawaga* (foreigner) and *khawagas* are always rich, so they are supposed to have *baksheesh* (literally: share wealth) for everyone. It is obvious that you tip a waiter, a porter, or a taxi driver, but the guard who opens a tomb or switches on the light "specially for you," or the friendly man who wants to show you a "special" mosque will also expect *baksheesh*. Children whose picture you took and even people who didn't do anything at all will ask for it, and alms for the poor are called *baksheesh*, too. It can be an annoyance as it will seem everyone wants something from you, but it is very much part of the culture. It is best to get used to paying something if someone makes your life easier—indeed, this form of bribery is often necessary to get something done—but resist giving it, apart from alms, to people who haven't done anything but are asking you because you are a *khawaga*.

Toilets

Public toilets, be it the squatting, sitting or stand-up type, are often filthy and do not provide toilet paper but a bucket of water or a squirter to splash yourself with. If you want to avoid these, look for toilets in the upscale hotels or restaurants.

Visitors with disabilities

There are no special facilities for people with disabilities and to visit the major sights may prove a real challenge, but it will be a rewarding one. Egyptians accept disabilities as God's will and are always ready to help out. If arrangements are made beforehand it should be possible to see a lot of Egypt. Check with your national support organisation before departure, who usually offer advice on traveling.

Women travelers

Some Egyptian men are convinced that foreign women come to Egypt to have sex, and their attentions can be annoying. The most important thing you can do is to dress modestly. Wear loose clothes, such as a long shirt over a long skirt or baggy pants, covering arms, legs, and curves. Be confident when you walk in the streets, don't react to verbal obscenities but shout as soon as someone touches you, and if you are dressed properly people will come to your aid. In public places, such as buses, there is often a section reserved for women. If not, sit near other women who will often protect you if there is any hassle.

... subjects are many and varied

EGYPTIAN TOURIST OFFICES
Abroad
Canada: Place Bonaventure, 40 Frontenac, P.O. Box 304, Montreal, Québec H5A IB4 (tel: 014/861-4420)
U.K. & Ireland: Egyptian House, 170 Piccadilly, London W1 (tel: 020-7493 5282; fax: 020-7408 0295)
U.S.A.: 630 Fifth Avenue, Suite 1706, New York, NY 10111 (tel: 212/332-2570; fax: 242/95664)

In Egypt
Don't expect to get too much help or information from tourist offices in Egypt, though they are a good place to check for the official rates of taxis, excursions, and *feluccas*.
Local tourist offices include:
Alexandria: Midan Saad Zaghlul (tel: 03/480-7985); Misr Station (tel: 03/492-5985)
Aswan: Corniche el-Nil, in the shopping arcade behind the little park at the northern end of the Corniche (tel: 097/323297)
Cairo: 5 Sharia Adly, downtown (tel: 02/391-3454); Pyramids of Giza, Giza (tel: 02/383-8823); Train station, Sharia Ramses, Ramses (tel: 02/579-0767); Cairo International

270

Airport, terminal 2 (tel: 02/291-4255 ext. 2223)
Hurghada: Sharia Bank Misr, beyond the Sheraton (tel: 065/446513)
el-Kharga (New Valley): Sharia el-Nasser, near the Fellahin Monument (tel: 092/901611)
Luxor: Corniche el-Nil, between the temple and the Winter Palace (tel: 095/383294) and at the airport (tel: 095/372215)
Port Said: Sharia Filasteen (tel: 066/235289)

Online
http://www.idsc.gov.eg/tourism is Egypt's tourism net, a directory of hotels, transportation, agents, etc.
http://interoz.com/egypt is the Ministry of Tourism's site.
http://163.121.10.41/tourism is the address of Egypt Has It All, a key to tourist attractions.
http://www.cairocafe.com.ep is a site devoted to what's on in Cairo, with restaurants, galleries, and nightlife.
http://Pharos.bv.edu/Egypt/Home.html is Egypt's worldwide web index.

The Alexandrian Mosque of Abu el-Abbas el-Mursi

Accommodations & Restaurants

ACCOMMODATIONS

$	= under $40
$$	= $40–100
$$$	= over $100

CAIRO
The telephone code for Cairo is 02.

Atlas Zamalek Hotel ($$)
20 Sharia Gama'a el-Duwal el-Arabiya,
Mohandeseen tel: 346-5782 fax: 347-6958
This modern and comfortable hotel has business facilities, a small swimming pool, and popular discotheque called Tamango.. Although it is some distance from downtown, it is close to restaurants and Western-style shopping.

Berlin Hotel ($)
4th floor, 2 Shawarby, off Sharia Qasr an-Nil
Downtown tel/fax: 395-7502
email: berlinhotelcairo@hotmail.com
Clean, air-conditioned rooms with shower are available in this hotel, in a relatively quiet backstreet of downtown Cairo. The owner is friendly and English-speaking.

Cairo Marriott ($$$)
Sharia Saraya el-Gezira, Zamalek
tel: 340-8888 fax: 340-6667
email: marriott@utsec3.com.eg
The main building is the splendid Gezira Palace, built to commemorate the opening of the Suez Canal (1869). Rooms are in two adjacent high-rises, but the hotel has retained some of the regal atmosphere. The Garden Promenade is a great place to recover from the Cairene heat and beat.

Conrad International Hotel ($$$)
1191 Corniche an-Nil Boulaq Maspero
tel: 580-8000 fax: 580-8080
email: conrad7@intouch.com
This is the most luxurious hotel in town with sweeping views over Cairo and the Nile. It is next door to the World Trade Center and within easy reach of downtown and Zamalek.

Cosmopolitan ($$)
1 Sharia Ibn Taalab, downtown
tel: 392 3845 fax: 393-3531
The Cosmopolitan is a grand art-nouveau building in a quiet backwater in the middle of downtown. All rooms are refurbished and offer all appliances, good value, and nostalgia with a capital N.

Flamenco ($$)
2 Sharia el-Gezira el-Wusta, Zamalek
tel: 340-0815 fax: 340-0812
email: flamencohtl@flamenco.com.eg
A modern Spanish-run hotel, the Flamenco offers spacious rooms, some overlooking the river and, on a clear day, the pyramids. There is a good Spanish restaurant.

Garden City House ($)
23 Sharia Kamal el-Din Saleh, Garden City
tel: 354-4969
The basic rooms are large and clean, some with a view of the Nile. Half board is compulsory, but the food is pleasant and breakfast conversations with resident archeologists and scholars are interesting. Reservations are a must.

Horus House ($$)
21 Sharia Ismail Muhammad, Zamalek
tel: 340-3977
This very friendly and clean hotel is in the heart of Zamalek, and also rents a few apartments for longer stays. People usually come back to this hotel or stay for awhile, so reservations are necessary. The restaurant serves cheap and good *prix fixe* lunches.

Al-Husayn ($)
Midan el-Husayn, Khan el-Khalili
tel: 591-8664
Definitely the best hotel in the old part of town, the Al-Husayn has clean but very basic rooms with good views over the medieval city. During religious festivals it is practically impossible to sleep because the party goes on all night.

Ismailiya House ($)
7th floor, 1 Midan Tahrir, downtown
tel: 356-3122
In this popular backpackers' hotel, rooms and dormitories are adequate. There is MTV and an excellent laundry service. The hotel overlooks the noisy Tahrir. It is best to book well in advance.

Lotus ($)
12 Sharia Talaat Harb, downtown
tel: 575-0627 fax: 575-4720
The staff are friendlyand the rooms are clean here. Some rooms have a bath and air conditioning. The Lotus has a good central location.

Mayfair ($)
9 Sharia Aziz Osman, Zamalek tel: 340-7315
The Mayfair has quiet, pastel rooms with balconies overlooking a tree-lined street. It has a relaxed, old-fashioned atmosphere, and a cafeteria on a pleasant terrace.

Mena House Oberoi ($$$)
Pyramids Road, Giza tel: 383-3222
fax: 383-7777 email: obmhobc@oberoi.com.eg
This is the hotel with The View: the Pyramids of Giza. Set in a 19th-century khedival hunting lodge with a splendid old wing; rooms here are deluxe, decorated with taste and some antiques. There is a less impressive modern wing in the garden. The swimming pool also has a pyramids' view and there is a fine Indian restaurant.

Mövenpick Heliopolis ($$$)
Cairo International Airport Road, Heliopolis
tel: 247-0077 fax: 418-0761
email: @movenpickhel.com.eg
The Mövenpick Heliopolis has a convenient location just outside the airport. This hotel offers good food and excellent service.

Nile Hilton ($$$)
Corniche el-Nil, downtown
tel: 578044/0666 fax: 578-0475
email: rhilton@brainy1.ie-eg.com
This was the first modern international hotel built in Egypt, opened by Nasser in 1959. Located in the heart of Cairo, next door to the Egyptian Museum and overlooking the Nile, it has become an institution in the city. Wealthy Cairenes and expatriates meet in the Ibis Café, Jacky's nightclub is one of the city's best, the casino is crowded till the early hours, and there are several other restaurants as well as the Taverne du Champ de Mars, a *fin de siècle* café imported from Brussels. There is also a pleasant swimming pool.

Odeon Palace ($–$$)
6 Sharia Abdel Hamid Said, downtown
tel/fax: 577-6637
This modern hotel has clean, no-nonsense rooms and friendly staff. The pleasant bar on the roof terrace is popular with local intellectuals and foreign correspondents.

Pension Roma ($)
169 Sharia Muhammad Farid, downtown
tel/fax: 391-1088
The best budget hotel in town has a Moorish façade and 1940s atmosphere. Clean, large rooms have high ceilings. Advance booking is advised.

President ($$)
22 Sharia Taha Husayn, Zamalek
tel: 340-0652 fax: 361-0874
A friendly, modern, good value hotel with good business facilities, the President is in a quiet, residential area close to shops and restaurants. The extremely popular Cellar Bar downstairs serves good *mezze* (appetizers).

Saqqara Country Club and Hotel ($$)
Saqqara Rd to Abu el-Nomros, Saqqara
tel: 384-6115 fax: 385-0577
This well-run hotel in the vibrant green countryside near the Saqqara necropolis, has excellent stables and riding facilities. You can obtain temporary club membership from reception.

Saqqara Palm Club ($$)
Saqqara Road, Badrashein
tel: 200791 fax: 201187
A small hotel, this is the perfect antidote to Cairo's crowds and pollution. Rooms are comfortable and there is a pool set in lush palm-shaded gardens. Far from central Cairo, but excellent for exploring Memphis, Saqqara, and Giza.

Tulip ($)
3 Midan Talaat Harb, downtown
tel: 393 9433
Another favorite old-style hotel, this has basic, clean rooms with bath; those iat front have a good view over the bustling square but tend to be noisy. Reservations are a must.

Victoria Hotel ($$)
66 Sharia el-Gumhuriya, Ramses
tel: 589-2290 fax: 591-3008
A renovated 1930s hotel with polished mahogany furniture and air conditioning, the Victoria has a pleasant terrace.

Windsor ($–$$)
19 Sharia el-Alfy, downtown tel: 591-5277
fax: 592-1621
Despite faded, high-ceilinged rooms with old wooden furniture and out-of-place posters of Austria, this is one of the only hotels that still feels like Cairo as it used to be, and a favorite for many who know the city. Book in advance. The lounge bar is wonderful—even more faded and old-fashioned!

LOWER NILE VALLEY

Asyut
Badr Hotel ($)
Sharia el-Thallaga tel/fax: 088/329811
This middle-range hotel is decorated in notorious bad taste. Rooms have fridge, and VCR, and at least one has TV. The only real restaurant in town, but it's expensive for what is to be had.

el-Faiyum
Auberge du Faiyum ($$)
Lake Qarun tel: 084/700002 or
Cairo reservation: 02/350-2356 fax: 700730
This former lodge of King Farouk offers pleasant rooms overlooking the lake. The hotel is slightly run down.

Montazah ($)
Sharia Ismail el-Medani tel: 084/328662
A simple hotel, the Montazah is more or less clean, and in the north part of town. Sometimes hot water and fans are available.

New Panorama Shakshuk ($$)
Qarun Lake tel: 084/701746
fax: 084/701757
This is the best resort hotel in the oasis, with modern air-conditioned rooms that have balconies overlooking the lake. Sports facilities include duck shooting, fishing, swimming, wind surfing and water skiing.

Oasis Motel ($)
Lake Qarun tel: 084/701565
This motel has very basic accommodations. It is on the lakeside, and staff are friendly.

Minya
Beach Hotel (el-Shati) ($)
31 Sharia el-Gumhuriya tel: 086/322307
fax: 086/366467   '
Clean and carpeted rooms are a feature here. There are fans or air conditioning.

Lotus ($)
1 Sharia Port Said tel: 086/324541
fax: 324576
Rooms in the Lotus have fans. The top-floor bar and restaurant, overlooking the Nile and valley, are good for dinner or just for a beer.

Mercure Nefertiti & Aton ($$)
Sharia Corniche el-Nil tel: 086/341515
fax: 366467
This is the most comfortable hotel in town, often used by tour groups. Slightly out of the center, it has good views over the Nile, and a swimming pool. Rooms may be noisy on Thursday nights when there is usually at least one wedding party taking place in the hotel.

Nag Hammadi
Aluminium Hotel ($$)
40km from Abydos tel/fax: 096/581320
This comfortable, but ugly, Soviet-style hotel, is part of an aluminum smelting plant. It is an ideal base for visiting the temples of Abydos and Dendara if the area is safe.

LUXOR
The telephone code for Luxor is 095.

Amon el-Gazira ($)
Geziret el-Bairat, West Bank (near the ferry landing, left at the Mobil petrol station)
tel: 095/310912
The Amon el-Gazira is a friendly, family-run hotel set amidst lush sugar cane fields. Rooms are very clean (with and without private bathrooms). The roof terrace has marvelous views over the West Bank, and there is a lovely garden where breakfast is served. Book in advance.

Accommodations and Restaurants

Club Med Belladonna ($$)
Sharia Khaled Ibn Walid tel: 380914
email: sales@cmme.com.eg
This is a traditional Club-Med style hotel in an Arabesque décor. The pleasant swimming pool overlooks the Nile, and there is a popular nightclub.

Emilio ($$)
Sharia Yusuf Hasan tel: 373570
Popular with tour groups, the Emilio has a rooftop swimming pool with breezy views over Luxor town and temple. Advance booking is recommended.

Habu Hotel ($)
opposite the Temple of Medinat Habu, Nag Lolah, West Bank tel: 372477
The rooms here are basic with traditional blue wash. A large terrace overlooks the temple and garden. This is strongly recommended if Luxor gets to you, or if you want to stay awhile and relax.

Horus ($)
Sharia el-Maabad, opposite Luxor Temple
tel: 372165
Modern, simple and clean rooms have air conditioning and spectacular views over the temple from the front. The back hangs over the *souk* (market).

Luxor Hilton ($$$)
New Karnak tel: 095/374933
fax: 095/376571
email: luxhitw@brainy1.ie-eg.com
This well-run hotel is on the northern outskirts of town, with rooms overlooking the Nile and gardens. A sundeck and heated swimming pool overlook the river. There are several good restaurants and a free courtesy bus into downtown.

Mercure Luxor ($$$)
Corniche el-Nil tel: 380944 fax: 374912
A four-star hotel, this offers all facilities and a heated swimming pool. Sip your aperitif at sunset on the front terrace. Rooms have views over the Nile and the Theban Hills.

Mersam ($)
Known as Sheikh Ali's Hotel, near the Noble Tombs, West Bank tel: 372403
Basic but pleasant mud-brick rooms have fans. There is a quiet garden. Sheikh Ali, who helped excavate Seti I's tomb, is one of the Abdul Rassul family, once notorious tomb robbers, but his son is now happy just to show people around.

Mina Palace ($)
Corniche el-Nil, opposite visitors' center
tel: 372074 email: mpluxor@intouch.com
The good-value rooms have air conditioning, TV, new bathrooms, and views over the Nile and Luxor Temple. A pleasant roof terrace serves cool beers.

Mövenpick Jolie Ville ($$$)
3mi. out of town, Crocodile Island
tel: 374855 fax: 374936
This is one of the best resort hotels in Egypt with deluxe bungalows set in beautiful gardens beside the Nile. Wonderful food is served in several restaurants, there is an excellent swimming pool, children's activities and zoo, and—above all—immaculate service. Recommended for a longer rest after seeing tombs and temples.

New Windsor ($$)
Sharia Nefertiti tel:
This modern hotel between the *souk* and the Nile, has a health club, and swimming pool on the roof. There is a good international phone and fax office.

Pharaoh's ($)
Between the ticket office and the Temple of Medinat Habu, Nag Lolah, West Bank
tel: 374924 fax: 376477
Slightly more stylish than other hotels this side of the river, Pharaoh's has clean rooms with air conditioning or fan, some with views of the temple. There is an Oriental restaurant and a beer garden.

Philippe ($)
Sharia Nefertiti tel: 372284 fax: 580060
This very well-run hotel has a roof garden. Rooms are clean with bathroom and air conditioning, views over the Nile and excellent atmosphere. The Phiippe is good value, so book in advance.

Sofitel Old Winter Palace ($$$)
Sharia Corniche el-Nil tel: 380422 fax: 374087
A beautiful and impressive building whose pretensions are let down by the service, the Old Winter Palace's ideal guest is someone with more money than taste. Only stay here if you have an exaggerated sense of romance. The new wing next door has modern facilities but no charm.

UPPER EGYPT AND NUBIA

Abu Simbel
Nefertari ($$)
Abu Simbel tel/fax: 097/400508/9
Between the temple and the airport, this hotel has clean, air-conditioned rooms, swimming pool, and tennis courts for those who brave the heat. Ideal if you want to watch the sun rise over the temple.

Nobaleh Ramses ($$)
Tourist City, Abu Simbel tel/fax: 097/400380
Less pleasant than the Nefertari, this state-run hotel is nearer to the temple.

Aswan
The telephone code in the Aswan area is 097.

Amoun ($$),
Amoun Island tel: 313800 fax: 317190
This Club Med resort, on its own island with a free ferry from the Corniche, overlooks Elephantine Island and the Old Cataract Hotel on one side, and the desert and more Nile on the other. It is small, but a great place to relax with good-size rooms, a pleasant swimming pool, and tasty meals. Recommended, and cheaper in summer.

Aswan Oberoi ($$$)
Elephantine Island tel: 314667 fax: 313538
The ugly tower of the hotel, which once supported a panoramic restaurant, has become a landmark. There are good views, efficient service, luxurious rooms, and an excellent swimming pool. A mock-pharaonic boat is used as a ferry to the Corniche.

Basma ($$–$$$)
In front of the Nubian Museum, Sharia el-Fanadik tel: 310901 fax: 310907
email: sst@ritsec1.com.eg
This is a newish resort hotel, decorated by two Egyptian artists. There is a beautiful pool to relax by in the patio.

Cleopatra ($$)
Sharia Sa'ad Zaghlul tel: 324001 fax: 314002
The Cleopatra has refurbished rooms with air conditioning, business facilities, and a swimming pool on the roof. The hotel is central with good views.

274

Horus ($)
98 Corniche el-Nil tel: 323323 fax: 313313
This popular, cheap hotel has basic rooms, some with a noisy air conditioner and a view of the Nile. There is a quite pleasant bar on the roof.

Kalabsha ($$)
tel: 302666 fax: 325974
The Kalabsha is next door to the two Cataract hotels. The rooms are modest, clean and comfortable. Guests can use the Cataract swimming pool.

Ramses ($)
Sharia Abtal el-Tahrir tel: 324000
A new building in the center of Aswan, this hotel is good value. Rooms are adequate with air conditioning, private bath, telephone, and views over the Nile.

Sofitel Cataract ($$$)
Sharia Abtal el-Tahrir, next to the Ferial Gardens tel: 316001 fax: 316011
This is one of the most romantic hotels in Egypt, now refurbished in the old style. The spacious rooms on the Nile side have splendid views over the river and the islands. The swimming pool is set in beautiful, perfumed gardens and breakfast is served by the friendly staff on your balcony or in the impressive Moorish Hall. For a splurge, stay in the vast Agatha Christie suite or in King Farouk's.

Idfu (Edfu)
Dar as-Salam ($)
Sharia el-Maglis, next to the Temple of Horus.
This very basic hotel is used by market traders. The cleanest hotel in town, it has the luxury of hot showers.

Kom Ombo
Cleopatra ($)
Near the service-taxi stop tel: 097/ 500325
The rooms, with fans, are not always clean and the bathrooms less so. Only stay here if you must.

WESTERN DESERT OASES
The telephone code for the New Valley Oases is 088; Siwa is 046.

Bahariya
Alpenblick ($)
Behind the police station, el-Bawiti.
This friendly hotel has an exotic name for its location, along with basic but clean rooms with shared bathrooms. The owner organizes trips to the springs and the White Desert and can tell you all you want to know about Bahariya.

El-Beshmo Lodge ($)
el-Bawiti, Bahariya tel/fax 802117
By far the most pleasant hotel in town (a 10-minute walk from the main street), this lodge is on the edge of a beautiful palm grove right opposite the Roman hot spring of the same name. The rooms are quite simple but spotless and comfortable with private or shared bathrooms.

Dakhla
Gardens ($)
Beside Hamdy's restaurant in Qasr
tel: 821577
Here you will find basic, clean rooms. All have mosquito screens and shared bathrooms.

Mebarez ($)
On the main road to Farafra, Mut
tel/fax: 821524
Modern, clean, and friendly, the Mebarez's rooms have fans and bathrooms, and breakfast is included. This is by far the best place to stay in Mut.

Mut Talata ($$)
between Mut and al-Qasr tel: 821530
This is a new three-star hotel with rooms, chalets and canvas tents all decorated with lack of style, but comfortable. A pleasant pool takes its water from the nearby warm spring.

Farafra
El Badawiyya Safari and Hotel ($)
main street, Farafra Reservations via Cairo
tel: 02/345-8524.
A rather impressive hotel for the isolated oases, this is owned by local Bedouin Saad and his brothers, but under Swiss management. Designed in a modern interpretation of the traditional mudbrick architecture, the rooms are domed and have private or shared bathrooms. Book well in advance.

Rest House One and Two ($)
Qasr Farafra.
Both rest houses offer spartan and fairly clean dormitories and, usually, cold running water.

275

Kharga
Hamad Alla ($)
Sharia Nada, off Sharia Nasser tel: 920638 fax: 925017
The clean rooms have private showers and fans (some with air conditioning). Service is friendly.

Kharga Oasis Hotel ($)
tel: 921500
This modern characterless structure has well-kept rooms (some with air conditioning). There is a lovely palm-shaded garden and a popular terrace.

Pioneers Hotel ($$$)
Kharga tel: 092/927982 fax: /927983
The recently opened Pioneers is the first four-star hotel in the oasis. The building looks rather detached from its surroundings (it is salmon pink) but the rooms are comfortable, air-conditioned and have satellite TV. Same owners as the three-star Mut Talata in Dakhla (tel: 092/821530).

Siwa
Adrere Amellal ($$$)
(just outside Siwa) tel: (in Cairo) 02/340-0052 fax: 02/341-3331
This blissful and expensive eco-lodge is built in traditional Siwan style with a natural spring pool and simple, comfortable rooms lit by oil lamps. Excellent food is served fresh from the organic farm. A new experience in Egypt, and recommended.

Palm Trees ($)
(off the main square) tel: 460-2204
A popular hotel, Palm Trees offers clean rooms equipped with hot water, fans and mosquito screens. There is a pleasant palm-shaded garden.

Siwa Safari Paradise ($$)
Siwa town tel: 046/460-2289/90 fax: 046/460-2286
Set in an idyllic palm grove, this hotel has clean and comfortable rooms, if rather on the tacky side. The architecture is less than inspiring.

ALEXANDRIA AND THE DELTA

Alexandria
The telephone code for Alexandria is 03.

Acropole ($)
*27 Rue Chambre de Commerce
tel: 480-5980*
A top-floor neighbor to the famous Cecil Hotel, haunt of royalty and stars, the popular Acropole has clean, simple rooms with high ceilings, old wood furniture, shared bathrooms, and an elevator that works most days. It is still run by Greeks, so you might get a sense of Alexandria of yesteryear. Book ahead.

Agamy Palace ($$)
el-Bittash Beach tel: 433-0230 or 433-0386
Spacious rooms with balconies overlooking the beach and a swimming pool make this a popular though run-down escape from noisy and crowded Alexandria.

Ailema ($)
21 Sharia Amin Fikry tel: 484-7011
Tucked away in a side street, the Ailema has basic, clean, old-style rooms, some with balconies overlooking the bay and Ramla tram station. It is a little quieter than most hotels in the area. The hotel restaurant does not serve alcohol.

Sofitel Alexandria Cecil ($$$)
*Midan Sa'ad Zaghlul tel: 483-7173
fax: 483-6401*
Alexandria's most famous hotel boasts names like Lawrence Durrell, Noel Coward, and Somerset Maugham in its guest book. Now run by Sofitel, it's no longer glamorous but is still the place to stay. Seaside rooms have magnificent views over the eastern harbor and the sweeping Corniche up to Qaytbay Fort. The coffee shop is a good place to hang out in the early evening; the new roof garden is perfect for sunset-watching with sea breezes at the end of a hot day.

El-Salamlik San Giovanni ($$$)
*Muntazah Palace gardens
tel: 547-7999 fax:547-3585
email: salamlek@sangiovanni.com*
Sleep in princely style in this small luxurious hotel, an Italianate chateau, once the guesthouse of the Muntazah Palace.

Paradise Inn Metropole ($$)
*52 Sharia Sa'ad Zaghlul tel: 482-1465
fax: 482-2040*
This period hotel has undergone a complete refurbishment, but retains much of its charm and is highly recommended. All rooms have high ceilings and old wooden furniture; some have sea views, and also noise from the tram station. The airy breakfast room has wonderful art-nouveau décor. This is a contender with the Cecil for the best central hotel. Reservations are advised.

Helnan Palestine ($$$)
*Montazah Palace tel: 547-3500 fax: 547-3378
email: neshp@helnan.com*
Not as old as the Cecil, but almost as much of an institution, this hotel's relaxing atmosphere makes it popular with Egyptian and expatriate families on weekends and holidays. All rooms have balconies overlooking the Mediterranean and/or Montazah gardens. The beach is cleaner than most.

San Giovanni ($$)
*205 Sharia al-Geish tel: 546-7775
fax: 546-4480*
Away from the center but near Sidi Gaber station, this mid-range hotel has sweeping views over Stanley Bay.

Sea Star (formerly Admiral) ($)
24 Sharia Amin Fikry tel: 483-1787
The rooms here are clean, comfortable, and modernized. This hotel is good value.

Windsor ($$)
*17 Sharia el-Shohada tel: 480-8123
fax: 418-9090*
This old hotel lost much of its old-world charm when it added modern conveniences. Some rooms have good views over the Corniche and sea.

Damietta
Al-Manshy ($)
*5 Sharia el-Nokrashy tel: 057/323308
fax: 333400*
The Al-Manshy is one of the only hotels in town, mostly of interest to bird-watchers. Most visitors prefer to stay in nearby Ras el-Bahr.

Mersa Matruh
Beau Site ($$)
*6 Sharia Osman Ahmed Osman
tel: 03/932011 or 932012*
A very popular Greek-run family hotel, the Beau Site has its own private beach. The addition of two towers has spoiled the beauty of the site, and made the beach crowded, but you'll find friendly service and good food. Full board is compulsory.

Negresco ($$)
Corniche tel: 493-3605 fax: 493-3960.
Rooms here are clean and adequate, some with a view over the sea. Half board can be compulsory in summer.

Reem ($)
Corniche tel: 493-4420
Spotless rooms with a balcony overlooking the Mediterranean Sea.

Sidi Abd al-Rahman
Alamein ($$)
*Sidi Abd el-Rahman tel: 03/492-1228
fax: 492-1232*
One of the best hotels west of Alexandria, this isolated, four-star resort with a beautiful private beach is often booked well in advance in summer. The restaurant is not very good, but it the only place to eat in the vicinity.

CANAL ZONE AND RED SEA COAST

Hurghada
The telephone code for Hurghada and El-Gouna, 12 miles north, is 065.

El-Giftun Village ($$)
Hurghada center tel: 442665 fax: 442666
A traditional family resort popular with windsurfers, divers, and sunbathers, the village offers comfortable bungalows set on the beach. There are several bars and restaurants.

Golden Sun ($–$$)
Sharia Sheraton, Sigala tel: 444403
fax: 443862
This is friendly hotel is recommended. It offers good-sized very clean rooms. Staff are attentive- and there is attention for detail.

Happy Land ($)
Sharia el-Sheikh el-Sebak tel: 574373
The rooms at the Happy Land are simple and clean with fans. Transportationis available to the nearby private beach.

Intercontinental ($$$)
Sheraton Road, Hurghada tel. 446911
fax: 446910
One of many new chain resorts along this coast, the "Inter" stands out for standards of service and cooking that were unimaginable in Egypt a couple of years ago. There is an excellent pool, beach and sports facilities, including a PADI 5-star dive center.

Mashrabia Village ($$–$$$)
(south of the port) Sharia Sheraton
tel: 443330 fax: 443904.
This excellent four-star hotel is designed in a pseudo-Moorish style. There are several swimming pools and very good watersports.

Moon Valley Village ($)
Sharia Sheraton tel: 442811
A pleasant hotel with a lovely garden, the Moon Valley Village has views over the Red Sea. There is a small private beach across the road.

Shedwan ($$)
Sharia el-Corniche tel: 544007 fax: 548045
This is a popular hotel for diving package vaca-tions. There is a good beach and swimming pool and lively resort atmosphere.

El-Gouna

Dawar el-Omda ($$)
El-Gouna tel: 545060 fax: 545561
This lovely hotel is built in a modern interpretation of traditional Nile-valley architecture, with domes and many niches. The rooms are tastefully deco-rated with antiques and modern furniture designed by young Cairene designers. Recommended.

El-Khan ($–$$)
El-Gouna tel: 549701 fax: 549701
email: El-Khan-info@threecorners.com
A small but charming hotel with stylish rooms set around a peaceful courtyard, the El-Khan overlooks the lagoon. It is popular with young Cairenes.

Miramar Sheraton ($$$)
El-Gouna tel: 545606 fax: 545608
A sort of Disneyland on the Red Sea, this hotel was designed by the star-architect Michael Graves on several islands around a lagoon, facing the sea. Comprehensive watersports facilities are available and there is a golf course.

Mövenpick ($$$)
El Gouna Resort, 12 miles north of Hurghada
tel: 545160
email: resort.elgouna@movenpick.com.eg
This is the best of the large hotels in El Gouna, Egypt's newest and smartest resort. There is a choice of restaurants and bars, and the beachfront rooms, friendly and attentive staff and the regular shuttle bus to neighboring restaurants and shops make this one of Egypt's most relaxing seaside resorts.

Isma'iliya

Al-Salaam ($)
Sharia al-Geish tel: 064/324401
The spotless spacious rooms here have a bath. Some also have air conditioning and TV.

Mercure Ismailiya ($$)
Fursan Island, Isma'iliya tel: 064/765322
fax: 338042
This hotel has fairly luxurious air-conditioned rooms with private bath. it is set on a quiet, shady island.

Marsa Alam

Red Sea Diving Safari ($–$$)
at Marsa Shaqara, (20 km north of Marsa Alam) tel: 065/3399942 fax: 065/3494219
Environmentalist and diver Helmy started this small eco-friendly resort with spotlessly clean and comfortable tents, huts and chalets. It is mainly aimed at divers, but non-divers looking for peace and quiet will love it too.

Port Said

Hotel de la Poste ($)
42 Sharia Gumhuriya tel: 066/224048
This is another 1940s hotel and a reminder of grander days. Rooms are spacious but recently renovated.

Mereland ($)
off Sharia Saad Zaghloul and Sharia an-Nahda tel: 066/227020
This hotel offers large and immaculate rooms with private or shared bathroom. It is good value.

New Regent ($$)
15 Sharia Muhammad Mahmoud, off Sharia el-Gumhuriya tel: 066/235000 fax: 224891
The rooms are modern and air-conditioned with TV and bath. They lack the atmosphere of the now totally decayed Regent Hotel around the corner.

Helnan Port Said ($$$)
(on the beach front) tel: 066/320-511
fax: 066/324-825.
Spacious rooms are on offer here. All have good facilities and excellent views.

El-Quseir

Mangrove Bay Resort ($$)
(30 miles south of el-Quseir)
tel: 065/3486748 fax: 065/3605458
The Mangrove Bay is a quiet, simple but charming resort. Diving and snorkeling facilities are excellent.

Mövenpick Sirena Beach Quseir ($$$)
El-Ouadim Bay tel: 065/432100
fax: 065/432128
email: resort@moevenpick-qusir.com.eg
This blissfully peaceful hotel is harmoniously designed, with Nubian-style domed rooms and excellent service. It is a perfect retreat to get away from it all, listening to the lapping of the waves. Some of Egypt's best snorkeling and diving is available off the hotel's private beach.

Helnan Port Said Hotel ($$$)
El-Corniche, Port Said tel:066/320890
fax:/323762
Undoubtedly the best hotel in Port Said, this offers all facilities. Rooms are spacious, overlooking the sea and an excellent private beach.

277

Accommodations and Restaurants

Nora's Tourist Village ($$)
El-Corniche, Port Said tel:066/329834
fax:/329841
This popular tourist village offers comfortable
rooms overlooking the beach. Service is friendly
and the food is good.

Suez
Red Sea Hotel ($$)
13 Sharia Riyad, Port Tawfiq
tel: 062/334302 fax: 334301
This is the only decent place to stay in Suez.
Rooms are clean with views over the Bay of Suez.

SINAI

el-Arish
Egoth Oberoi ($$$)
Sharia el-Fateh, el-Arish tel: 064/351321
fax: 352352
With luxurious rooms on the beach and a swim-
ming pool for residents, this is the only five-star
hotel in town. It is also the only place selling alco-
hol—at wildly inflated prices—and often the only
place where foreigners stay.

Moonlight ($)
Sharia Fouad Zikry, el-Arish Beach tel: 341362
If you're looking for simple, inexpensive rooms,
this is the place. This hotel is just off the beach,
and some rooms have private bath.

Sinai Beach ($)
Sharia Fouad Zikry, el-Arish Beach
tel: 064/341713
This is a characterless, modern building. Rooms
are clean and air-conditioned, however, and
have balconies.

Dahab
Mirage Village ($)
(north of the lighthouse) tel: 062/640341
The Mirage Village is a friendly hotel and camp.
Rooms are clean and are equipped with a fan and
mosquito nets.

Nesima Hotel & Diving Centre ($$)
Mashraba tel: 062/640320
fax: 062/640321 email: nesima@intouch.com
A highly recommended, beautiful domed hotel, the
Nesima has simple but comfortable rooms and a
great relaxed atmosphere. There is an excellent
dive club, too.

Sphinx House ($)
Masbat tel: 062/640032
Here you will find adequate rooms with fans,
mosquito screens, and some with private bath and
air-conditioning. There is a good big pool and a
popular billiard table.

Nuweiba
Basata ($)
(14 miles north of Nuweiba) tel: 062/500481
or Cairo 02/350-1829
Basata means 'simplicity' in Arabic and this is
what visitors come for. The environment-friendly
camp offers basic bamboo huts or a place under
the stars on the beach. Guests recycle their
garbage and cook their food, some organically
grown on the spot, in the communal kitchen.
Book well in advance.

Elsebay Villagen ($)
Tarabin tel: 062/500373
This small well-kept hotel has spotless rooms all
with fan or air conditioning and private or shared
bathrooms.

Helnan Nuweiba ($$)
Nuweiba tel: 062/500401 fax: 500407
Air-conditioned bungalows with modern features,
are set in a garden. On the beach is a campsite
and clean huts with fans.

Hilton Coral Resort ($$$)
Nuweiba Port tel: 062/520320 fax: 520327
Currently Nuweiba's best hotel, the Hilton Coral
Resort serves good food. The beach is clean, and
water sports are available.

Al-Waha Tourist Village ($–$$)
Nuweiba tel/fax: 062/500420
These simple, clean, air-conditioned bungalows
are on the beach. There are also tents with the
use of hot showers.

St. Catherine
Monastery Hostel ($)
Monastery of St. Catherine
tel: 062/770221 or 770456
The rooms here are almost monastic, some with
showers. Gates close at 9:30 PM, but it's convenient for an early ascent. Three plain, solid
meals are included in the price. Book in advance
or check-in early morning.

St. Catherine Tourist Village ($$$)
Wadi el-Raha, St. Catherine (reservation in
Cairo, tel: 02/470333 fax: 470323)
This is an ugly, modern, deluxe complex, half a
mile from the monastery.

Sharm el Sheikh
The telephone code for Sharm el Sheikh is
062.

Camel Dive Club ($$)
Naama Bay tel: 600700 fax: 600601
This pleasant hotel has tastefully decorated rooms
attached to the excellent diving club. A beautiful
pool and a totally relaxed atmosphere provide a
welcome change from the other big resort hotels.

Clifftop Hotel ($$)
Sharm el Sheikh tel: 650251
The air-conditioned bungalows in a pleasant gar-
den are no longer modern, but the atmosphere is
peaceful and quiet.

Fayrouz Hilton Village ($$$)
Na'ama Bay tel: 600137 fax: 601040
email: fayrouz@sinainet.com.eg
Some of these luxurious bungalows have sea
views. All sports facilities, including stables for
horseback riding are provided on site. A delicious
pizza and pasta buffet is served in the Beach
BBQ restaurant.

Mövenpick Jolie Ville ($$$)
Na'ama Bay tel: 600100 fax: 600111
email: hotelmail@movenpicksharm.com
The classiest resort hotel in the area. Five-star,
air-conditioned bungalows are set in a beautiful
garden. There are two swimming pools, a good
beach and water sports, and a child-care facility.
Try the excellent restaurants, and the best disco
in the bay.

Pigeon House ($)
Na'ama Bay tel: 600996 fax: 600905
This is the least expensive place to stay with clean rooms. It is a good place to hang out if you want to go trekking with Bedouins.

Red Sea Diving College ($$)
Na'ama Bay tel: 600313 fax: 600312
email: college@sinainet.com.eg
The comfortable, air-conditioned rooms are usually rented to people on a diving course. The diving club is recommended.

Safety Land ($)
Sharm el Moya tel/fax: 600395
This is a camp with huts and tents. There is a private beach.

Sanafir ($$)
Na'ama Bay tel: 600197 fax: 600196
There is traditional architecture, a laid-back atmosphere, a good seafood restaurant and the hippest bar in town in this hotel run by an eccentric Egyptian. Motorbikes and horses are for rent. This is excellent value, so book in advance.

Shark Bay Camp ($–$$)
Shark Bay, 6 miles north of Na'ama Bay tel: 600943
This peaceful, excellent resort village has rooms, and tents on the beach. There are no sharks these days, but a beautiful coral reef.

Taba

Taba Hilton ($$$)
Taba Beach, Taba tel: 062/530300
A typical Hilton, the Taba is away from it all. This is a good place for a beach-only vacation.

RESTAURANTS

Cairenes dress up in a big way to go to an expensive restaurant and advance reservations are recommended. Inexpensive Egyptian restaurants tend to be for men only, but they usually have a family room at the back or upstairs, where couples or single women can eat in peace.
See also pages 100–103.

$	= under $15
$$	= $15–30
$$$	= over $30

Prices for a three-course meal for one person excluding alcoholic drinks and tips.

CAIRO

The telephone code for Cairo is 02.

Absolut ($$)
10 Midan Amman, Mohandiseen tel: 336-5583
The Absolut is one of the city's trendiest hangouts, serving good snacks, with loud funky music. The décor is contemporary Oriental and the clientele young, wealthy and beautiful.

Abu Shakra ($)
69 Sharia Qasr el-Aini, Garden City tel: 364-8111
Known as the best kebab and kofta place in town, meat is sold by weight here. Alcohol is not served.

Alfi Bey ($)
3 Sharia el-Alfy, downtown tel: 577-1888 or 577-4999
A wonderful, old-style albeit slightly faded restaurant with chandeliers, where over-helpful waiters serve traditional Egyptian and Levantine fare, but no alcohol.

Americana Fish Market ($$)
26 Sharia el-Nil, Giza tel: 570-9693
This excellent fish restaurant is in a large boat moored on the Nile. Choose your fresh fish or seafood from the 'Fish Market'—then tell chef how you want it cooked in the open kitchen. Salads are well prepared and the dessert trolley is a must.

Andrea ($–$$)
59–60 Marioutieh Canal, Giza tel: 383-1133
Try simple but excellent food (grills, vine leaves, salads) in a garden setting off Pyramids Road. Good for lunch when you're visiting the pyramids.

Arabesque ($$)
6 Sharia Qasr en-Nil, downtown tel: 574-7898
Oriental and continental specialties are served in a simple but classy décor. Popular with Egyptian film stars and French expatriates. The *mulukhiya* and *Umm Ali* are excellent.

Ataturk ($$)
20 Sharia Riyadh, off Sharia Shihab, Mohandiseen tel: 364-8811
A good selection of *mezze*, with vast slabs of hot, fresh bread is served in this cool but cozy Turkish restaurant. The entrées are include *hagi baba*, rice pilaf with veal liver and pine nuts, or *babas yakhni*, meat, potatoes, and vegetable stew.

Aubergine ($$)
5 Sharia Said el Bakri, Zamalek tel: 340-6550
This simple but good vegetarian bistro kitchen is known for its laid-back service and good jazz music. The upstairs bar, Curnonsky, is good for meaty snacks, a beer and a chance to eavesdrop foreign correspondents, who often hang out here.

Bua Khao ($$$)
9 Road151, Maadi tel: 340-6550
An excellent and very popular Thai restaurant, the Bua Khao serves authentic Thai cuisine. Check out their delicious crispy fried chicken with cashews and excellent dim sum.

Cairo Jazz Club ($–$$)
197 26th July Street, Agouza, opposite the Balloon Theatre tel: 345-9939
Lively, particularly late evening, the Cairo Jazz Club has live music every night—jazz, reggae, rock and even classical. Good *mezze*, salads and simple pastas are served in a dark, smoky atmosphere.

Cortigiano ($$)
44 Sharia Michel Bakhum, Dokki tel: 337-4938
Cortigiano is a pleasant Italian restaurant, filled with interesting antiques, that serves traditional Italian fare like thick pizzas and fresh pastas, as well as some French meat classics, and *soupe à l'oignon*.

Egyptian Pancake House ($)
Between Sharia el- Azhar and Midan el-Husayn.
Try the excellent but inexpensive *fateers* (Egyptian pizzas, sweet or savory) that are a specialty here. No alcohol is served.

279

Accommodations and Restaurants

Estoril ($$)
12 Sharia Talaat Harb (in the passage), downtown tel: 574-3102
Tucked away in a passage, Estoril has a casual interior, friendly waiters, and European–Levantine menu. It is often crowded with regulars, politicians, and actors. Strongly recommended.

Felfela ($)
*15 Sharia Hoda Shaarawi, downtown
tel: 392-2833*
Felfela is popular with tourists and locals for typical Egyptian food, served in an exotic setting with birds and aquariums. Now Felfela has restaurants everywhere, usually good places to take kids.

Fishawi ($)
In the same alley as the el-Husayn Hotel, Khan el-Khalili.
This is the oldest tea house in Cairo and the family claims that they have never closed since 1773. It is a wonderful place to sit and watch the world go by. No alcohol is served.

Flying Fish ($$–$$$)
166 Corniche el-Nil, Dokki tel: 349-3234
This is actor Omar Sharif's favorite fish restaurant. The fresh fish, shrimps, and lobster are excellent.

Four Corners ($$$)
*4 Sharia Hasan Sabry, Zamalek
tel: 341-2961*
This is a collection of four high-quality restaurants. La Piazza serves good Italian dishes and is very popular. Matchpoint gathers the young crowd for snacks and to watch the latest music videos. Chin Chin serves expensive Chinese food. The star restaurant is Justine, serving excellent French food.

Grillon ($$)
*8 Sharia Qasr an-Nil, in alleyway
tel: 574-3114*
A pleasant enclosed terrace out back, serves Mediterranean and oriental food. It is particularly popular with local intellectuals wanting a beer.

Jounieh ($$$)
Corniche el-Nil, opposite the World Trade Center, Boulaq tel: 575-9709
This Lebanese restaurant and bar has views over the Nile and Zamalek from its outdoor terrace, and swinging Arabic live entertainment inside. Slick service and excellent food especially the *mezze* menu, tender meat grills, and succulent *kibbeh*.

Khan al-Khalili ($$$)
*5 Sikkat el-Badistan, Khan el-Khalili
tel: 590-3788*
This pricey restaurant run by the Oberoi, serves Egyptian and European food, in the heart of the bazaar. Tea, coffee, and fresh juices, are served in the café and on the terrace. It's good for a snack and notable for the cleanest toilets in the area.

Kushary at-Tahrir ($)
169 Sharia el-Tahrir, Bab el-Luq
The waiter claims that the one who eats *kushari* here is like the one who drinks water from the Nile: he always comes back for more. Typical, good and clean *kushari* place. There is no alcohol.

Moghul Room ($$$)
Mena House Oberoi Hotel, Sharia el-Haram, near Giza Pyramids tel: 340-6550
Recover from a hectic Cairo day in this elegant, beautifully decorated restaurant that serves the best and most authentic Indian food in town.

Al-Omdah ($)
6 Sharia el-Gazair (next door to Atlas Hotel), Mohandeseen tel: 345-2387
This is one of the best *kushari* places in town, serving a superior version of the national dish with the right proportions of rice, noodles, lentils, and spicy sauce as well as other Egyptian dishes such as *fateer*, *shaweima* kebab and pigeon

Peking ($$)
14 Sharia Saraya el-Ezbekiya (behind Cinema Diana) tel: 591 2381
Try this tasty, fresh Chinese food in a pleasant setting. The specialty of the house is, strangely, Irish Coffee— with accompanying taped bird song.

Raoucha ($$$)
3 Sharia Gamaat ad-Duwal al-Arabiya, Mohandiseen tel: 303-0615
Raoucha is a sophisticated restaurant where you can enjoy authentic Lebanese cuisine in elegant surroundings, accompanied by live music at night. There is a wide range of fine Lebanese *mezze*, as well as excellent meat dishes, including *laban ummuh*—tender lamb cooked in yogurt.

Rigoletto ($)
3 Sharia Taha Husayn, Zamalek tel: 340-8684
Good ice cream, delicious iced cakes and cheesecake are the specialties here.

Samakmak ($$)
*92 Sharia Ahmed Orabi, Mohandiseen
tel: 347-8232*
Select a fish or seafood caught that day and have it fried or grilled, with rice, bread and fresh salads. Do as locals do: eat at a pavement table, ending with a sweet *sheesha* (waterpipe). Recommended.

Simmonds Coffee Shop ($)
12 26th July Street, Zamalek.
Cappuccino and espresso, fresh juices and croissants are recommended for a stand-up breakfast. Foreign journalists use it as a meeting place while real habitués use it as an unofficial office—the charming cashiers take their phone messages! Amm Arabi behind the counter remembers exactly how his regulars take their coffee, and gives in to most of their whims. No alcohol.

Sushiyama ($$$)
World Trade Center, 1191 Corniche el-Nil, Boulaq tel: 580-4066 /578-5161
Sushiyama is one of the best Japanese restaurants in Cairo. It offers a large menu of authentic *sushi*, *sashimi*, *tempura* and grills.

Tabasco ($–$$$)
8 Midan Amman, Mohandiseen tel: 336-5583
This chic, hugely popular bar/restaurant has loud music, good food, and Cairo's most fashionable patrons. Booking is essential.

Tandoori ($$)
*11 Sharia Shehab, Mohandiseen
tel: 348-6301*
Good Indian curries are served in this cool, marble setting. No alcohol.

LOWER NILE VALLEY

el-Faiyum
Auberge du Lac Coffee Shop ($$)
Lake Qarun tel: 700002
This pleasant restaurant looks onto the overgrown garden. Its specialty is wild Faiyumi duck.

Café Gabal el-Zinah ($)
Lake Qarun
This pleasant café-restaurant has wonderful views over the lake. The house specialty is fish. There is a children's playground, and colorful row-boats can be rented from the boat landing.

Kebabgi ($)
Sharia Mustapha Kamil, Madinat el-Faiyum.
The usual kebab and kofta is served here, and a good choice of vegetable dishes. No alcohol.

Said ($)
Near the sluice on Bahr Sinuris, Madinet el-Faiyum
Try the best *kushari* in town. No alcohol.

Sherif's ($)
Sharia Mustapha Kamil, Madinat el-Faiyum.
Sherif's serves excellent ice cream and sweets. It is famous locally as the home of the best *beleela* (hot milk, wheat, nuts, raisins, and sugar) in Egypt.

Luxor

Aboudi Internet Café ($)
Between Luxor Temple and the Winter Palace Hotel tel: 372390
email: aboudi@access.com.eg
You won't find a big choice of food here, but Aboudi offers convenient and inexpensive Internet access from 9 AM to 10 PM.

Cafeteria Mohamed ($)
Beside Pharaoh's Hotel, West Bank
tel: 311044
Hard to find—there's no sign—but this is the best place to look for local cooking. Give him warning and Mohamed will prepare excellent stuffed pigeons and grills. Cold beer available.

1886 Restaurant and the Royal Bar ($$–$$$)
Winter Palace Hotel, Sharia Corniche el-Nil
tel: 095/3580422
Luxor's classiest restaurant and bar, this is part of the old hotel's refurbishment. Neither the food nor the service live up to expectations, but the rooms are as calm and elegant as a *fin de siècle* boudoir.

Kings Head Pub ($–$$)
Sharia Khaled ibn el-Walid tel: 371249
This is a slice of England newly imported to Luxor: darts, billiards, pub food (no closing time, though).

Kushari Sayyida Nefisa ($)
Sharia Mustapha Kamel near the souk
Renowned for its *kushari*, this establishment attracts a mostly male crowd. No alcohol.

La Mamma ($$)
In the Sheraton Hotel at the far end of Sharia Khaled Ibn el Walid tel: 374544
La Mamma is a good, outdoor Italian restaurant, set in a garden with a pond and atmospheric Neapolitan live music. Fresh pastas and pizzas are served.

Maratonga Café-Restaurant ($)
Opposite Medinet Habu Temple, West Bank
Enjoy the lovely shaded terrace to watch the sun set behind the mountains and the magnificent temple. Just have a drink or you can try the simple, but well-prepared, Egyptian dishes.

Marhaba ($–$$)
Sharia Corniche el-Nil, above the tourist office.
You will find average, often overpriced food, here, but you can drink cool local Stella beers on the excellent roof terrace overlooking the Nile.

Marsam Hotel Restaurant ($)
Opposite the Valley of the Nobles, West Bank
tel: 372165
Simple but well-prepared Egyptian dishes are served on the terrace by talkative waiters. Here you may run into archaeologists excavating in the neighborhood. This is best visited in spring and fall.

Mövenpick Restaurants ($$–$$$),
Crocodile Island tel: 095/374855
The terrace restaurant beside the Nile serves fresh salads and pastas for lunch, homemade ice cream and sherbets, as well as a fantastic breakfast buffet in spring and autumn. There are two indoor restaurants, one serving a good buffet and the other pricey but good French cuisine *à la carte.*

Tutankhamun ($)
Near the ferry landing on the West Bank
tel: 310118
It's worth crossing the river for some of the best food in Luxor. The friendly, chatty owner was head chef in a deluxe hotel for several years. Excellent chicken with rosemary, spinach casserole, and good oriental rice are worth trying. No alcohol.

Minya

Cafeteria Ali Baba ($)
Corniche el-Nil past the Governorate Building
Good Egyptian fare is served here—kebab and chicken are specialties. No alcohol.

Lotus ($)
Top floor of the Lotus Hotel.
Good meals are complimented by fine views. This is one of only two places that serve alcohol.

UPPER EGYPT AND NUBIA

Aswan

1902 Restaurant ($$$)
Old Cataract Hotel, Sharia Abtal el-Tahrir
tel: 316000
Disappointingly bland international cuisine is served in this elegant restaurant, but the turn-of-the-century Moorish dining hall is an experience in itself. Nubian dancers and musicians will add spice to the evening.

Aswan Moon ($)
Corniche el-Nil tel: 097/316108
This lively place has a mock-castle entrance gate and a restaurant on a floating extension. It's a favorite for *felucca* captains who come for the least expensive beer in town, the nostalgic Nubian songs, and for foreign women. An amusing place for dinner, with fresh juices and "oriental" food.

Darna ($$)
New Cataract Hotel, Sharia Abtal el-Tahrir
tel: 316002
This is a pleasant restaurant, designed as an Egyptian house in the countryside. A buffet is served featuring traditional Egyptian dishes.

Al-Misri Tour Restaurant ($)
Sharia el-Matar, off Sharia el-Suq tel: 302576
Tucked away, but popular with the locals, the Al-Misri Tour serves excellent kebab and kofta with salads and cold drinks, amid much Islamic kitsch. There is a family room at the back.

Old Cataract Hotel Terrace ($)
From 4 PM until dusk English tea is served, with cakes and sandwiches, and a splendid view.

Accommodations and Restaurants

Panorama ($)
Corniche el-Nil, Aswan tel: 097/326169
This pleasant terrace along the Nile serves a huge variety of Egyptian and Europeanized dishes. The Panorama is good for breakfast, lunch, and dinner or just for a fresh juice or herbal tea. No alcohol.

La Trattoria ($)
In the Isis Hotel on the Corniche
tel: 097/315100
This is a fairly boring Italian restaurant, but good enough if you're tired of Egyptian fare.

WESTERN DESERT OASES

Bahariya
Oasis Cafeteria ($) and
Paradise Motel Restaurant ($)
On the main road
Both places serve basic menus to undemanding backpackers. A good meeting place if you want to share transportation with someone.

Popular Restaurant ($)
(el-Gash) opposite the police station
The owner gets angry if people ask the price of the food in advance. He is known to overcharge if he doesn't like your face.

Dakhla
Al-Dakhla Café ($)
Opposite the new mosque
Good for sandwiches only.

Hamdy's ($)
Off the main road.
A hangout for every tourist in town, with the best food and, for the oases, an amazingly varied menu. It plays 1970s pop music, some of which you won't have heard for a while.

Siwa
Abduh's ($)
Opposite the Yusuf Hotel
Food here is good and inexpensive. It serves three meals a day and is also a good place for picking up information about the oasis.

Adrere Amellal ($$$)
You can find some of the best and most innovative food in Egypt here. The restaurant uses local produce from its own organic farm and garden.

East–West ($)
On the main road.
Excellent food is served here, mostly Egyptian fare influenced by backpackers' tastes.

ALEXANDRIA AND THE DELTA

Alexandria
The telephone code for Alexandria is 03.

Athineos ($)
21 Midan Sa'ad Zaghlul tel: 482-0421
This is a pâtisserie, nightclub, and a vast restaurant with gilded friezes serving a Levantine menu. In summer, large windows open onto the bay.

Baudrot ($)
23 Sharia Saad Zaghlul tel: 482-5687
Pastries are bland in this once-famous pâtisserie, but the romantic garden makes it all worthwhile.

Brazilian Coffee Store ($)
Sharia Saad Zaghlul, behind the tourist office
Founded in 1929, this Greek-owned stand-up café still serves one of the better *cappuccinos* in town beneath the Brazilian flag.

Cap d'Or ($)
4 Sharia Adib, off Sharia Saad Zaghlul
tel: 483-5177
An old art-nouveau bar-restaurant, this is worth the trouble of finding for its fried fish and tasty squid casseroles. Popular with locals who pop in for beer and 1970s French music. Wild décor.

Denis ($–$$)
1 Sharia Ibn Bassam tel: 482-1709
One of the simpler fish restaurants around the Corniche, Denis lacks a sea view, but has excellent fish and shrimps to choose from an iced cabinet.

Fish Market ($$–$$$)
El-Kashafa el-Bahariya Club, 26 Corniche el-Nil
tel: 480-5114
This is a slightly grand fish restaurant, with excellent seafood and fish. Service is good, and the views of the lovely bay and harbor are sweeping.

Hassan Bleik ($–$$)
Opposite 18 Sharia Saad Zaghlul
tel: 484-0880
This wonderful, old-fashioned and cheap Lebanese restaurant is open only for lunch. A plentiful choice of dishes includes stuffed pigeon,fish and chicken with grilled almonds. Leave room for homemade Oriental sweets. No alcohol. Highly recommended.

Mohamed Ahmed ($)
17 Sharia Shakour tel: 483-3576
Calling itself the Great Pyramid of Alexandria, this place is always packed. It serves a great *fuul* and *falafel*. No alcohol.

Pastroudis ($–$$)
39 Sharia el-Hurriya tel: 492 9609
The dark, red-plush restaurant is a good place to hide when history and crowds get the best of you. Another typically Alexandrian menu with dishes from all sides of the Mediterranean served on a popular terrace. There is also a pâtisserie.

Samakmak ($$)
42 Qasr Ras et-Tin, el-Bahry tel: 480-9523
This unpretentious restaurant has both indoor and outdoor seating near to the fish market. The fish is as fresh as it gets, and is grilled or fried to order. Recommended

Santa Lucia ($$)
40 Sharia Safia Zaghlul tel: 482-0332
This is one of the most expensive restaurants in town specializing in seafood and European cuisine. The old waiters do their best to keep up the grand style. Very lively floor show.

Spitfire Bar ($)
7 Sharia el-Bursa el-Qadima tel: 480-6503
One of Egypt's most unusual bars, its walls are covered with memorabilia. It is generally smoky and crowded, playing loud rock 'n' roll. If the U.S. Navy is in town you'll most likely find sailors here.

Trianon ($$)
Midan Saad Zaghlul
tel: 482-0986 or 482-0973
Live piano music adds to the atmosphere in this stylish, wood-paneled restaurant serving good steaks and oriental specialties. The excellent café-pâtisserie serves good-value breakfast.

Venous ($)
12 Sharia el-Hurriya and 37 Sharia Nabi Danyal
tel: 482-0956
Resist if you can the beautiful pâtisserie with mounds of pralines, cookies, and a wide variety of cakes.

Zephirion ($$)
41 Sharia Khalid Ibn Walid, Abu Kir
tel: 560-1319
A large, blue-and-white family taverna overlooking the beach is well worth the excursion to an otherwise seedy suburb. There is a wide variety of fresh fish and Egyptian wine. After over 60 years' in business it's very popular, so reserve on weekends.

Mersa Matruh
Beau Site ($$)
6 Sharia Osman Ahmed Osman
tel: 03/493-8555
Beau Site is a long walk from town but it's worth it to sample Mersa Matruh's best food. There's a fixed-price menu and a bar overlooking the sea.

SUEZ CANAL AND RED SEA COAST

Hurghada
Chez Pascal ($$)
Next door to Three Corners Village
tel: 02/336-5205
This occasionally excellent Belgian-run restaurant serves homemade pasta, pizza, and seafood. The ice cream and pancakes are good. Next door, the same owners run one of Hurghada's hottest night spots, the Cha Cha Disco.

Felfella ($)
Tariq el-Sheraton tel: 065/442411
Part of the Cairene chain, Felfella serves good Egyptian food in a rustic setting. There are good views of the sea.

Portofino ($$)
Tariq el-Mustashfa tel: 065/546250
Good Italian food is served in a pleasant atmosphere. The specialty is seafood fondue for two.

Scruples Steak House and Pub ($$$)
Sharia Nasr tel: 065/444636
European food is on the menu here. Specialties include imported beef and seafood.

Isma'iliya
George's ($$)
Sharia Sultan Hussein, Isma'iliya
tel: 064/288363
George's is so famous for its fresh fish and seafood that Cairenes come for the day just to eat at this restaurant.

King Edward ($$)
171 Sharia el-Tahrir tel: 325451
King Edward offers a fairly good, moderately priced, and varied Egyptian and "European" menu. The restaurant is air conditioned.

Port Said
El-Borg ($–$$)
Near the beach
Try some of the best fish in Egypt. Seafood soup is a specialty; the sole and sea bass are perfectly grilled. No alcohol, but you can bring your own.

Cecil Reana House ($$)
5, Sharia el-Gumhuriya, opposite Akri Hotel
tel: 066/223911
Korean food isn't what you would expect to find in Port Said and the staircase to the first floor isn't encouraging, but everyone from honorary consuls to passing sailors comes to Mr. Pak's for a taste of the East. Spicy here means tongue-burning.

Galal ($)
Sharia Gaberti and Gumhuriya
Very good fish and seafood specialties are served in a plain setting here.

Nora's Floating Restaurant ($$)
Sharia Filistine, opposite the National Museum, Port Said tel: 066/329834
You can choose between lunch or dinner cruises in this floating restaurant. Enjoy good Egyptian food, accompanied by excellent views of the Nile.

Pizza Pino ($$)
Intersection of Sharia Gumhuriya and 23rd of July Street tel: 239949
This is the place to be seen. Good, simple Italian cuisine and excellent ice cream.

Suez
al-Magharbel ($$)
Sharia el-Gheish
The best food in town, which isn't saying much.

SINAI

el-Arish
Oberoi Restaurant ($$–$$$)
Oberoi Hotel tel: 351321
A mixed menu of Indian, Egyptian, and European cuisine is served here. Equally appealing whether you dine alone or in a crowd.

Samar ($)
On 23rd July Street, el-Arish
Simple, good chicken, kofta, and not much more. No alcohol.

Dahab
Tota ($)
el-Masbat.
This boat-shaped restaurant serves a varied menu. Vegetarian dishes and pizza are good. Tota is famous for its delicious chocolate cake.

Sharm el Sheikh
Beach BBQ ($$–$$$)
Fayruz Hilton, Na'ama Bay
If you like Italian food, try this buffet of fresh pasta, and a grill with fish and meat, all for a fixed price. In the evening it is served on the beach.

Beach BBQ ($$)
Mövenpick Jolie Ville, Na'ama Bay
This pleasant beach restaurant is open for lunch. Choose from the excellent salad bar, good grills, and sandwiches.

Hilton Fish Restaurant ($$$)
Near the Hilton Diving Center
An outdoor restaurant, the Hilton serves expensive but excellent French-inspired fish dishes.

Pirates Bar ($$)
Hilton Fayrouz, Na'ama Bay tel: 660136
A popular venue for an evening drink, Pirates is set in a beautifully lit garden with bridges over ponds.

Index

Index

286

Index

Acknowledgments

The Automobile Association would like to thank the following photographers, libraries, and associations for their assistance in the preparation of this book.
JIM MORRIS/AXIOM 54/5 Nightview of Cairo **BRITISH MUSEUM** (copyright) 30 Menthuhotpe II; 36a/37a Roman mummy case; 131 Temple of Isis, Philae. **CORBIS** top cover picture **EYE UBIQUITOUS** 110/1 Traffic in Cairo **MARY EVANS PICTURE LIBRARY** 41a Salah ad-Din; 41b Salah ad-Din; 48 Anti-British riots; 96a British soldiers 1882; 96c Picnic on the Great Pyramid of Cheops, Giza; 182a and 182b Aswan Dam; 232a Opening of Suez Canal. **S FRANQUET** 8a. **P GODEAU** 10/11 The Nile; 16b el-Muallaqa Church, Cairo; 23a Bab-el-Wagin; 24b Naguib Mahfouz; 46b British Embassy gates; 72a Mihrab of Qajmas el-Ishaqi mosque; 74/5 City of the Dead; 77b el-Qa'ah reception hall, Gayer Anderson House; 85a Sultan Barquq's tomb; 86a World Trade Centre, Cairo; 109 Marriott Hotel; 146a and 146b Siwa; 192 Dakhla Oasis; 193a Dakhla Oasis; 194a el-Kharga; 194/5 Dakhla Oasis; 195a el-Qasr; 196/7 Black Desert; 196 White Desert; 198a el-Qasr; 198b View el-Qasr; 199 Roman Fort, el-Kharga Oasis; 224 Irrigation system, Nile Delta; 227a Suez Canal; 229 Red Sea Coast; 250b Dive site, Sinai. **PETER GUTTMAN** cover silhouette **J HENDERSON** 63 Step Pyramid of Zoser, Saqqara; 72c Muhammad Ali Mosque, Cairo; 152 Mortuary Temple of Hatshepsut, Luxor; 161 Valley of the Kings, Luxo; 188 Lake Nasser cruise, 188/9 Temple of Ramasses II, el-Sebua, 189 Reliefs on wall of Maharraka temple. **HULTON DEUTSCH COLLECTION LTD** 26 Umm Kalthoum; 50/1 Sadat, Carter and Begin; 232b Suez Canal dredgers. **IMAGOS/C COE** 20b Boy and cart, Cairo; 81 Cairo grain market; 217a Qaytbay Fort, Alexandria. **B IVERSON** 167 Nefertari's tomb, Valley of the Queens. **THE MANSELL COLLECTION LTD** 36b Emperor Augustus; 45b Tourists at the Pyramids of Giza; 60a Great Pyramid of Cheops; 96b James Bruce; 125 Akhenaton; 164b Howard Carter in Tutankhamun's tomb. **JAMES H MORRIS PICTURE LIBRARY** 4a Nile scene; 5c Relief from tomb of Seti I; 6 Spices; 38 Cairo Muslims; 126 Coptic School, White Monastery; 127 White Monastery; 160 Tomb of Rameses IV, Valley of the Kings; 163 Tomb of Tuthmosis III, Valley of the Kings. **NATURE PHOTOGRAPHERS LTD** 228 Blackspotted grunt (D A Smith); 250a Diver, Red Sea Coast (J Sutherland); 250b Clown fish (D A Smith). **REX FEATURES LTD** 13 Islamic Conference, 50/1 Nasser and Tito. **A SATTIN** 8c; 31b Ramses II, Abu Simbel; 156 Ramses III, Madinet Habu. **N SCHILLER** 147 Moulid of el-Husayn, Cairo; 171a and 177 Daraw camel market; 234b Red Sea Mountains. **SPECTRUM COLOUR LIBRARY** 14b Cairo el-Azhar Mosque; 28a Abydos Temple reliefs; 71 el-Azhar Mosque; 133 Roman Column, Dandara; 162 Seti I's tomb, Valley of the Kings. **WORLD PICTURES** 233 Hurghada **ZEFA PICTURES LTD** 104 Cairo restaurant; 105 Casino, Cairo.

The remaining pictures are held in the Association's own library (AA PHOTO LIBRARY) and were taken by CHRIS COE with the exception of pages: 3, 5b, 8b, 10, 18a, 21, 27b, 30a, 33, 35, 39, 40b, 42/3a, 42/3b, 44b, 46a, 47, 52/3, 53, 55, 56, 60b, 61b, 73, 80, 82b, 84, 86b, 88b, 92, 100, 101, 102b, 103b, 108, 113a, 113b, 114a, 114/5, 114b, 118, 119a, 119b, 121, 123, 128, 129, 130, 132, 134, 135b, 137, 138, 140a, 140b, 141, 142, 143, 148a, 148b, 151, 153, 154/5, 156, 158, 169b, 171b, 172, 173a, 173b, 174b, 175, 176a, 180/1, 191, 193b, 200/1, 201, 204, 205, 206a, 207, 211, 212a, 212b, 217b, 220a, 222, 231, 234a, 235, 237a, 239a, 239b, 241a, 241b, 244, 245b, 246a, 248, 249, 252b, 255, 259, 260, 261, 265b, 266, 270 and 271a which were taken by RICK STRANGE.

Contributors

Revision copy editor: Julian Rowe   Original copy editor: Donna Dailey
Revision verifiers: Anthony Sattin and Sylvie Franquet